Peter Norton's Visual Basic for DOS
The Accessible Guide to Professional Programming

Who This book is For

Introductory to intermediate Visual Basic for DOS programmers who want to develop and extend their programming expertise and add new performance to their programs.

What's Inside

- How to bring all the visual elements of Windows to DOS with pull-down menus, scroll bars, and text boxes

- Porting your VB/Windows applications easily to VB/DOS

- Connecting VB/DOS with assembly language for extra programming speed and compactness

- File and Error Handling

- Hints, tips, and tricks to increase programming proficiency

- Advanced Databasing with ISAM

Disk Contents

The Visual Basic for DOS disk contains all the programs described in the book (and three more programs which do not appear in the book). This means you can start advancing your skills immediately. You will be able to add these three BONUS programs to your repertoire:

- Altfont.Mak

- Animate.Mak

- Hyper.Mak

Peter Norton's
Visual Basic for DOS

Steven Holzner

**The Peter Norton
Computer Group**

Brady Publishing

New York   London   Toronto   Sydney   Tokyo   Singapore

Brady Publishing

A Division of Prentice Hall Computer Publishing
15 Columbus Circle
New York, NY 10023

Manufactured in the United States of America

10 9 8 7 6 5 4 3 2 1

Library of Congress Cataloging-in-Publication Data

Holzner, Steven.
Peter Norton's Visual Basic for DOS/Steven Holzner.
        p.   cm.
  Includes index.
  ISBN 1-56686-026-1 : $39.95
  1. BASIC (Computer program language) 2. Microsoft Visual BASIC.
3. MS-DOS (Computer file) 4. PC-DOS (Computer file)   I. Peter
Norton Computer Corporation II. Title.
QA76.73.B3H685 1992
005.26'2--dc20   92-31623
                                               CIP

ISBN 1-56686-026-1

Limits of Liability and Disclaimer of Warranty

The authors and publisher of this book have used their best efforts in preparing this book and the programs contained in it. These efforts include the research and testing of these programs to determine their effectiveness. The authors and publisher make no warranty of any kind, expressed or implied, with regard to these programs or the documentation contained in this book. The authors and publisher shall not be liable in any event for incidental or consequential damages in connection with, or arising out of, the furnishing, performance, or use of these programs.

Trademarks

Most computer and software brand names have trademarks or registered trademarks. The individual trademarks have not been listed here.

Contents

Introduction

Why Visual Basic for DOS?

Visual Basic for Windows has brought about a revolution in the way programmers program for Windows. Programming for Windows used to be an enormously unpleasant task, involving many support files and page after page of arcane code. Visual Basic for Windows changed that. It added the programming tools that have been lacking for so long in Windows. Working with it for the first time, experienced Windows programmers can hardly believe their eyes. The ideas are simple—if you want a window of a certain size, you simply draw it that size. If you want a text box at a particular point in your window, simply select the correct tool and draw it there. That is, Visual Basic does what programs excel at—it handles the details for you. That's useful because, at last, the aid of the computer itself is being enlisted in the programming process.

Now, at last, Visual Basic is available for DOS as well. We'll be able to do just about anything that Visual Basic for Windows lets us —but now we'll be developing Visual Basic programs in DOS. We'll start by adjusting a window to the size we want, and then we'll be able to add the type of items that normally only appear in Windows: Listboxes, buttons, combo boxes—whatever you want. When we're through, we'll write a few (often a very few) lines of BASIC code to make things work, and Visual Basic creates the working .exe file for us. That's all there is to it. Now the power of Visual Basic for Windows comes to DOS.

Our Approach

This is a book for would-be Visual Basic programmers, so we're going to spend a lot of time seeing Visual Basic at work. In other words, we're going to see what the software is capable of—and to do that, we'll have to see plenty of examples, which is always the best way to learn about software. We'll start almost at once in Chapter 1, by getting a window on the screen and working with it. As the book progresses, we'll see many other examples: an alarm clock, a text editor, a database program, a paint program, calculators, and many others.

In addition, as the name Visual Basic itself implies, we'll spend some time looking at windows on the screen and learning what makes them tick. This book is unlike other programming books that you might have read in that much of what we'll cover has to do with using Visual Basic to Design our software—visually—instead of working through long programs. If you're unfamiliar with Visual Basic programming, you'll also find that the code we develop is different from what you might expect; in particular, Visual Basic programs are *event-driven*, which means that our code will be divided up into many small sections to handle specific events. This method is a contrast to the linear, continous programs that you might be used to, and can take some getting used to; but after a while, thinking in terms of events like mouse clicks or key presses comes naturally. We'll see more about this method in Chapter 1. In a nutshell, then, our approach is the programmer's approach: task- and example-oriented, without a great deal of unecessary theory. In this book, we'll put Visual Basic for DOS to work for us.

What's in This Book

Visual Basic is a tremendous toolbox of programming resources, and we're going to explore them in this book. We'll work our way up, from the most basic examples to the most polished. In the beginning of the book, we'll get the essentials down, and then we'll be able to progress beyond them. We'll follow the natural course of Visual Basic programming development—starting with just a blank window. Then we'll embellish it a little with a caption and size it the way we want. Next, we'll start to add buttons and text boxes—what Visual Basic calls controls. When we become comfortable with the idea of controls, we'll add dialog boxes, and then the menus themselves. As we work our way throughout the book, we'll get into the kinds of topics that real Visual Basic applications deal with, such as file handling, graphics, and error handling. We'll even have a chapter on debugging and one on advanced databasing with the ISAM system that comes with Visual Basic for DOS Professional Edition.

As mentioned above, our orientation will be on seeing our programs work and on getting functional results. To do that, however, we'll have to understand what we're doing. That means that we'll have to take the time to understand all the concepts involved in Visual Basic: concepts like forms and methods, projects and modules.

For that reason, part of the first chapter will get us started by exploring the concepts we'll need. We'll begin with fundamental Visual Basic concepts—such as windows and buttons themselves—and then we'll work through some Visual Basic programming concepts. Since this will form the foundation of all we do in the book, we'll make sure that we get all the beginning ideas down before continuing.

From then on, our coverage will be task-oriented as much as possible. Most of the successive chapters are purposely designed to cover one specific type of Visual Basic "control"—for example buttons, listboxes, combo boxes, dialog boxes, or menus. In this way, we'll build our expertise by building our DOS windows—piece by piece, steadily adding more and more power to our applications. This will allow us to handle the complexities that might arise in a gradual, systematic way.

All this makes for quite an ambitious plan: learning how to design and put serious Visual Basic applications to work with a minimum amount of trouble. Normally this would mean a book full of ten or twenty page programs, as well as a great deal of work. However, we'll see that Visual Basic is a whole different story. Getting our windowed programs working—and producing real results—will largely be a matter of simply designing what we want on the screen and then letting VB handle the details.

What You'll Need

To read this book profitably, you should have some knowledge of BASIC. However, you won't need much; the programming here is generally not very advanced, and we'll introduce new BASIC constructions as we need them. Even so, you should be familiar with BASIC (such as BASICA or QuickBasic) to the point of being able to write your own simple programs in it. If you find yourself lost in the first chapter, you should probably become familiar with BASIC before continuing. The Best BASIC review is Micrsoft QuickBasic, because as far as straight programming goes, Visual Basic for DOS is a subset of QuickBasic.

Finally, you'll need Visual Basic for DOS itself; any version will do. If you haven't installed it yet, just run the Setup program explained in the Visual Basic documentation. Visual Basic itself is all the software you need—you'll be able to enter programs directly without the assistance of a word processor or text editor.

That's it; we're ready to begin. Our first task will be to get a simple window on the screen as soon as possible—but to do that, first we'll need to understand a few things about Visual Basic, so let's dig in immediately with Chapter 1.

NOTE: *We should also note that you'll need a mouse (or other pointing device) for the work we'll do in this book. While Visual Basic applications are supposed to run with either the mouse or the keyboard, it's very difficult to do real work with a mouse—and it's certainly almost impossible to program in Visual Basic without one. That is, casual users may be able to get along without a mouse—but for the more serious Visual Basic programmer, the mouse is an essential tool.*

Our First Windows

Welcome to Visual Basic for DOS, one of the components of a revolution in programming. This powerful package is one of the new generation of tools that are beginning to open up programming as never before. No longer will it take a great deal of patience, experience, and expensive software to produce valuable windowed applications. Under Visual Basic (and programs like it), developing windowed programs is easier than ever. In this chapter, we'll put together our first Visual Basic programs, which will run under DOS. We'll see that it's easier than you might expect to do this, because Visual Basic handles most of the details for us automatically.

You can think of Visual Basic as an immense box of tools and resources, waiting for us to use it. To use these tools and resources, however, we'll have to understand them. In other words, we'll have to know what's available before we can take advantage of what Visual Basic has to offer us.

Accordingly, we'll begin our tour of Visual Basic by examining what's in a Visual Basic window—the kind that we'll be able to produce in our programs. Next, we'll see how Visual Basic works, and what tools it offers us. Then, when we're ready, we'll put Visual Basic to work

and get some results. Let's begin now by examining the kinds of
windows Visual Basic produces so that we know the names of all its
parts before we start the programming process itself.

A Visual Basic for DOS Window

A typical Visual Basic for DOS window appears in Figure 1-1, and
you should be familiar with its parts before starting to program Visual Basic applications. Before starting to program, then,
let's spend a little time reviewing Visual Basic window terminology
ourselves; this will help us later in the book. At the upper left of the
window in Figure 1-1 is a system menu box, which, when selected,
displays a menu that typically allows the user to move the window,
close it, or minimize it. At the top center is the title or caption bar
(Visual Basic refers to the text as the window's caption, not its title),
and this provides an easy way of labeling an application.

Figure 1-1 A Visual Basic Window

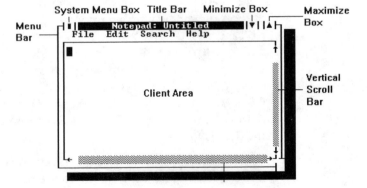

To the right of the title bar are the minimize and maximize boxes,
which allow the user to reduce the window to an icon (called an
application's *iconic* state), or expand it fully, usually to the whole
screen. Under the title bar is a menu bar offering the currently available menu options for the application. In almost every stand-alone
application, there will be a menu bar with at least one menu item in it:
the File menu. This is the menu that usually offers the Exit item at the
bottom, as shown in Figure 1-2.

Figure 1-2 A Visual Basic Window with Menu

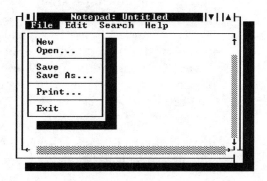

NOTE: *The Exit item is the usual way for users to leave an application, so if your application supports file handling, you should include the Exit item at the bottom of your File menu.*

Under the menu bar is the *client area*; in fact, the *client* area makes up the whole of a window under the menu bar except for the borders and scroll bars (it's the area that the window is designed to display). This is our drawing area, the area we will work with directly in Visual Basic; that is, this is the part of the window on which we'll place buttons, list boxes, text boxes, and the other parts of our programs.To the right of the client area is a vertical scrollbar, which is a common part of a window that displays text. If there is too much text to fit in the window at once, scrollbars let you look at some subsection of the whole, moving around in the document. (By the way, the small square that moves up and down and which you use to manipulate your position in the scroll bar is called a *thumb*.).

On the bottom of the window is another scroll bar, a horizontal scroll bar, which scrolls the text in the client area horizontally. Everything in the window but the client area is called the *nonclient area*; even the border is part of the nonclient area. Visual Basic will be responsible for maintaining the nonclient area of the window, and we'll be responsible for the client area.

The Feel of Visual Basic Programs

Before programming in Visual Basic, we should be very familiar with the way the user expects Visual Basic programs to work and feel. This is similar to what they would expect from a Windows program, so if you use Windows, you're all set. In particular, you should be at home with the language of mouse clicks and double clicks, and of anticipating what the user might expect from your application.

For example, the fact that the File menu usually has an Exit item, and that item—if present—is always last, is part of the Visual Basic interface you'll be programming in. There are many other aspects of the way users expect Visual Basic applications to work that you should be familiar with before producing applications yourself. Although we'll discuss these conventions as we reach the appropriate topics, there's no substitute for working with existing Visual Basic (or Windows) applications to get the correct feel for the interface.

After some practice, these conventions become quite automatic; for instance, in file list boxes (where the program is showing you which files are available to be opened), one click of the mouse should highlight a filename (called *selecting*), and two clicks should open the file (called *choosing*). On the other hand, it is also supposed to be possible to use windowed programs without a mouse at all—just with the keyboard—so you must provide keyboard support at the same time (in this case, the user would use the Tab key to move to the correct box, the arrow keys to highlight a file name, and the Enter key to choose it).

There are other conventions that users of Visual Basic applications expect; if there's some object that can be moved around the screen, users expect to be able to drag it with the mouse. They expect accelerator keys in menus, system menus that let them close a window, and windows that can be moved, resized, or minimized. As mentioned, the best way to know what will be expected of your program is to work with existing Visual Basic applications, or with Windows.

NOTE: *For the purposes of program design in this book, we are assuming that you have a mouse to go along with Visual Basic. Although it is possible to use windowed* **applications** *without a mouse, Visual Basic* **programmers** *are severely hampered without one, to the point of seriously crippling their productivity.*

About Visual Basic Programming

Now let's take a look at one program application for Visual Basic, and what makes it different from normal programming under DOS. To start, standard DOS programs are written sequentially; that is, one event follows the other. In a standard DOS program, control goes down the list of statements, more or less in the order that the programmer designed. For example, this is the way an introductory program from a BASIC book might look:

```
WHILE INKEY$ = "": WEND

PRINT "Hello from Basic."
```

In the first line, we're simply waiting until the user presses a key. When they do, control goes sequentially to the next line, and the message "Hello from Basic." appears on the screen. If there were more statements, control would continue with them, looping and progressing in the way that the programmer designed it to work. However, Visual Basic is different.

Visual Basic Events

An application under Visual Basic typically presents all possible options (in the form of visual objects) on the screen for users to select for themselves. In this way, it represents an entirely new kind of programming—*event-driven* programming. That is to say, the programmer is no longer completely responsible for the flow of the program— the user is. The user selects among all the options presented, and it is up to the program to respond correctly. For example, there may be three buttons on a window, as shown in Figure 1-3. Clearly, we can't just write our program assuming that the user is going to push them in some sequence.

Figure 1-3 Clicker Window

Instead, we'll have to write separate code for each button. That's going to be the case in general, and it will have significant consequences for us in this book. Instead of monolithic programs that you can read from beginning to end, our code will necessarily be divided up into smaller sections, one section for one kind of event. For example, we may add a text box to the window, in which we want the message "Hello from Visual Basic." to appear when the user clicks the button marked Click Me. In that case, our program might look like this:

```
Sub ClickMe_Click ()

        Message.text = "Hello from Visual Basic."

End Sub
```

This code is specifically designed to handle one type of event—clicking the button marked Click Me. Our programs will typically be collections of code sections like this, one after the other. That's how event-driven programming works: we'll largely be designing our code around the *interface* (the way we've set up the window) at least in the early part of this book. Our programs won't have "modes", the way that an editor can have modes (e.g., insert mode, marking mode, and so on); instead, all the options available at one time will be represented on the screen, ready to be used. We'll soon see how this works.

Besides being event-driven, Visual Basic programming is also *object-oriented* (although not in the strict C++ sense). That is easy enough to see on the screen: just pick up an object such as an icon or paintbrush and move it around. This corresponds closely to what's called *object-oriented programming*. This type of programming breaks a program up into discrete objects, each of which has its own code and data associated with it. In this way, each of the objects can be somewhat independent from the others.

Using object-oriented programming is a natural for event-driven software, because it breaks the program up into discrete, modular objects. It turns out that that's the way we'll be treating our windows and all the buttons, text boxes, and so on that we put in them: as objects. Each of these objects can have both data and code associated with it, as we'll see. You may have heard of object-oriented programming, and you may suspect that it's difficult to implement, but it turns out that Visual Basic takes care of all of the details for us. In fact, let's look into that process in Visual Basic next; now that we've gotten our background down, we're ready to look at the programming tools we'll be using in this book.

About Visual Basic Programming

There are three major steps to writing an application in Visual Basic, and we'll follow them throughout this book. Here they are:

NOTE: *Although Visual Basic programming does resemble object-oriented programming in many ways, it is not really true object-oriented programming. Languages such as C++, which are true object-oriented languages, include several programming constructs that Visual Basic does not (e.g., classes and class inheritance).*

▼ Design the window(s) you want

▼ Customize the properties of buttons, text boxes, and so on

▼ Write the code for the associated events (e.g., button pushes)

The first step—drawing the window you want, complete with buttons and menus—is where Visual Basic really shines. Before, it was a tedious process to design the appearance of windows, where the buttons would go, how large they would be, and many other considerations. Adding or removing features was also very difficult. Under Visual Basic, however, this whole process has become extraordinarily easy. VB allows us to simply draw, just as in a paint program, the window(s) we want, as well as all the buttons, boxes, and labels we want. In other words, we'll see the actual appearance of our application at design time. Adding or removing buttons or boxes works just as it would in a paint program, as we'll see; there's no difficult programming involved at all. The next step involves customizing the properties of what we've drawn—for example, we might give a window or button a certain caption, or change its color (or even whether or not it's visible). Finally, we write the code that responds to the events we consider significant. That's how it works in outline; now let's see it in practice.

Our First Window

Let's put together a one-window application that simply has one button and one text box. When the user clicks or chooses the button, the words "Welcome to Visual Basic." should appear in the text box, as shown in Figure 1-4.

Start programming by starting Visual Basic for DOS. The VB display appears in Figure 1-5. As with any new software, there are new terms and concepts to learn here. (In fact, there are only about ten major terms to learn in Visual Basic.) What we're seeing now is the

7

Programming Environment, and we'll be able to write and debug our window's code here. However, to do that, we have to design our window first, and we do that in Visual Basic's *Form Designer*.

Figure 1-4 Our First Program

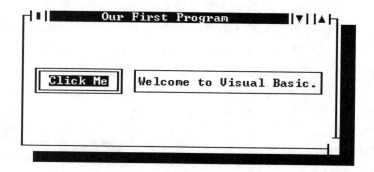

Figure 1-5 The Visual Basic Programming Environment

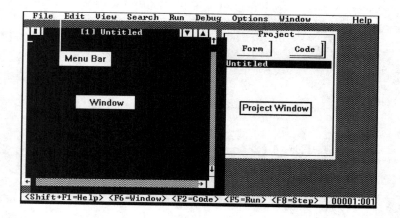

The Visual Basic Form

In Visual basic, windows under design are called *forms*. To switch to the Form Designer, select the New Form... item in the Programming Environment's File menu, as shown in Figure 1-6. The New Form dialog box opens, as shown in Figure 1-7, asking us for the name of our new form. Type, say, Click.Frm (when we save forms on disk, we'll give the standard VB extension.Frm), and click the OK button. When you do, the Visual Basic Form Designer opens, as shown in Figure 1-8.

Figure 1-6 The Programming Environment's File Menu

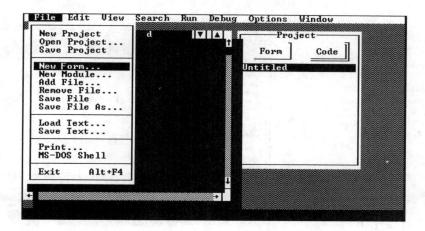

Figure 1-7 The New Form Dialog Box

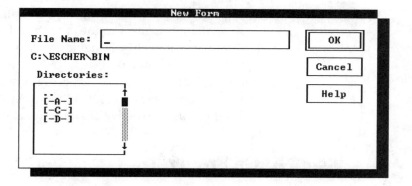

Let's go over the parts of the Form Designer, each of which will be important to us as we design our windows. To begin, there is a window that appears in the center of the screen, labeled Click. This is the window that we're designing (keep in mind that Visual Basic refers to windows that you customize as *forms*). As you can see, the form we begin with has the appearance of a normal Visual Basic window. In fact, this is the way our window will look when the application we're writing starts. Notice that Click already has a system menu box, a title bar, both minimize and maximize boxes, a border, and a client area.

Figure 1-8 The Visual Basic Form Designer

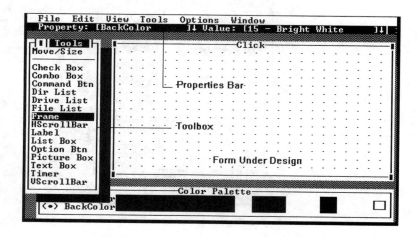

As you can see, the client area is filled with dots at regular intervals. These dots form a grid which will help us to align buttons and boxes when we're designing our window(and they'll disappear at run time). In fact, our window is already viable as it stands; as a program, it will work, but it won't do much. If we tell Visual Basic to run this program, this window, labeled Click, will appear on the screen. The parts of the window that you already see, including the system menu and maximize and minimize boxes, will all be active.

Visual Basic Properties

The window—that is, the form—that we're designing so far is pretty plain. Right now all we have is a single window named Click; let's start customizing it.Visual Basic treats windows under design—forms—as well as boxes and buttons as *objects*, and each different type of object can have certain *properties*. For example, our *object* named Click has *properties* associated with it that are normal for

NOTE: *If you're familiar with object-oriented programming, then you'll already know that objects such as these not only have data associated with them, but built-in procedures too, which can be used to, say, move a button around the window. In C++, these object-connected procedures are called member functions; in Pascal and Visual Basic they're called methods, and we'll meet them soon.*

The toolbox will play a big part in this book, because it allows us to draw all the controls we'll need. Since we want to draw a text box at this point, select the text box tool—the thirteenth tool down in the toolbox. There are two ways to draw controls in Visual Basic. The first way is to select a tool from the toolbox (click it once). When you do, you can then position the mouse cursor anywhere on the form, click once to anchor that end of the control (the top-left end), then move the pointer to the other end of the control (the bottom left end), and click again; the control appears. The second method, which we'll use more often, is simply to click twice on the tool in the toolbox; when you do, the control you want appears in the center of the form, ready to be moved and shaped.

Since our goal now is to create a text box, click twice on the text box tool. A default-sized text box appears in the middle of the form, as shown in Figure 1-10.

Figure 1-10 Default Text Box

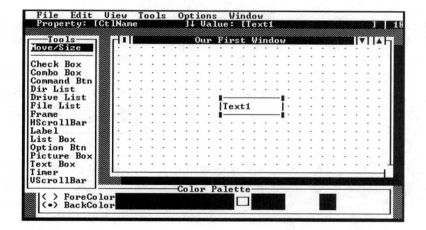

Note that the properties bar now displays CtlName and Text1. The CtlName is the name of a control (i.e., CtlName is a contraction of Control Name), and it's the way we'll refer to it in our program. That is, the CtlName is the name of our control as far as Visual Basic is concerned. In this case, the default name for our text box is Text1. As you can also see, there are four small black squares on the periphery of our new text box. These squares, *sizing handles*, allow you to manipulate the size of the controls that you're designing. Using them, you can stretch a control in any of the four directions. Also, you can move the control itself simply by pressing (and holding) the mouse button down when the mouse cursor is over the control, then dragging it with the mouse.

Move the text box and resize the window until it corresponds roughly to Figure 1-11. Since the text box is selected, the properties bar is ready to display the properties of the text box that we can set. As mentioned above, not all properties associated with an object are available at design time, but we'll find that many useful ones are.

Figure 1-11 Text Box Moved

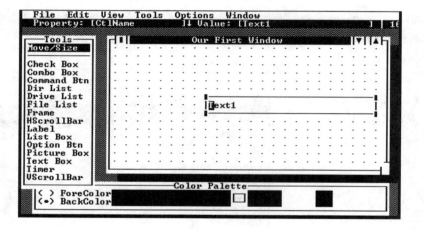

Let's take a look at the properties (i.e., the data items) that we can set for our text box now. Click the arrow to the right of the box in the properties bar marked CtlName, and a list appears, as in Figure 1-12. This list presents all the properties of an object that you can set at design time. You can scroll through to see what's available, such as BackColor (the background color behind the text),FontName, Left, and Top (the position of the top left corner of the text box), Width, and Height. If you select a property such as Width, the current width of the text box appears in the middle box in the properties bar.

Figure 1-12 Properties List

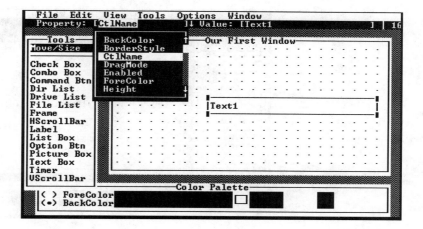

That's how it works; you select a property of the object you're dealing with first, and the current setting of the property appears in the right hand box. The downward pointing arrow in the right-hand box opens up to display a list of all the possible options that you can set the current property to. This way, you don't have to remember long lists of numbers or codes: just select an object, select a property in the leftmost box (from the list provided if you forget what properties are available), and then set the property as you want it to be when your program starts. In fact, if you do check the Width property, you may be surprised to find that your text box has a width of something like 31—which corresponds to 31 screen columns.

We can take advantage of this flexibility to change the text that appears in our text window. Right now, it simply reads Text1, which is not very interesting. Let's change it to read Welcome to Visual Basic. To do that, make sure the textbox is selected (i.e., the sizing handles appear around it),and then move up to the properties bar. Click the down arrow in the first box, the *properties list*. The property we want to change is called Text; find and select it.

When you do, the properties list box displays the wordText, and the box next to it, the *settings box*, displays the current setting of that property which is Text1, as in Figure 1-13.

Figure 1-13 Setting Text in a Text Box

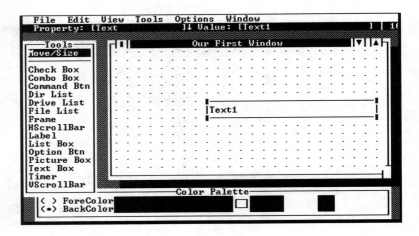

Now just edit the text in the Settings box (i.e.,Text1), changing it to Welcome to Visual Basic. As you type, the text in the text box automatically changes, following each keystroke. Now we've changed a property of the text box—that is, we've changed the text in it from Text1 to Welcome to Visual Basic. This new data becomes part of the object, and, when we make this into a program, this new text will appear in the text box. As we'll see in a few pages, we can also reach the properties of controls like this textbox from our programs. If we were to run our program so far, we'd get something like the window in Figure 1-14.

Figure 1-14 Initialized Text Box

The new text would appear in the text box: Welcome to Visual Basic. That's still not very interesting; let's add a command button now that we can click to display the text in the text box, instead of having the text appear immediately when we run the program.

Command Buttons

C hoose the command button tool in the toolbox. When you double-click this tool, a command button appears in the center of our form, as shown in Figure 1-15. Note that Visual Basic gives it the default CtlName of Command1.

Figure 1-15 Creating Command Buttons

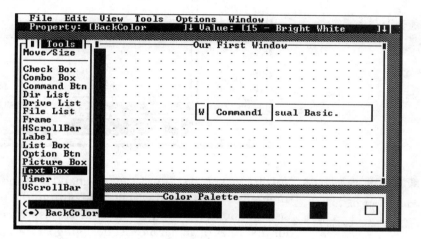

Using the mouse, move the command button to the left side of the form so that it doesn't obscure the text box. Because the command button is selected, the properties bar contains all of its properties that we can work with at design time. As you can see by looking through the properties list, this includes CtlName, the name of this control, Left, Top, Height, and Width as before, FontName and other properties having to do with fonts, and a number of other properties we haven't seen before, such as TabStop (whether or not you can reach this command button using the Tab key on the keyboard), and Index (which will let us coordinate the actions of several buttons by giving

17

them all index numbers). In this case, let's change the caption of this button so that it says Click Me. Just select the Caption property for this command button in the properties bar, and edit the text in the Settings box to Click Me, as shown in Figure 1-16. As you do, Click Me appears on our new command button. Next, erase the text in the text box by selecting it, choosing the Text property in the Properties List box, and deleting all the characters there so that the text box is blank.

Figure 1-16 Click Me Graphic

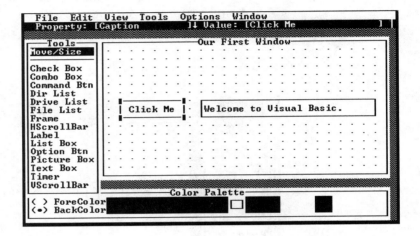

Now we've got to connect the command button to the text box somehow so that when we click the button, the text, Welcome to Visual Basic appears in the text box. This is where we'll start writing our first lines of actual *Basic* code. Our goal is to reach the text property of the text box from inside our program. To do that, we have to know how Visual Basic refers to the properties of the various controls we have in our program. It turns out that if we have a text box whose name (that is, whose CtlName) is Text1, then we can simply refer to the text in it (its Text property) as Text1.Text. In other words, the usual way to refer to a property in a Visual Basic program is Object.Property, where Object is the name of the object—form or control—that has this property, and Property is the name of the property itself.

We should note that it's important not to get a control's caption or some other text confused with its actual control name. The control name is the internal name of that control for a Visual Basic program, and the default control name for our text box is Text1 (a second text box would automatically be named Text2, and so on). You can see this by checking the CtlName property of the text box, as in Figure 1-17.

Figure 1-17 Text Box Control Name

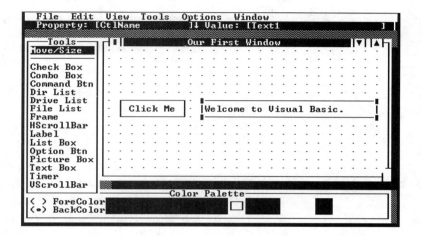

We want to set Text1's Text property in our program, and we can do that in a Visual Basic statement when the Click Me button is pushed like this:

```
Text1.Text = "Welcome to Visual Basic."
```

If we delete the text in the text box at design time, when the program starts, the text box will be empty. When we execute the above statement, however, the text "Welcome to Visual Basic." will appear in it. As you know, our programs are going to be event-driven—that is, broken up into sections specifically written to handle certain events, such as button pushes. This means that we have to connect our single line of code to the correct event; in this case, when the user clicks our command button. To write such code, we have to return to the Programming Environment, which we do by selecting the Event Procedures...item in the Form Designer's Edit menu. A dialog box will open, asking if you want to return to the Programming Environment;

click Yes. A second dialog box will then appear, with the message: "Project or source files have changed. Save them now?" Since we do want to save the changes we've made to our form, Click.Frm, select yes again. When you do, we switch back to the Programming Environment, and the Event Procedures dialog box opens, as shown in Figure 1-18.

Figure 1-18 The Event Procedures Dialog Box

This is the dialog box that we can use to select which event we want to add code for. Note that the available file is Click.Frm, the one we've just saved. The objects in that file (as you can see in the Objects box) are the form itself, a text box named (i.e., CtlName) Text1, and a command button named Command1. Since Form is the object currently highlighted, the Events box shows all possible events we can associate code with the form. Since we want to add code to our command button, click Command1 now and then double-click the top event in the Events box: the Click event. When you do that, the code window appears in the Programming Environment, as shown in Figure 1-19 (the code window contains the line Sub Command1_Click ( ) in it).

Using the Code Window

The code window has a template for every event procedure (i.e., connected with a specific object) that we can write. This is exceptionally handy for two reasons: (1) it will save us some time setting up the outlines of the procedures we want to write; (2) the Code Window indicates what kind of events there are that we can respond to. As you can see in Figure 1-19, this outline is already prepared for us:

```
Sub Command1_Click ()

End Sub
```

Figure 1-19 The Code Window

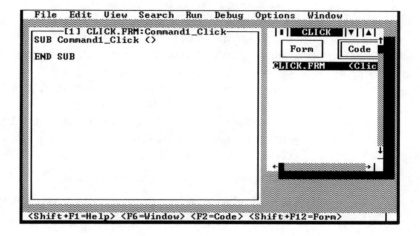

There are two types of procedures in Visual Basic: Sub procedures and Function procedures. The two differ in that function procedures can return values, and Sub procedures cannot, just as in normal Basic. For example, Inkey$ is a popular Basic function (which, incidentally, is not supported in Visual Basic unless you're using graphics, as we'll see); it returns a value that we can check like this:

```
WHILE INKEY$ = "": WEND

PRINT "Hello from Basic."
```

Just as in standard BASIC, Sub procedures and Function procedures take arguments passed to them in Visual Basic:

```
Sub MySub (A As Integer, B As Integer)

    :

    :

End Sub
```

```
Function MyFunc (C As Integer, D As Integer)

    :

    :

End Function
```

We'll see how to set up our own Sub procedures and Functions later, including what kind of data they can handle. For now, however, let's take a look at the Sub procedure that's already set up for us, in outline, in the code window: Command1_Click(). Command1 is the default control name of our command button Click Me (as you can see by checking its CtlName property in the properties bar)—just as the default control name of our text box was Text1, so the default control name of a command button is Command1. The name of the Sub procedure Command1_Click () indicates that this event procedure is connected with button Command1, and that this is the Sub procedure that gets executed when the user clicks that button. In our case, our code is entirely I/O related, and it consists of this single line:

```
Text1.Text = "Welcome to Visual Basic."
```

We can place that line in the Command1_Click Sub procedure like this:

```
Sub Command1_Click ()

    Text1.Text = "Welcome to Visual Basic."

End Sub
```

To do that in Visual Basic, we only have to position the insertion point (in Visual Basic, the place where new text will go is called the insertion point or caret; the term cursor is reserved for the mouse cursor) in the code window, and enter the text as shown in Figure 1-20.

Note that we indented the single code line by pressing the tab key first. While not necessary, it's good programming practice to indent code lines like this, and, when our code gets more complex and includes multiple levels of control, we'll see that indenting helps make the code much easier to understand. That's it as far as the code necessary for Command1_Click() is concerned.

Now we're ready to run; to do so, simply choose the Start option in Visual Basic's Run menu. The window we've been creating appears on the screen along with the command button (labeled Click Me) and the text box (now empty). Just click the button, and the text Welcome to Visual Basic. will appear in the text box, as shown in Figure 1-21. End the program before continuing by clicking Close in our window's System Menu box and then typing any key to return to the Programming Environment.

Figure 1-20 Entering Basic Code

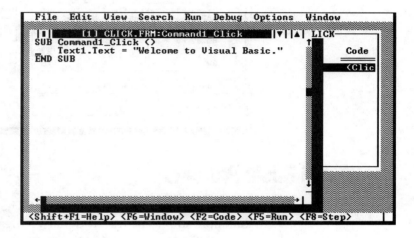

Figure 1-21 Running Our First Program

In fact, we don't need to run our program under Visual Basic; we can make it into a stand-alone Visual Basic application. All we need to do is choose the Make ExeFile... option in Visual Basic's File menu. When you choose this option, a dialog box opens, as shown in Figure 1-22. Click the Make EXE button, and Visual Basic creates a file called Click.Exe, which you can run in DOS directly—and which will produce our fully functioning window. Congratulations; you've created your first complete Visual Basic application.

Figure 1-22 Make Exe File Dialog Box

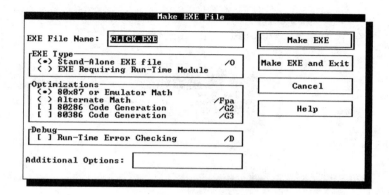

Visual Basic Projects

You may wonder why Visual Basic gave the name Click.Exe to our application. The reason is that VB organizes tasks by *projects*, not by forms, and it took the name from the only form in the current project, Click.Frm. An application can have a number of forms associated with it—i.e., multiple windows—and collecting everything together into a single project wraps it up into one easily managed package. Visual Basic only allows one project to be open at one time, and each project can have three different parts; now that we've run our first program, let's take the time to explore what makes up a Visual Basic project.

Visual Basic Forms

You already know what a form is; it's a window that we design in Visual Basic. Applications usually have at least one form (but it's not technically necessary):

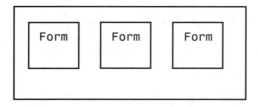

Visual Basic Modules

A Visual Basic *module* is made up of BASIC code—but it's code that's not directly associated with a particular form. The procedures in a module can be reached from anywhere in the application. For example, you might want to define a Sub procedure that sorts data. This procedure is not directly concerned with input or output, but it can be vital to some applications. To avoid the necessity of having all code tied to some form, Visual Basic introduced the idea of a module, which was designed only to hold code. To create a module, as we'll do later, use the New Module... item in Visual Basic's File menu. Usually, larger applications use modules to store procedures that are used throughout the application:

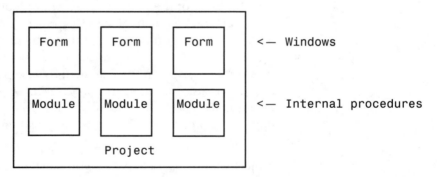

Visual Basic Global Variables

Global variables are shared by the entire application. That is, you can declare variables in BASIC, as well as constants, and you can also define types. Making these declarations global (by declaring the Common Shared keywords) makes them accessible to the rest of the application:

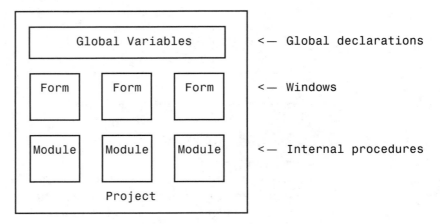

This has a great deal to do with the scope of constants and variables, and we'll put off that discussion until the next chapter, when we discuss what variable types are available.

Using Visual Basic Projects

When you create the first form in a project, Visual Basic uses that name as the name of the project you're working on. When you leave, it will ask you what name to give to the project you've just created, and, unless you tell it otherwise, it will use the name of the first form you created. To work on some project that already exists, you can use the Open Project... item in the File menu. To keep track of the current project, Visual Basic maintains the *project window* (the other window besides the code window in the Programming Environment); the contents of the project window for our application are shown in Figure 1-23.

The project window is useful when you have multiple forms or code modules; here, we only have a single form, so we haven't made much use of it. You might also notice in the project window that our form Click.Frm, is the currently active one; we can jump back and forth between looking at the form itself and looking at the code window (which holds all the code associated with the objects in this project) by choosing the buttons in the project window: Form or Code.

Finally, projects themselves are saved as .Mak files (although the associated .Frm and .Bas files are stored separately). Initially, when you create a new project, including new forms and even modules, Visual Basic doesn't automatically create the corresponding files on disk. Instead, it's up to you to save the files you want (although Visual Basic will prompt you to save files when you leave, if you haven't already done so). Now that we've created our own project, let's make sure that we can save it to disk so that nothing is lost.

Figure 1-23 The Project Window

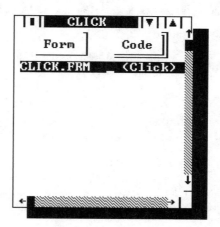

Saving Your Work On Disk

TIP: *If you have BASIC code because you're moving over from QuickBasic or the Microsoft Basic Professional Development ment System, the best two options for importing and checking it are the Load Text... and Save Text... pair.*

There are four different Save items in the Visual Basic menu system: Save Project, Save File, Save File As...,and Save Text.... The Save Project item saves all the files associated with the current project in Visual Basic's binary format on disk (if the project you're working on doesn't have a name yet, Visual Basic asks you for one). In addition, you can use the Save File item to save the currently selected form or module (as opposed to the current project), but you should give it a name before doing so, which you can do with the Save File As... item. This menu item opens a dialog box, and you must specify the name of the file you want to save. Storing files this way makes them inaccessible to you outside Visual Basic, because VB stores them in its own binary format.

However, you might want to edit the code files yourself outside Visual Basic. This is a common thing to do, especially when the code you're writing is long and not directly I/O connected. To do that, use the

Save Text...option. In this case, all the code connected with the object-oriented events you've written, as well as modules (application wide procedures) can be stored as normal text, which is easy to work with and edit.

To save our current project, then, just select Save Project in the File menu and save it as Click.Mak.

Adding More Power to Our Text Box

TIP: *If you don't want the user to change the text that you display on a form, use a label instead; as we'll see, you can write to a label at run time, but the user can't change the displayed text, which means labels can act as read-only textboxes.*

Before we finish with our first application, you might notice that, since the text (Welcome to Visual Basic.) appears in a text box, the user is actually free to edit it, even after we've displayed our message (this corresponds to a normal text box in Windows). However, we can modify our program so that we're appraised if any change is made to the text; it turns out that changing the text in a text box is one of the events we can write code for.

When the text in a text box is edited, a text box change event occurs. Because our text box is named Text1, this event will be called Text1_Change(). We can intercept that change by selecting Event Procedures... from the Edit menu of the Programming Environment (both the Programming Environment and the Form Designer have an Event Procedures...item in their Edit menus, but Event Procedures... in the Form Designer will only switch you back to the Programming Environment). Once again, the Event Procedures dialog box opens, as shown in Figure 1-18. This time, we can select Text1 in the Objects: box, and then double click Change in the Events box. The code window for the text box opens up, as shown in Figure 1-19. The text change event procedure appears in the code window, like this:

```
Sub Text1_Change()

End Sub
```

TIP: *Keep in mind that if you want to make a change in the form's appearance itself, you can click the Form button in the project window to switch back to the Form Designer.*

If the text is edited, a text box change event is generated, and we might want to allow the user the option of restoring it to the original welcome message. We can do that by changing the caption of the command button from Click Me to, say, Restore Msg. This is easy because the caption of the command button is simply a property of the command button, which we can reach from our program. In particular, since the button's control name is Command1, we can simply make this Visual Basic assignment: Command1.Caption = "Restore Msg", where we assign the string Restore Msg to the caption property of the button. We do that by making this change to the Sub procedure Text1_Change():

```
Sub Text1_Change()

    Command1.Caption = "Restore Msg"

End Sub
```

Now, when we run the program, the usual window appears, along with the Click Me button and the empty text window. However, as soon as the user changes the text in the text box, the caption of the button changes to Restore Msg, as shown in Figure 1-24, indicating that the original message can be restored by pressing this button.

Figure 1-24 Restore Msg Button

That's it for this chapter; in it, we've gotten many of the essentials of Visual Basic down, including the terms form, control, object, module, project, and others. And we've put our first working Visual Basic application together. In the next chapter, we'll start to dig into Visual Basic in more depth; in particular, we'll explore all there is to know about two of its most popular objects—in fact, two objects that we've already been introduced to: buttons and text boxes.

Using Buttons and Textboxes

Two of the most common Visual Basic controls are text boxes and buttons. In fact, we've already used both of these controls in the first chapter. Text boxes are the important text I/O controls in Visual Basic, and buttons are one of the chief command I/O controls (the other being, of course, menus, which we'll see in Chapter 3). For those reasons, we'll see how to use both text and buttons in this chapter in some depth.

It's important to realize that text boxes are the primary means of character string input in Visual Basic, and that means that they take the place of the standard Basic instructions Inkey$, Line Input, Input$, and Input (except in graphics mode, as we'll see). Here, we have to use the Visual Basic method of reading text, which is with text boxes. The user will be able to type character input into our text boxes for our program to read. In addition, they are a primary means of character string output, which means they can take the place of other Basic instructions such as Print or Print Using. Given this importance to both user character input and output, they make up one of the first topics we should cover in this book.

The whole idea of text I/O—that is, character string input and output—brings us closer to the heart of programming in Visual Basic; that is, to understand handling text, and how to display data from our programs, we'll have to examine how to store it in the first place. That will bring us to the topic of variables. In fact, our first application in this chapter will be a simple calculator that operates in its own window so that we can learn how to accept and display numeric values in text boxes.

It turns out that text boxes also have some fairly advanced capabilities that we should look into as well: for example, we can set up text boxes with more than one line—what VB calls multiline text boxes—which include word wrap and scroll bars, and we can also retrieve specific text that the user has marked. Later on, in our file handling chapter, we'll put together a small file editing program, and we can get that started here by writing a notepad application that takes keystrokes and lets you store text. That's the plan for this chapter, then: handling all kinds of character string input and output with text boxes and getting commands from the user with command buttons. Let's begin the chapter now with our calculator example.

A Calculator Example

Our calculator is going to be remarkably simple, since we're focusing on text boxes and not on how to write larger applications. We'll just have two text boxes, one for the first operand and one for the second, a button marked with an equals sign, and a text box to hold the result of adding the two operands together. When the user clicks the equals button, the result of the addition will appear in the result text box.

To begin, start Visual Basic and switch to the Form Designer by selecting New Form.in the Programming Environment's File menu. When Visual Basic asks you for a name for this new form, call it Calc.Frm. Next, change the caption property of the form (which now reads Calc) to Calculator by editing its Caption property in the properties bar.

Now choose (that is, double-click) the text box tool. A text box appears in the center of the form; move it up to the top of the form and change its control name (CtlName in the properties bar) to Operand1. In addition, remove the text in it (which is now Text1) by editing its Text property, as shown in Figure 2-1.

This text box, Operand1, is going to receive the first operand; the next text box will receive the second, then there will be a button marked with an equals sign, and a result text box. For simplicity's sake, this calculator will only perform addition, adding Operand1 + Operand2 to get a result, but it's a simple matter to add buttons for subtraction, multiplication, and division if you want.

Figure 2-1 Calculator Form

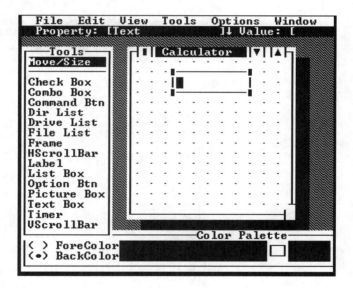

Next, double click the text box tool again, and place the second text box under the first one, changing its CtlName to Operand2 and clearing the text in it, as shown in Figure 2-2 (note that VB gives it the default CtlName Text1 just as it did for the first text box, since we've renamed the first box Operand1). Now place a command button under the two boxes, and give it an equals sign for a caption. Finally, place one last text box under the command button, and give it a control name of Result, as shown in Figure 2-3.

Figure 2-2 Calculator with Second Text Box

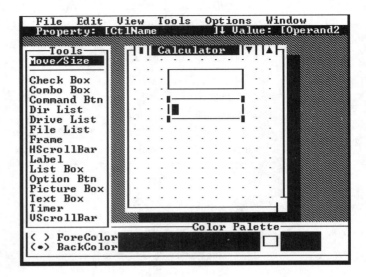

Figure 2-3 Calculator Template

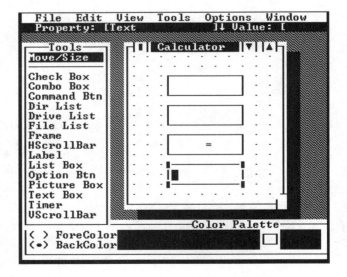

There is one last thing to do, and we will have designed the calculator's appearance completely; add a plus sign, +, in front of the second text box (Operand2) to indicate what operation we're performing, like this:

TIP: *While labels often appear only as text, you can also put a box around them, making them look just like a text box. You do that by setting the BorderStyle option to 1 (recall that all possible settings for a property are displayed in the settings box in the properties bar). However, you should note that it's only possible to set the value of this property at design time; that is, a program cannot add or remove a label's border at run time.*

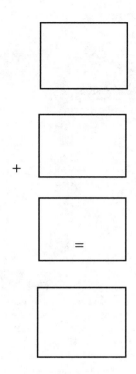

To do that, we can place a *label* on the form.

Visual Basic Labels

Labels are usually used, as their name implies, to label other controls on a form. Although your program can change the text in a label by referring to its caption property, the user cannot.

The label we want to add to our calculator is very simple—only a plus sign. We can do that by choosing the label tool, which is the ninth down in the toolbox. A label appears in the middle of the form; change its caption property from "Label1" to "+" in the properties bar, and move it next to the Operand2 text box, as shown in Figure 2-4.

Now the calculator template is complete; all that remains is to write the code. The action here is simple; when the user clicks the command button (the bottom text box). However, to do this poses a problem: so far, we've only dealt with text in text boxes. How do we interpret the text as a number? For that matter, how do we display numbers? And how do we store them in our program?

Figure 2-4 Completed Calculator Template

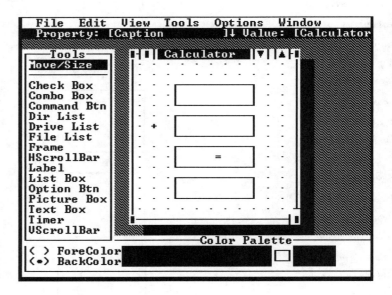

This is going to be very important for us: how can we manipulate the input we recieve from the user in our text boxes, especially if that input is supposed to represent numbers and not just text? In other words, our job now is to translate the text in the text boxes Operand1 and Operand2 into numbers, add them in our program, and then display the results. And all this internal handling of data brings up our next topic, variables, which we'll need to explore before proceeding.

Variables in Visual Basic

The types of variables Visual Basic uses are much like the variables in QuickBasic, or in the Microsoft Basic Professional Development System. Like those compilers, variable names can be up to 40 characters long (including letters, numbers, and underscores), and they have only two naming rules: the first character must be a letter (so VB doesn't assume this is a numeric value), and we cannot use VB reserved words (such as Sub or Function) as variable names. The data types that are built into Visual Basic are shown in Table 2-1, along with their ranges of allowed values.

Table 2-1 Visual Basic Data Types

Type	Number of bytes	Character	Range
Integer	2	%	–32,768 to 32,767
Long	4	&	–2,147,483 to 2,147,483,647
Single	4	!	–3.37E+38 to 3.37E+38
Double	8	#	–1.67D+308 to 1.67D+308
Currency	8	@	–9.22E+14 to 9.22E+14
String	varies	$	[Not applicable]

Type Conventions for Variables

If you're a QuickBasic user, you might have not seen the currency type before. Although originally designed to hold the currency values, it's attractive for other reasons as well—it stores numbers with fifteen-place accuracy to the left of the decimal place, and four places to the right. These numbers are fixed-point numbers; that is, they always have four places to the left of the decimal point.

Like other Basic compilers, there are certain characters (e.g., !, or %, as indicated in Table 2-1) that you can use to indicate what type of variable you intend when you first use it. For example, if you want to use an integer value named the_int, you can indicate to VB that the_int is an integer by adding a % character to the end of it like this: the_int%. Similarly, if you want to use a single precision floating-point number called the_float, you can call it the_float!. In fact, you can even leave it as the_float, since the default type for variables is single in Visual Basic (as it is in QuickBasic and the Basic Professional Development System).

In fact, there are two ways of indicating to Visual Basic that you want to use a certain name as a variable name. The first is simply to use the name where you want it, like this:

```
the_int% = 5
```

If Visual Basic hasn't seen the_int% before, this becomes an *implicit declaration*. As we've seen, the last character of the variable can determine the variable's type; if the last character is not a special type-declaration character (i.e., %, &, !, #, @, or $), then the default type is single.

The other way (and more proper from a programming point of view) is to use the Dim statement to specifically declare a variable at the beginning of a procedure. Here are some examples:

```
Dim the_int As Integer
Dim the_double As Double
Dim the_variable_string As String
Dim the_fixed_string As String * 20
```

Note in particular the last two variables, the_variable_string and the_fixed_string. The first one, the_variable_string, is a string with variable length (up to 65,535 characters in Visual Basic), and the second one is explictly declared as fixed length by adding "* 20" to the end of the declaration, which makes it a string of exactly 20 characters, just as in other Basic compilers. (We'll take a closer look at strings later in this chapter, when we deal with the built-in string statements and functions in Visual Basic.)

There are several places to put such declaractions, and the placement of a variable's declaration affects the variable's *scope*—which refers to the portion of the program that the variable is visible to. Let's look into that next, and then we'll be ready to complete our calculator example.

Scope of Variables in Visual Basic

As mentioned, a variable's scope refers to the regions in the application that can access it. It turns out that there are four different levels of variable scope, because there are four different places to declare variables.

The first place to declare variables, either with the Dim statement or implicitly (i.e., just by using it), is at the procedure level. There are two kinds of procedures in Visual Basic, the Sub procedures and Function procedures, and each can have variable declarations in them. When you declare a variable in a procedure, however, that variable is *local* to that procedure; in other words, its scope is restricted to the procedure in which it's declared. Such variables are called *local variables* in Visual Basic:

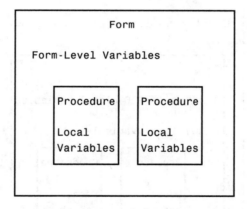

TIP: You can, however, make local variables permanent by declaring them static. Visual Basic will not reinitialize a static variable at any time. To make a variable static, declare it with the keyword Static instead of Dim (e.g., Static the_int As Integer).

One important note is that local variables don't outlast the procedure they're defined in; that is, every time you enter the procedure, the local variables are reinitialized. In other words, don't count on retaining the value in a local variable between procedure calls.

The next two places where you declare variables are at the form and module levels (recall that a module can hold the general, non-I/O code associated with an application). If you declare a form-level variable, that variable is accessible to all procedures in that form. The same goes for code modules. If you declare a module-level variable, that variable is accessible to all procedures in that module:

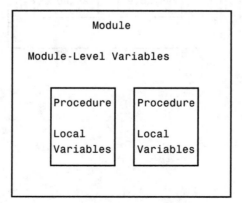

In particular, you might notice that this lets you share information between procedures. The way to declare a variable at the form or module level is to place it into the declarations part of the general object that we saw before, in the code window (we'll see this later). And, the way you create new modules is simply by selecting the New Module... item in Visual Basic's File menu (as we'll also see later). These new variables are static variables by default—that is, although procedure level variables are reinitialized each time the procedure is entered, variables at the form and module (and global variables as well) are static. The final level, of course, is the global level. Every procedure or line of code in an application has access to these variables (i.e., these variables are application-wide). To make a variable global, we have to use the COMMON SHARED statement to declare variables (COMMON SHARED must appear in the declarations part of each module and form):

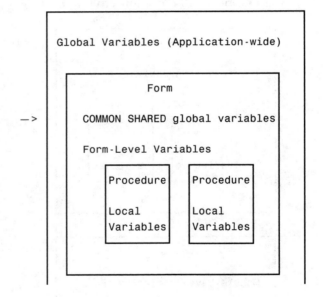

```
|-----------------------------------------------|
|                                               |
|   |-------------------------------------|     |
|   |             Module                  |     |
|   |                                     |     |
|-->|   COMMON SHARED global variables    |     |
|   |                                     |     |
|   |   Module-Level Variables            |     |
|   |                                     |     |
|   |   |-----------|  |-----------|      |     |
|   |   |Procedure  |  |Procedure  |      |     |
|   |   |           |  |           |      |     |
|   |   |Local      |  |Local      |      |     |
|   |   |Variables  |  |Variables  |      |     |
|   |   |-----------|  |-----------|      |     |
|   |                                     |     |
|   |-------------------------------------|     |
|                                               |
|-----------------------------------------------|
```

In general, there are six statements for declaring variables in Visual Basic for DOS. Using these statements, we can declare variables at the four possible levels: the procedure, form, module, or global levels:

DIM	Local variables
DIM SHARED	Variable is shared between the module where it is declared and any sub procedures in the module
SHARED	Like DIM SHARED, except that duplicate SHARED statements must appear in the declaration section of each procedure in a module
COMMON	Variable is shared between multiple modules at the module level (only). Duplicate COMMON statements must appear in each module you want to use the variable in
COMMON SHARED	Global variable. Shared between a number of modules and all their procedures

$FORM	For form properties only; allows you to share form properties between multiple modules. Added automatically by Visual Basic.

In our case, in our calculator example we'll be able to use procedure level (i.e., local) variables. Let's get back to that application now.

Storing the Calculator's Data

I f we wish, we can store the calculator's data—that is, the numbers typed by the user and the result—as single precision numbers. The way we've designed things, all action takes place when the user clicks the = button. Let's take a look at that procedure. To do that, select Event Procedures... in the Form Designer's Edit menu, switching back to the Programming Environment (clicking Yes when VB asks if you want to save the changes we've made to Calc.Frm). The Event Procedures dialog box appears in the Programming Environment; click our = button's CtlName, Command1, in the Objects: box, and select its Click event in the Events: box. This brings up the code window and displays the Sub procedure for a click event associated with our = button, Command1:

```
Sub Command1_Click()
End Sub
```

So far, there's nothing in this procedure. Let's begin by reading the text in the text box Operand1 (i.e., Operand1.Text) and storing it in a single precision variable named Op1 which we can declare like this:

```
Sub Command1_Click()
    Dim Op1 As Single
        :
End Sub
```

To convert the text Operand1.Text into a number, Visual Basic provides the Val( ) function, which works like this:

```
Sub Command1_Click()
    Dim Op1 As Single
—>  Op1 = Val(Operand1.Text)

        :

End Sub
```

Val( ) will take a string and, starting from the left and working towards the right, convert as much of it as it can into a numeric value (if it reaches illegal characters, it simply stops converting the text into a number). Next, we do the same for Operand2, calling the resulting variable Op2:

```
      Sub Command1_Click()
            Dim Op1 As Single
 —>         Dim Op2 As Single

            Op1 = Val(Operand1.Text)
 —>         Op2 = Val(Operand2.Text)
                :

      End Sub
```

Besides the Val( ) function, Visual Basic also has the Str$( ) function, which goes the other way, converting a number into a text string. In other words, we can add the two numbers and display the results in Result.Text like this:

```
      Sub Command1_Click()
            Dim Op1 As Single
            Dim Op2 As Single

            Op1 = Val(Operand1.Text)
            Op2 = Val(Operand2.Text)

 —>         Result.Text = Str$(Op1 + Op2)
      End Sub
```

And that's all the code we'll need; our calculator is ready (if not powerful). Just select the Start item in the Run menu, and the calculator will function, as in Figure 2-5. You can type in floating point numbers for the first two operands, and, when you click the = button, the two will be added (it might even be a good idea to make the Result text window into a label so that the user can't modify it). In fact, the user can even modify the two operands after typing them (i.e., to correct mistakes), since we're using text boxes.

At this point, it's a good idea to save our whole project in case we want to work on it later; do that with the Save Project item in the File menu. Visual Basic will suggest a name of Calc.Mak for the project file; click OK.

Figure 2-5 Calculator Running

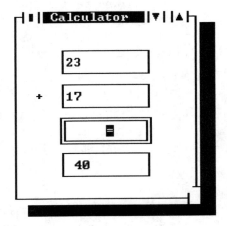

As is usual in Visual Basic, the user can switch from text box to text box in our calculator by pressing Tab (not Enter), in addition to using the mouse. However this includes the Result box—that is, the user can tab to the result box. Since that's not convenient for data entry, one change we might make to the program is to make sure that the Tab key will not move the *focus* to the Result box. When a control has the insertion point in Visual Basic, it's called having the focus. The way to make sure that the Result box no longer gets the focus by tabbing around the text boxes is to set its TabStop property to False (the default for text boxes and command buttons is True).

We can do that by selecting the TabStop property for the Result text box in the properties bar and by setting it to False, as in Figure 2-6 (note that the two options offered by the settings list are True or False, so the choice is easy).

There's one more change that we might make here—which will also indicate another capability of command buttons. Since the user won't use the Enter key for anything else here, we can make the equals button the *default button*. In other words, when the user presses the Enter key, it will be the same as clicking the equals button. As is standard in Visual Basic for DOS, the default button is surrounded by a double black border so that the user knows exactly which button is the default.

Figure 2-6 The TabStop Property

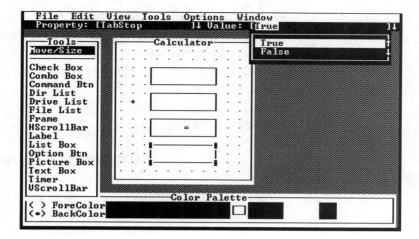

We can make the equals button into the default button simply by setting its Default value to True at design time, as in Figure 2-7. Now when the user runs the program, the equals button may be selected simply by pressing the Enter key.

Figure 2-7 Calculator Button Design

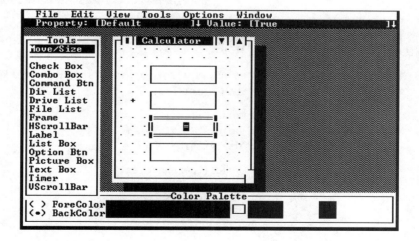

The full version of the calculator, then—complete with the default equals button (note the double black border)—appears in Figure 2-8. We've made a good deal of progress as far as numeric I/O is concerned, but there's more that follows. In particular, since text boxes are so important for displaying data (in addition to reading it), and since this is our text box chapter, we should explore some of that added capability next.

Figure 2-8 Calculator Application

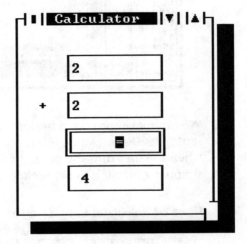

Formatting Text

As we've seen, one way to display numbers as text in a text box is to use the Str$( ) function:

```
Sub Command1_Click()
    Dim Op1 As Single
    Dim Op2 As Single

    Op1 = Val(Operand1.Text)
    Op2 = Val(Operand2.Text)

—>     Result.Text = Str$(Op1 + Op2)
End Sub
```

Here, we set the Text property of the Result object to Str$(Op1 + Op2). The Str$( ) does a good job of formatting numeric data in most cases;

that is, it adds a space before and after the number it is to print out, and it even handles floating point numbers (i.e., if numbers get too big, it will print them out with an exponent, such as: 1.2E+07). However, this is essentially unformatted output—we have no real control over the format of the text in our Result text box.

To give us more control, Visual Basic includes the Format$( ) function. With Format$( ), we can indicate the number of decimal places that a number must have, the number of leading or trailing zeros, as well as the capability of formatting currency values. The way to use Format$( ) is as follows (the square brackets indicate that the format string is optional):

```
text$ = Format$(number [, format_string$])
```

The format string here can be made up of any of the characters in Table 2-2. Let's take a look at some examples like this to get an idea of how Format$( ) works:

```
Format$(1234.56, "######.#")    =    1234.5
Format$(1234.56, "00000.000")   =    01234.560
Format$(1234.56, "###,###.0")   =    1,234.56
Format$(1234.56, "$#,000.00)    =    $1,234.56
```

As you can see, the # symbol is a placeholder, telling Format$( ) how many places you want to retain to around the decimal point. The 0 symbol acts the same way, except that if there is no actual digit to be displayed at the corresponding location, a 0 is printed. In addition, you can specify other characters, such as $ or commas to separate thousands.

Table 2-2 Format String Characters

Character	Means
0	Digit placeholder; print a digit or a 0 at this place
#	Digit placeholder; do not print leading or
.	Decimal placeholder; indicates position of the decimal point
,	Thousands separator
-+$( )Space	A literal character—displayed literally

Let's add thousands of separators to our calculator. We can do that simply by changing the Str$( ) statement to a Format$( ) statement like this:

```
Sub Command1_Click()
    Dim Op1 As Single
    Dim Op2 As Single

    Op1 = Val(Operand1.Text)
    Op2 = Val(Operand2.Text)

    Result.Text = Format$(Op1 + Op2, "###,###,###.#####")
End Sub
```

To use Format$, however, we must also load in the Quick Library dtfmt.qlb, and we do that when we first start Visual Basic for DOS by using the /L (Library) switch; that is, we add these characters to the command line when we first start Visual Basic for DOS: "/L dtfmt.qlb". Now when we run the program, the resulting change to the calculator is shown in Figure 2-9.

Figure 2-9 Calculator with Thousands Separator

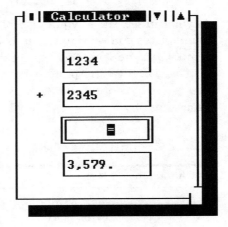

Displaying Date and Time

Visual Basic also makes it easy to display the time and date with the Format$( ) function. In fact, we can use the function named Now to return the current time and date in numeric form, and use Format$( )

to display that date and time. In this case, we can use special formatting characters: h, m, s and m, d, y. Format$( ) is capable of producing text strings from Now in many different ways, depending on how you use these characters, and how many you use. Here are some examples:

```
Format$(Now, "m-d-yy")                   ="4-5-92"
Format$(Now, "m/d/y")                    ="4/5/92"
Format$(Now, "mm/dd/yy")                 ="04/05/92"
Format$(Now, "ddd, mmmm d, yyyy")        ="Thu, April 5, 1992"
Format$(Now, "dddd, mmmm d, yyyy")       ="Thursday, April 5, 1992"
Format$(Now, "d mmm, yyyy")              ="5 Apr, 1992"
Format$(Now, "hh:mm:ss mm/dd/yy")        ="16:00:00 04/05/92"
Format$(Now, "hh:mm:ss AM/PM mm-dd-yy")  ="4:00:00 PM 04-05-92"
```

As you can see, there is a variety of formats available. In fact, if you use "ddddd" for the day and "ttttt" for the time, you will get the day and time in an appropriate format for the country that the computer is in (as set in the Visual Basic control panel). For example, Format$(Now, "ttttt ddddd") might be "4:00:00 PM 04-05-93" in the United States, but in some European countries, it would be "93-04-05 16.00.00".

At this point, we've had a good introduction to the use of text boxes and control buttons with our calculator, but we can move on to even more powerful applications. For example, our next project is to build a windowed notepad, complete with text boxes that include scroll bars.

A Notepad Example Complete with Cut and Paste

Putting together a functioning notepad application might be easier than you think in Visual Basic. In fact, a notepad is really just a multiline text box—and VB supports multiline text boxes automatically. To see how this works, start Visual Basic (or, if you're already in Visual Basic, select New Project from the File menu) and create a new form (using the New Form... item in the File menu) with the name Pad.Frm. A form labeled Pad appears in the Form Designer.

To produce our multiline text box, simply double-click the text box tool and stretch the resulting text box until it takes up most of the form (leaving room for a row of buttons at the bottom), as shown in Figure 2-10. Now find the Multiline property in the properties bar; there are two settings allowed for this property, as indicated by the settings list (which drops down from the arrow next to the settings box): True and False. The default is False, which means that textboxes can only handle a single line of text. Set this property to True, which gives our pad multiline capability.

Figure 2-10 Pad Prototype

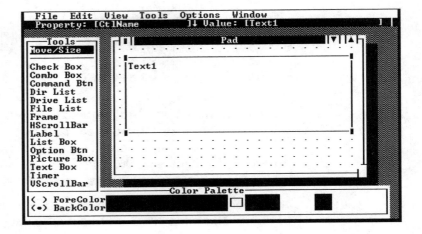

At this point, our pad is already functional; just delete the text in the text box (i.e., "Text1") using the properties bar, and run the program (switch back to the Programming Environment by selecting Event Procedures..., and select Start from the Run menu). The pad appears, as in Figure 2-11, and you can write in it. In fact, it comes complete with word wrap—when you get to the end of a line, the current word gets "wrapped" whole to the next line instead of being broken in the middle.

However, there's a great deal more that we can do here; for example, we can add a vertical scroll bar to the text box just by changing its Scrollbars property. In fact, we can add horizontal scroll bars as well, but if you add horizontal scroll bars to a multiline text box, word wrap is automatically turned off, so we won't. Unlike the scroll bars that we'll see later in this book, multiline text box scroll bars are managed entirely by Visual Basic. And adding them is easy; to add vertical scroll bars, just find the Scrollbars property in the properties bar.

Figure 2-11 Pad at Run Time

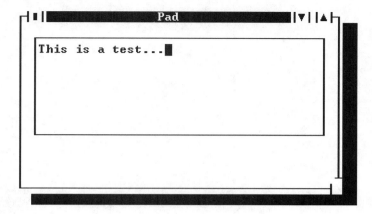

The settings list indicates what's available—horizontal scroll bars, vertical scroll bars, or both, as indicated in Figure 2-12. To add vertical scroll bars to the text box in our notepad, just select the Vertical option, and a vertical scroll bar appears as in Figure 2-13. Now we can scroll through a much larger document in our new notepad—up to 64K in fact, which is the maximum length of strings in Visual Basic. So far, all we've done has been quite easy, so let's press on and add more capabilities to the pad; specifically, let's add cut and paste, where the user can select text, cut it, and paste it back in somewhere else.

Figure 2-12 Scroll Bar Options

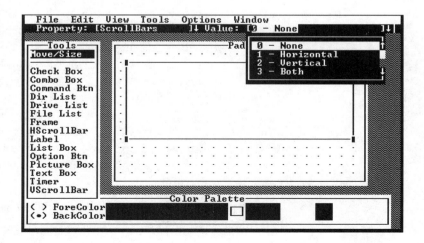

Figure 2-13 Pad with Vertical Scroll Bar

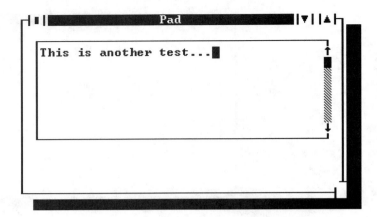

Using Selected Text in Text Boxes

As is usual for a text box, the user can mark, or select text in Visual Basic text boxes; for example, they can simply place the (mouse) cursor at some location, hold down the left button, move the cursor to another location, and release it. In that case, the text between the two points is automatically highlighted—i.e., Visual Basic has already given this capability to our text boxes. We already know that we can refer to the text in a text box as, say, the_text.Text (i.e., the_text is the name we gave to the text box control), but how can we refer to selected text?

It turns out that this is also easy under Visual Basic. There are three properties associated with text boxes that keep track of selected text for us: SelStart, SelLength, and SelText. The first of these, SelStart, is the location in the the_text.Text string at which the selected string starts. If there is no text selected (which you can check with the next property, SelLength), this property indicates where the insertion point is. If SelStart is 0, the selected text starts just before the first character in the text box; if SelStart is equal to the length of the text in the text box, then it's indicating a position just after the last character in the text box. Note that SelStart is a long integer (because it has to be able to handle numbers up to 64K).

The next property, SelLength, is also a long integer, and it indicates the number of characters that are selected. Finally, SelText is a string that contains the selected characters from the text box (if there are no characters selected, this is the empty string, ""). In fact, your program can set these properties at run time (e.g., SelStart = 0 : SelLength = 5 would highlight the first five characters).

We'll use these properties to add cutting and pasting capablities to our notepad by adding some command buttons. In particular, we can add three specific functions: Clear All, which deletes everything in the notepad's text box; Cut, which cuts the selected text; and Paste, which pastes the selected text at the insertion point.

TIP: *If you change the name of a control part way through the design process, you should know that Visual Basic does not go through your code and change the names of the procedures you've already written to match—you're responsible for doing that.*

The first button, Clear All, is easy; all we have to do is set the Text property of the text box to the empty string, "". To start, let's change the name of the pad's text box to PadText in the properties bar. (We'll find as programs get longer and longer that it's advisable to end an object's name with an indication of what type of object it is.) Next, add a command button with the caption "Clear All" and the name (i.e., CtlName) ClearButton. Position the button in the lower right-hand corner of the form and switch to the Programming Environment, opening the Click procedure for the button in the Event Procedures dialog box. The code window opens, displaying a template for that event (i.e., ClearButton_Click( )). Now add this line:

```
Sub ClearButton_Click()
    PadText.Text = ""
End Sub
```

— >

Now you can run the program; when you do, the button becomes active, and clicking it deletes the text in the text box. However, once you've selected an object in Visual Basic—by clicking it, for example—the focus (i.e., the active control, and the location of the insertion point) is transferred to that object. This is always the default action in Visual Basic—if you click on an object, that object gets the focus. In our case, that means that the Clear All button retains the focus even after clearing the pad (and it is surrounded by a double border to indicate that it still has the focus). To get back to the pad, the user has to press the Tab key or click on the text window, which seems less than professional.

We can fix that problem, however, with the SetFocus *method*. Programmers familiar with object oriented languages know that there are two types of programming constructions that you can associate with an object—both data and procedures. In Visual Basic, an object's data items are referred to as properties, and the procedures connected with it are called its methods. What concerns us here is the SetFocus method that is built into most controls. With it, we can give the focus back to the text box simply with the statement PadText.SetFocus.

You refer to methods the same way you refer to properties—with the dot (.) operator. (Later on, we'll see that some methods take arguments.) When we transfer the focus back to the text box, the insertion point appears there again and starts blinking. Here's how ClearButton_Click( ) should look:

```
Sub ClearButton_Click()
    PadText.Text = ""
—>    PadText.SetFocus
End Sub
```

That's all there is to it; your pad should now look like the one in Figure 2-14. Now, let's move on to cutting selected text in a text box.

Figure 2-14 Pad with Clear All Button

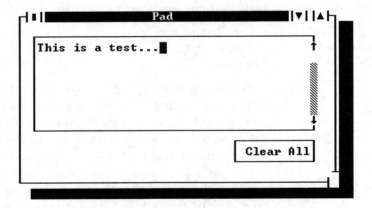

How to Cut Selected Text

To start the process of cutting text, add another command button in the lower left corner of the form—which we can name CutButton—and give it the caption Cut. When the user presses this button, they want the text that is selected in the text box to be cut; actually, we'll place it into a temporary buffer so that we can paste it later if required. Let's begin by creating this temporary buffer, which should itself be a String type, and which we can call CutText. Since we want both the Cut and Paste procedures to have access to this buffer, let's make CutText a form-level variable, making it accessible from all parts of our form (i.e., all procedures in it).

To make a form-level declaration, click the Code button in the Project Window and the Code dialog box appears, displaying the name of the procedure we've already written: ClearButton_Click( ). (If you want to see all available procedures, select the Event Procedures... item in the Programming Environment's Edit menu instead.) In addition, the name of our form, PAD.FRM, also appears. To declare a form-level variable, we need to click the form itself, PAD.FRM. When we do, the code window displays PAD.FRM. This is the declarations area of the form; add the following line there, as shown in Figure 2-15:

Dim Shared CutText As String

Figure 2-15 Pad's Form-level Variables

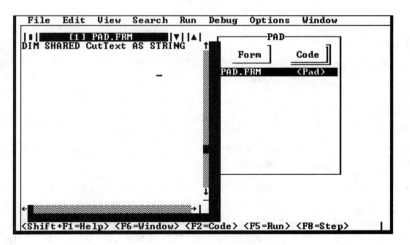

Using Dim Shared shares CutText among all of pad's procedures (we could have used Shared Cutext As String instead, but then we'd have to repeat that declaration in each procedure as well). Now that our buffer, CutText, is ready, we are prepared to cut the string itself in the pad's text box. Before we do, however, we should save the selected text in the CutText string. Open this Sub procedure template in the code window (i.e., select the Event Procedures... menu item and select CutButton's Click event):

```
Sub CutButton_Click()

End Sub
```

Then save the cut text like this:

```
Sub CutButton_Click()
    CutText = PadText.SelText
        :
End Sub
```

The next step is to cut the selected string itself. That turns out to be surprisingly easy; all we have to do is to replace PadText.SetText, the selected text, with an empty string, "" (if no text was selected, no text is cut) like this:

```
Sub CutButton_Click()
    CutText = PadText.SelText
—>  PadText.SelText = ""
        :
End Sub
```

Finally, we give the focus back to the text window using the SetFocus method:

```
Sub CutButton_Click()
CutText = PadText.SelText
    PadText.SelText = ""
—>     PadText.SetFocus
End Sub
```

That's it; the Cut button is now functional. At this point, you can make a stand-alone application out of our pad by choosing the Make Exe File... item in the File menu; when you run Pad.Exe under DOS, the pad appears. When the user selects text, they can cut it with the Cut button. However, that's only half the story of a full notepad application; the next step is to allow the user to paste the text back in.

This can happen in two ways. First, the user can select some additional text in the text box, and when they paste, we're supposed to paste over that text. Second, the user might simply position the insertion point at a particular location, and then we're supposed to insert the text there.

As it happens, Visual Basic takes care of these two cases almost automatically.

To begin, we'll have to introduce another button, which we can call PasteButton, and which we might give the caption Paste. Place this button in between the other two, and open its Click event in the code window, PasteButton_Click( ).All we have to do here is to replace the selected text in the text window, PadText.SelText, with CutText (the global string that holds the cut text). Visual Basic handles the details: if there is some text selected, it is replaced with CutText; if no text was selected, then CutText is inserted at the insertion point, exactly as it should be. Here's the code for PasteButton_Click( ) (note that we return the focus to the text box here, too):

```
Sub PasteButton_Click()
    PadText.SelText = CutText
    PadText.SetFocus
End Sub
```

We're almost done with the Paste button; the working pad application so far appears in Figure 2-16. However, there are still a few problems; one is that when the application is first started, there's nothing to paste yet, but the Paste button can still be pushed. Even though it does nothing, it would be better still if we could gray the button caption out—that is, disable the Paste button in the standard Visual Basic fashion before there is something to paste.

Figure 2-16 Pad Application with Paste Button

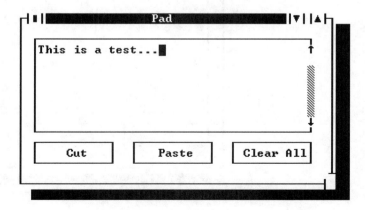

In fact, we can do this too. One of the properties associated with a command button is the Enabled property. When set to True, the button is enabled and can be clicked; when set to False, the button does not respond to the user, and its caption is grayed. We can take advantage of this immediately. First, set the Enabled property of the Paste button to False in the properties bar. We want to enable this button only when text has been placed in the CutText buffer. Since that's only done when the Cut button has been clicked, we can simply add a line to CutButton_Clicked( ) like this:

```
Sub CutButton_Click()
    CutText = PadText.SelText
    PadText.SelText = ""
—>  PasteButton.Enabled = -1 'Set to True
    PadText.SetFocus
End Sub
```

You might be suprised to learn that True has a value of –1 in Visual Basic. That's because in Visual Basic (as in most computer programs), True is stored as the integer &HFFFF, which equals 1111111111111111 in binary—all ones, the exact opposite of 0, which is False. Now, when you start the application, the pad appears as in Figure 2-17, with the Paste button grayed and disabled. However, as soon as you cut some text with the Cut button, Paste becomes active once again.

Figure 2-17 Pad with Paste Button Grayed

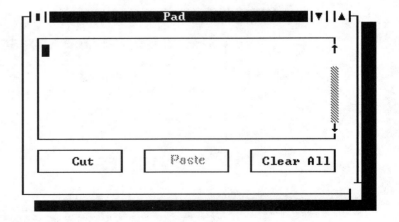

Loading CONSTANT.BI

We set PasteButton.Enabled to –1, which is the value Visual Basic uses for True. On the other hand, the constant True is defined in the file CONSTANT.BI already, and we can simply load that file into our form declarations (as we'll do throughout the book). To do that, open the form declarations by clicking the Code button in the Project Window and by clicking PAD.FRM as before. We already have declared CutText here:

```
Dim Shared CutText As String
```

Now we include CONSTANT.BI as well to get the definition of many constants, including True (= –1) and False (= 0) with the include *metacommand*::

```
    Dim Shared CutText As String
—>    ' $include: 'constant.bi"
```

The quotation mark (') is important here; all metacommands (which begin with $) must be preceded by either a single quotation mark and a space, or the word REM and a space (using ' or REM is also the way to precede comments—i.e., remarks that Visual Basic doesn't read). Now we're free to use the constant True instead of –1, like this:

```
    Sub CutButton_Click()
        CutText = PadText.SelText
        PadText.SelText = ""
—>      PasteButton.Enabled = True
        PadText.SetFocus
    End Sub
```

In fact, since we've gone this far, we might as well enable the Cut and Clear All buttons only when it makes sense. In particular, we can enable these buttons after the user has started typing something into the pad (i.e., at which time there is text available to cut or clear). In this case, we can work with the text box's Change event, which is one of the primary programming events of a text box, as we saw in the last chapter. Whenever the contents of a text box change (e.g., when characters are typed in it, or if your program affects the text box's Text property), a corresponding Change event is generated. We can take advantage of that here to enable the Cut and Clear All buttons in our pad after text has been typed for the first time.

To begin, set the Enabled property for both CutButton and ClearButton to False at design time; now, when the notepad appears for the first time, all three buttons, Cut, Paste, and Clear All will be grayed. Next, open the text box's Change event in the code window; this Sub procedure appears:

```
Sub PadText_Change()

End Sub
```

Now just put this code in:

```
Sub PadText_Change()
    CutButton.Enabled = True
    ClearButton.Enabled = True
End Sub
```

That's it; the first time the user types, the two buttons will be enabled. Our notepad is getting to be quite a polished application. While we're on the topic of command buttons, however, we should note that we can supply our buttons with *access* keys.

Using Access Keys

An access key is used in a menu or command button as a shortcut key that you can press along with the Alt key. For example, if we made C the access key for our Cut button, the user could press Alt-C to click the button.

Adding access keys is very easy; all we have to do is to specify which letter we want to stand for the access key by placing an ampersand (&) in front of it in the control's caption. For example, to make C the access key for the Cut button, change the button's caption to &Cut. To make P the access key for the Paste button, change the Paste button's caption to &Paste. Finally, to change the Clear All Button's access key to A (since we've already used C with the Cut button—each access key should be unique among the currently available buttons or menu items), change its caption to Clear &All. When you do, Visual Basic changes the caption of each button, highlighting the access key, as shown in Figure 2-18. It's that easy to set access keys in Visual Basic.

That's it for our pad for now (we'll come back to it later); the code, event by event, appears in Listing 2-1. Next, we can turn to another application: a windowed alarm clock.

Figure 2-18 Pad with Access Keys

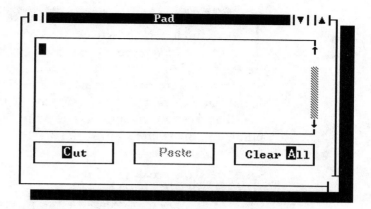

Listing 2-1 Pad Application

```
Dim Shared CutText As String

Sub ClearButton_Click ()
    PadText.Text = ""
    PadText.SetFocus
End Sub

Sub CutButton_Click ()
    CutText = PadText.SelText
    PadText.SelText = ""
    PasteButton.Enabled = True
    PadText.SetFocus
End Sub

Sub Pastebutton_Click ()
    PadText.SelText = CutText
    PadText.SetFocus
End Sub

Sub PadText_Change ()
    CutButton.Enabled = True
    ClearButton.Enabled = True
End Sub
```

An Alarm Clock Example

There is still a good deal to learn about text boxes and buttons. For example, we can actually read keystrokes as they're typed in a text box, or even change display fonts. For that matter, we can use an entirely different kind of button: the option button. Let's take advantage of some of those capabilities with a new application: a digital alarm clock that lets you display the time and which will notify you when a certain amount of time is up. The application we're aiming for, then, appears in Figure 2-19.

Figure 2-19 Alarm Clock Application

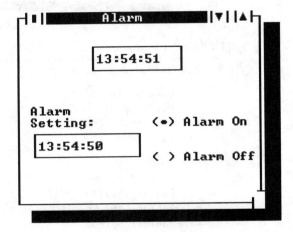

Start Visual Basic and give the name Alarm.Frm to a new form. The first thing we can do is set up the text box which will accept the alarm setting (e.g., the alarm setting in Figure 2-19 is 13:54:50). That's easy enough; just double-click the text box tool in Visual Basic's toolbox and place the text box in a position roughly corresponding that in Figure 2-19 (i.e., the lower left-hand corner of the form).

We can call this text box, say, AlarmSetting. In addition, you should clear the default text in the text box ("Text1") so that the text box is clear when the user starts the application. To keep this example relatively simple, we're only going to accept the time in this box in a restricted format, like this: "hh:mm:ss", the same way that the Time$

function of Basic will return it. (In a professional application, of course, we'd have to be more forgiving.) We haven't restricted user input before, but Visual Basic allows us to do so by reading each keystroke as it's typed.

Interpreting Individual Keystrokes

There are three events that occur each time the user types a key in a control or form that has the focus: KeyDown, KeyUp, and KeyPress. The KeyPress event is the one we'll be using here, because it returns the standard type of character values that we're used to dealing with in Basic. The KeyDown and KeyUp events are generated when the user presses and releases the key, and each event procedure receives two arguments: *KeyCode* and *Shift*. The key code here is the *ANSI* code (not ASCII) for the key that was pressed or released, and Shift holds the state of the Shift, Alt, and Ctrl keys. It turns out that ANSI, not ASCII, is the standard Visual Basic character set, and, while the two character sets have considerable overlap, they are not the same—however, they're the same for letters (like "a") and numbers (like "5").

In addition, KeyDown and KeyPress do not differentiate between lower case (z) and upper case (Z) except in the Shift argument; that is, the only way to tell if a character is lower or upper case is to look at Shift. This argument has a value of 1 if the Shift key is down, 2 if the Ctrl key is down, 4 if the Alt key is down, or a sum of those values if more than one of those keys are down (e.g., Shift+Alt would give a value in the Shift argument of 5).

The reason that KeyDown and KeyUp are useful is that they can read keys that have no standard ASCII value, such as the arrow keys or the function keys. For example, if the user pressed the F1 key, KeyCode will be equal to Key_F1 as defined in CONSTANT.BI; if the user pressed F2, KeyCode will equal Key_F2 and so forth. You can read which letter was typed by comparing KeyCode to the letters Key_A to Key_Z, as defined in CONSTANT.BI. However, both KeyDown and KeyUp are advanced events, so we'll stick with KeyPress here.

Our intention is to restrict the user's keystrokes to those allowed in the AlarmSetting text box. Those characters are: "0"– "9" and ":", and we'll check to make sure that the typed key is in that range. To set up our procedure, select AlarmSetting's KeyPress event from the Event Procedures dialog box and open AlarmSetting_KeyPress( ) in the code window. The following procedure template appears:

```
Sub AlarmSetting_KeyPress (KeyAscii As Integer)

End Sub
```

TIP: *Although we're restricting the user to the characters 0 to 9 and ":", it's a good idea in practice to allow text editing characters as well, such as the Backspace and Del keys (just get their ASCII codes from the Visual Basic documentation). Also, it's worth pointing out that the opposite of Chr$( ) is Asc( ); that is, Asc( ) returns the ASCII value of the first character of its argument string. It is also useful when checking to see if characters are in a certain range.*

As you can see, Visual Basic passes one argument to a KeyPress event— KeyAscii, the typed key's ASCII value. While KeyDown and KeyUp use ANSI key codes, KeyPress uses the ASCII set that most DOS programmers are used to. In other words, this is just like a normal Sub procedure with one argument passed to us—KeyAscii. That means we can make use of it immediately, checking the value of the just-typed key like this:

```
Sub AlarmSetting_KeyPress (KeyAscii As Integer)
    Key$ = Chr$(KeyAscii)
    If((Key$ < "0" OR Key$ > "9") AND Key$ <> ":") Then
        :
End Sub
```

First, we convert the ASCII code in KeyAscii to a character (i.e., a string of length one) using the Basic Chr$( ) function like this: Key$ = Chr$(KeyAscii). Then we check the value of that character against the allowed range—recall that the symbols < and > work for string comparisons as well as numeric comparisons in Basic; that is, they compare strings in alphabetic order, so "0" is less than "1" and "c" is greater than "b".

If the key that was typed is not in the allowed range, we should do two things: delete it and beep to indicate an error. We can beep with the Basic Beep statement, and it turns out that deleting the key is easy—we just have to set KeyAscii to 0:

```
     Sub AlarmSetting_KeyPress (KeyAscii As Integer)
         Key$ = Chr$(KeyAscii)
         If((Key$ < "0" OR Key$ > "9") AND Key$ <> ":") Then
  —>         Beep
  —>         KeyAscii = 0
         End If
     End Sub
```

That's it for checking the typed keys, so that's it for Alarm-Setting_KeyPress(); in addition, we should place the label "Alarm Setting:" above the text box to indicate what it's for. To do that, just click the label tool in Visual Basic's tool box, and place the label above the text box, setting its caption to "Alarm Setting:" (see Figure 2-19). Now we're set as far as recording and storing the alarm setting goes; our program will be able to read the alarm setting directly from the text box's Text property.

Displaying the Time

The next step in assembling our alarm clock is to set up the clock's display itself. Since we don't want the clock display to be edited from the keyboard (that is, it will use system time), we can use a label, not a text box here. Click the label tool once again, and enlarge the label until it is roughly the size of the one in Figure 2-20. Delete the characters in the caption property, and then take a look at the BorderStyle property in the properties bar.

Figure 2-20 Clock Template

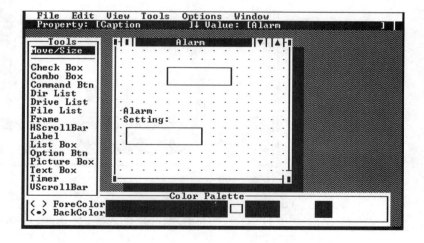

Normally, labels do not have a border, but they can have the same type of border that text boxes have. If you open the settings list next to the settings box, you'll see that the two options for BorderStyle are None and Fixed Single. Select Fixed Single to give the clock's display a border. In addition, we can give this label a name; let's call it Display. To display the time, then, we can just use the Basic function Time$ like this: Display.Caption = Time$.

The question, however, is how to keep the time updated. In other words, what kind of event occurs often enough, and regularly enough, to make sure that the time in Display.Caption is current? Visual Basic has another type of control for exactly this kind of use: timers.

Visual Basic Timers

A timer is just that: it can produce a specific event, called a Timer event, at a predetermined interval. Double-click the Timer tool in the toolbox now and position the timer roughly in the same position as in Figure 2-21. Visual Basic gives the timer a default name of Timer1.

Figure 2-21 Clock Template with Timer

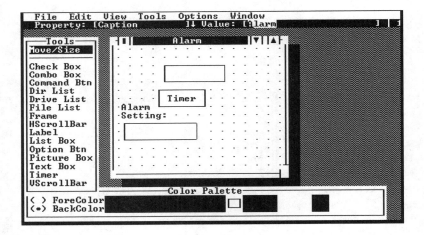

The next step is to set the timer's interval property—that is, how often the Timer event occurs. Make sure the timer is selected and open the properties list in the properties bar. Highlight the Interval property, and move over to the settings box. The interval property is measured in milliseconds—that is, in thousandths of a second. Since we don't want to put a significant burden on the rest of the system, we'll update the clock only once a second, so choose 1000 for the interval property of the timer.

Now we're ready to write the actual procedure that will be run every time the timer ticks (i.e., once a second). Open the Timer1_Timer() procedure in the code window, like this:

```
Sub Timer1_Timer()

End Sub
```

We can start by checking if the time is up—that is, if the string returned by the Basic function Time$ is greater than or equal to AlarmSetting.Text, like this:

```
Sub Timer1_Timer()
    If (Time$ >= AlarmSetting.Text) Then
            :
End Sub
```

If the condition is true, then we can just use the Beep statement this way:

```
        Sub Timer1_Timer()
            If (Time$ >= AlarmSetting.Text) Then
—>              Beep
            End If
        End Sub
```

That's it; when the time has elapsed, this procedure will make the clock beep—and since it's called once a second, the clock will keep beeping, once a second. However, this procedure is incomplete as it stands; alarm clocks usually have two settings: alarm on and alarm off (i.e., now that the alarm is on, we've got to shut it off).

For that reason, we can add two option buttons labeled Alarm On and Alarm Off (see Figure 2-19). The procedure connected with those buttons can communicate with the current procedure, Timer1_Timer(), through a form level variable that we might call AlarmOn. In other words, if AlarmOn is True *and* Time$ >= AlarmSetting.Text, then we should beep, which we can do as follows:

```
        Sub Timer1_Timer()
—>          If (Time$ >= AlarmSetting.Text AND AlarmOn) Then
                Beep
            End If
        End Sub
```

The last thing to do here is to update the display (i.e., because this procedure is called when the time changes), and we can do that as follows:

```
Sub Timer1_Timer()
    If (Time$ >= AlarmSetting.Text AND AlarmOn) Then
        Beep
    End If
—>  Display.Caption = Time$
End Sub
```

As mentioned, since this procedure is called once a second, the beeping will continue until the Alarm Off button is clicked (which will make AlarmOn False). Now let's set up AlarmOn itself; we can make it a form level variable by clicking the Code button in the Project Window and selecting ALARM.FRM. The declarations section of our form appears in the code window. Declare AlarmOn like this:

```
Dim Shared AlarmOn As Integer
```

At this point, then, our timer is ready, and our clock is almost ready to function; we compare the alarm setting to the current time, and we update the display on the screen: everything is ready—except for the AlarmOn variable. When we start, AlarmOn is 0, so we can add this line in AlarmSetting_Change() to make sure that AlarmOn is set to True (–1) when the user enters a time for the alarm to go off:

```
Sub AlarmSetting_Change()
    AlarmOn = -1
End Sub
```

However, we've asked the program to beep whenever Time$ >= AlarmSetting.Text AND AlarmOn, like this:

```
Sub Timer1_Timer()
—>  If (Time$ >= AlarmSetting.Text AND AlarmOn) Then
        Beep
    End If
    Display.Caption = Time$
End Sub
```

This means that the alarm will start beeping as the user enters the time character by character (i.e., Visual Basic treats "13:54:51: as greater than "13:5"), so we should wait until the user has typed in the full time that they want the alarm to be set to, like this:

```
Sub AlarmSetting_Change()
    If Len(AlarmSetting.Text) >= Len(Time$) THEN
        AlarmOn = -1
    End If
End Sub
```

The last step is designing the two option buttons that turn AlarmOn on and off, because without them, the user cannot turn the alarm off.

Using Option (Radio) Buttons

TIP: *Another way of making option buttons work as a group is to enclose them in a frame, by using the frame tool in the VB toolbox. The option buttons in such a frame are separate from the rest of the option buttons on the form.*

Option buttons—often called radio buttons—work in a group; that is, only one of the option buttons that appear on a form can be selected at once. You use option buttons to select one option from among several mutually-exclusive choices (i.e., choices where it's either one or the other, such as Floating and Not Floating).

Visual Basic takes care of the details of turning option buttons on and off for us; if one of a group of option buttons is clicked, the other one that was on (i.e., with a black dot in the center) will automatically be turned off. We can add two option buttons to our alarm clock easily; just double-click the option button tool in the toolbox and position the two option buttons under the Display label, giving them the captions Alarm Off and Alarm On as in Figure 2-22.

Figure 2-22 Alarm Clock Template with Option Buttons

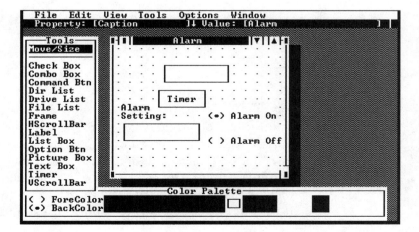

Together, these two make up an option button group. Because they are part of the same form (and not enclosed in separate frames), VB will turn them on and off so that only one is selected at a time. Each option button has a Value property associated with it, indicating whether or not the button is selected—True if selected (i.e., with a black dot in the center), False if not.

In addition, we need names for these new buttons. We can give them their own names, such as AlarmOnButton and AlarmOffButton and then write the corresponding procedures when one of them is clicked—that is, we can set the variable AlarmOn to True or False by checking the values of AlarmOnButton.Value and AlarmOffButton.Value. However, groups of buttons (in fact, groups of controls) like these are usually handled in a different way in Visual Basic, and that is by making the group of buttons into a *control array*.

Arrays of Controls

Control arrays are the way to handle groups of controls in Visual Basic. For example, imagine that you have a number of buttons like this:

ButtonA

ButtonB

ButtonC

ButtonD

In this case, you would have to write separate event handler for each button. For example, if you were interested in the Click event, you'd have ButtonA_Click( ), ButtonB_Click( ), ButtonC_Click( ), and ButtonD_Click( ). This can be awkward if the buttons perform essentially the same action with a few variations (as groups of controls usually do). The easier way to handle such groups of buttons like these is to give them all the same name. If you do, Visual Basic automatically gives them separate *Index* numbers (you might have noticed the Index property associated with most controls in the properties bar). For example, if you called each button MyButton, VB gives the first one an index of 0, the next an index of on, and so on:

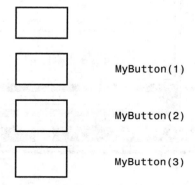

MyButton(1)

MyButton(2)

MyButton(3)

Now, instead of four separate event procedures (like ButtonA_Click() to ButtonD_Click()), there is only one procedure for each event, and VB automatically passes the Index corresponding to the button that was clicked: MyButton_Click(Index As Integer).

Let's see this in action. Name the top option button (Alarm Off) say, OnOffButton—that is, make its CtlName OnOffButton. Next, do the same for the other option button (Alarm On). When you do, Visual Basic pops up a box saying: "You already have a control named 'OnOffButton'. Do you want to create a control array?", as in Figure 2-23. Answer yes, then open the OnOffButton Click event in the code window.

This is the procedure template that appears:

```
OnOffButton_Click(Index As Integer)

End Sub
```

Notice the first line—because we've set up OnOffButton as a control array, Visual Basic passes the Index of the button pushed. That is, since we named the Alarm Off button as OnOffButton first, it will have Index 0. The Alarm On button will have Index 1 (if you wonder what a control's Index value is, just check it in the properties bar).

TIP: *If you had designed the clock in a slightly different order than we have here and put the alarm setting text box on the form after the option buttons, then there would be a small problem; when the application started, the option button placed on the form first would have the focus, not the alarm settings box. To give the alarm settings box the default focus, set it first in the tab order. That is, one of the properties of controls that can get the focus is called TabIndex. The control with a TabIndex of 0 gets the default focus, and you can tab around the form to the other controls.*

Figure 2-23 Control Array Box

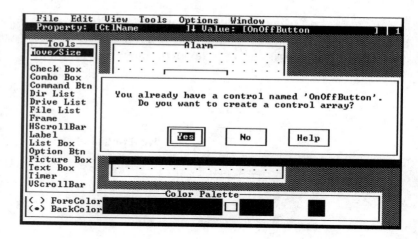

This means that if we check the value of Index, we'll be able to determine which button was pushed, letting us write one procedure for both buttons—precisely the idea behind creating groups of controls. When a set of controls handles similar functions, you should try to make them into a group and create a control array (since Visual Basic handles all the details, it's easy). All the current procedure has to do is determine which button was clicked by checking Index (0 —> Alarm Off, 1 —> Alarm On), and then set the global variable AlarmOn correctly (i.e., the job of these option buttons is to set the global variable AlarmOn). We can do that as follows:

```
OnOffButton_Click(Index As Integer
    If   (Index = 1) Then
         AlarmOn = True
    Else
         AlarmOn = False
    End If
End Sub
```

And that's all there is to it; our alarm clock is done. The working application appears in Figure 2-19, and the code, event by event, appears in Listing 2-2.

Listing 2-2 Alarm Application Code

```
Alarm.Frm ──────────────────────────────────

    Dim Shared AlarmOn As Integer

Sub Timer1_Timer ()
    If (Time$ > AlarmSetting.Text And AlarmOn) Then
        Beep
    End If
    Display.Caption = Time$
End Sub

Sub OnOffButton_Click (Index As Integer)
    If (Index = 1) Then
        AlarmOn = True
    Else
        AlarmOn = False
    End If
End Sub

Sub AlarmSetting_KeyPress (KeyAscii As Integer)
    Key$ = Chr$(KeyAscii)
    If ((Key$ < "0" Or Key$ > "9") And Key$ <> ":") Then
        Beep z
        KeyAscii = 0
    End If
End Sub

Sub AlarmSetting_Change()
    If Len(AlarmSetting.Text) >= Len(Time$) THEN
        AlarmOn = -1
    End If
End Sub
```

We'll continue our exploration of I/O under Visual Basic for DOS in the next chapter, when we start really digging in—by using menus in our programs.

Menus

The next step in creating useful applications is to add menus. In fact, we've already used many menus in Visual Basic. For example, Visual Basic's File menu appears in Figure 3-1, with the various parts labeled.

There are a number of elements in a menu that we should be familiar with before starting our own discussion of how to build them. The first is the *menu bar*, which indicates all the currently available menus in an application. Selecting a name in the menu bar pops down (or up if you're at the bottom of the screen) the associated menu. Each line in a menu lists a unique *menu item*; if that item is highlighted, it is selected.

Releasing the mouse button while an item is selected chooses that item; if the item has an *ellipsis* (that is, three dots: ...) after it, it opens a dialog box that can read more information from the user. In addition, items can be *grayed* (that is, disabled), or *checked* (with a dot next to them) indicating that a certain option has been turned on (for example, making the text bold in a word processor). Finally, menu items can be grouped together with a *separator bar*, as shown in Figure 3-1; in other words, all the menu items having to do with, say, text color can fit into one group, and all the items having to do with file handling can appear in another. We'll see all these parts—menu bars, menu items, disabled items, checked items, separator bars, and more in this chapter (however, we'll save the ellipsis items, which usually open a dialog box, for our dialog box chapter, Chapter 4).

Figure 3-1 Visual Basic's File Menu

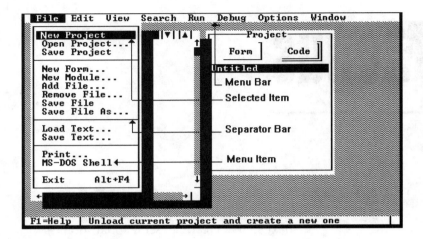

Designing and implementing menus in Visual Basic is not difficult. In this chapter, we'll see a number of examples; in particular, we'll start a small file editing program that we'll be able to finish later on (after we've covered the mechanics of loading and saving files), as well as updating our alarm clock into a menu-driven program. However, our first example will be a game—tic-tac-toe. We don't have the space here to develop the code necessary to let the computer play—games can be long programs to write—so this will be a game for two (human) players.

A Menu-Driven Tic-Tac-Toe Game

We can begin the tic-tac-toe game by beginning a new project (i.e., start Visual Basic or choose the New Form... item in VB's File menu). Name the form tictac.frm, give it the caption Tic-Tac-Toe, and place nine command buttons on it as shown in Figure 3-2 (we'll use command buttons rather than text boxes, because there is no click event for text boxes, which means the user would have to type "x" or "o").

Figure 3-2 Tic-Tac-Toe Template

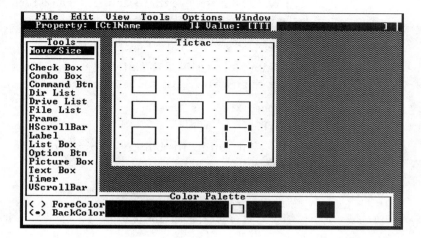

Clear the caption property of each command button, and name them all, say, TTT for Tic-Tac-Toe. When Visual Basic asks you whether you want to set up a control array, answer yes; writing one click procedure is going to be easier than writing nine. In fact, we can write that procedure immediately—open the code window. Exit the Form Designer either by selecting the Event Procedures... menu item, or the Exit menu item in the File menu, and open TTT_Click( ) in the code window:

```
Sub TTT_Click(Index As Integer)

End Sub
```

Because we've put the TTT buttons together into an array, Visual Basic passes an Index argument as well. If you've arranged the buttons in random order on the form, don't worry—it doesn't matter which index belongs to which button, because we can set the caption of a button like this: TTT(Index).Caption = "x." You can change the text or caption of a control when you're working with a control array—simply refer to the name of the array and afterwards add the index in parentheses. In our case, that means that we'll be able to refer to the caption of each button as TTT(Index).Caption.

However, we have to know whether we should put an x at the current place, or an o. Let's declare a form-level variable named XTurn: when it's True, it's x's turn; when False, it's o's turn. We can declare that variable by opening the form-level declaration section (i.e., TICTAC.FRM in the Event Procedures... dialog box) and making this declaration:

```
Dim Shared XTurn As Integer
```

In addition, load CONSTANT.BI with the metacommand $Include so that we can use the constants True and False:

```
       Dim Shared XTurn As Integer
—>     ' $Include: 'CONSTANT.BI'
```

At this point, setting the button's caption to x or o is easy; we can do it as follows:

```
Sub TTT_Click(Index As Integer)
    If (XTurn) Then
        TTT(Index).Caption = "x"
        XTurn = False
    Else
        TTT(Index).Caption = "o"
        XTurn = True
    End If
End Sub
```

This will keep the characters that appear alternating when the user clicks the various command buttons (notice that in this simple program we did not check whether the button had already been clicked, or whether someone has won the game—two things you should do if you intend to develop this into a tournament level Tic-Tac-Toe game).

Now we have to provide the user with some way of starting over—that is, adding a New Game option, which involves initializing the XTurn variable and clearing all the command buttons that make up the places on the Tic Tac Toe board. This is where we'll start working with menus, because New Game is exactly the kind of item that you might find in a menu. In addition, we'll add an Exit item to our menu, since all applications that have menus should have an Exit item.

Adding a Menu to the Tic-Tac-Toe Game

Designing menus in Visual Basic is not as hard as you might expect. In fact, each menu item is a control itself, and the primary event associated with it is the Click event. However, to get these new types of controls onto our form, we have to design them first, by using the

Menu Design Window (i.e., we can't just paint them with toolbox tools).

To pop that window onto the screen, open the Form Designer's Window menu and select the Menu Design Window item. That window appears, as shown in Figure 3-3.

Figure 3-3 The Visual Basic Menu Design Window

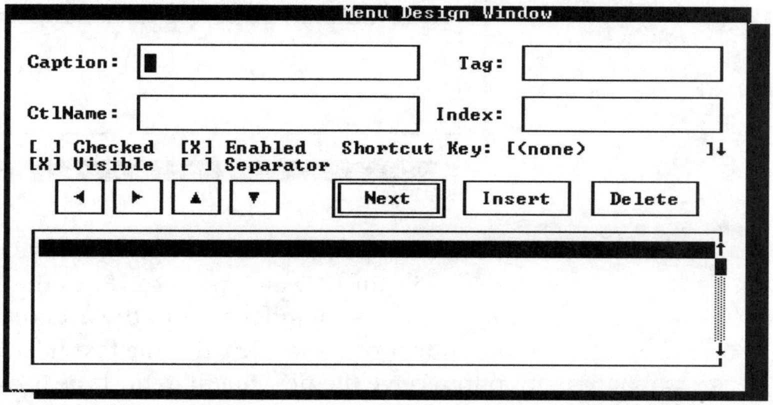

We can start by specifying the caption of our menu; in particular, we can call it File, because applications often have a File menu, and because that's where the user expects to find the Exit item (and, if you wish, you can modify the Tic-Tac-Toe game to save the current game to a file after we learn about file handling). To create a File menu (i.e., "File" will appear in the menu bar), type File in the Caption text box at the top of the Menu Design Window, as shown in Figure 3-4. In addition, each menu has to be given a control name (CtlName) so that the program can refer to it (which will allow us to switch menus around or in the menu bar, or change them altogether, as we'll see later). In our case, we can give the File menu the CtlName FileMenu, which we should type in the CtlName text box.

You might note that as we typed File in the Caption box, the same word appeared in the main list box below it. This is where the menu(s) that we are designing will appear. So far, we only have the caption of one menu: File. The next step is to add the New Game and Exit items.

Figure 3-4 Menu Design Window with File Caption

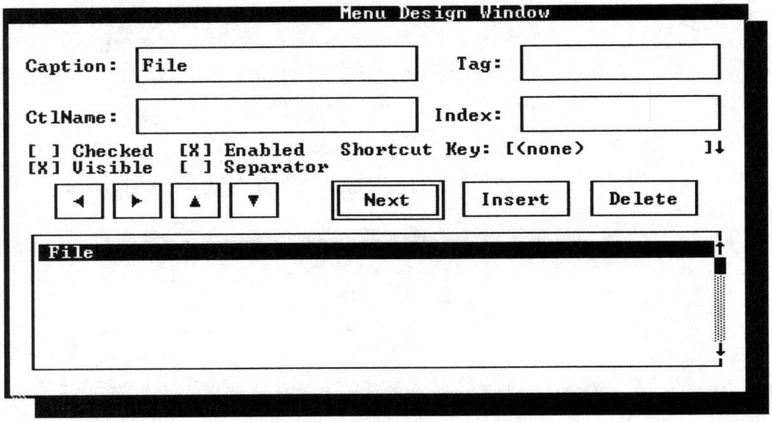

The insertion point should be right after the last name you typed—FileMenu in the CtlName text box. Press the Enter key to end this item and to move the highlight bar in the list box down one line; the Caption text box and the CtlName text boxes are cleared in preparation to receive the new menu item. Type New Game in the Caption text box, and, say, NewItem (meaning the New Game item in this menu) in the CtlName text box. Again, the text—New Game—appears in the list box at the bottom of the window. If we left it this way, however, New Game would be a menu name just like File, and would appear in the menu bar. Instead, we want this to be the first menu item in the File menu, so click the right arrow in the bar above the list box (i.e., the second arrow from the left in the group of four). When you do, the New Game entry is indented two spaces in the list box, as shown in Figure 3-5.

This means that New Game is an *item* in the File menu, not a menu itself; in fact, New Game is the first item. Next, press the Enter key again so that the highlight bar in the list box moves down one more line. Again, the Caption and CtlName text boxes are cleared.

Since the next item in the File menu is Exit, type Exit as the Caption and ExitItem as the CtlName. Notice that you did not have to click the right arrow again to indent Exit in the list box; it was automatically indented now that we're adding names to the File menu (to remove the automatic indentation, click the left arrow above the list box). The menu design is now complete, as shown in Figure 3-6.

TIP: *Visual Basic even allows you to have menus within menus, where selecting a menu item will pop open a new menu. You do this by successive levels of indentation—and you can have five such levels.*

Figure 3-5 Menu Design Window, New Game Indented

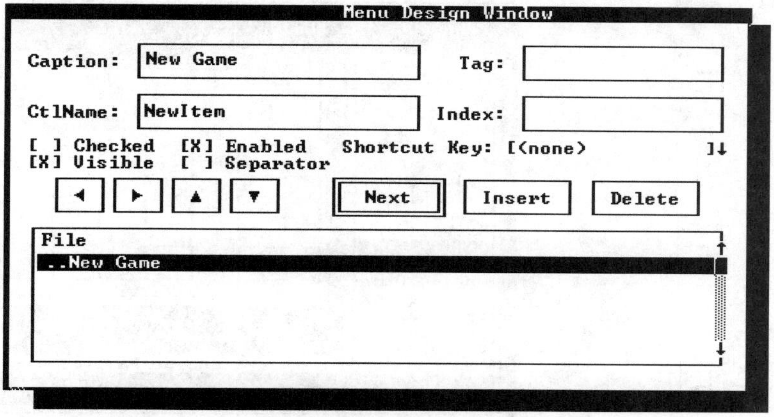

Figure 3-6 The Completed Menu Design Window

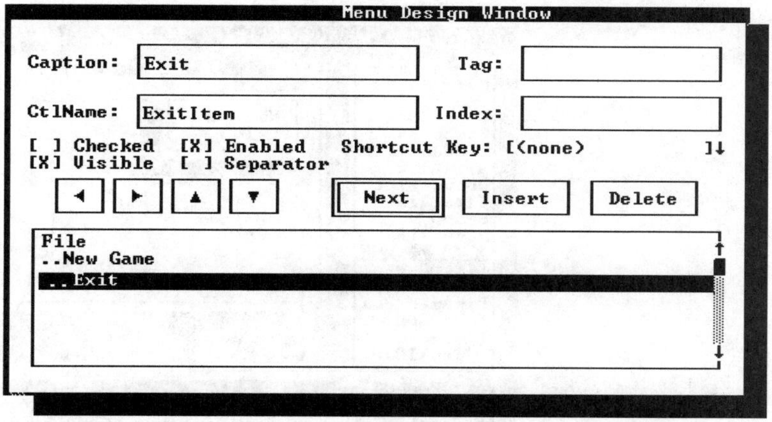

Close the Menu Design Window by clicking on the Done button; when you do, you'll see that a File menu has been added to our Tic-Tac-Toe game template, as in Figure 3-7.

As mentioned, the design process is primarily to add controls to our template; now that we've added the controls, we can treat them like any others—that is, we can attach code to them as easily. Let's see how this works: for example, click the File menu in the Tic-Tac-Toe menu bar. The menu opens, showing the two items we've put in it, New Game and Exit, as shown in Figure 3-8.

Figure 3-7 Tic-Tac-Toe Template with File Menu

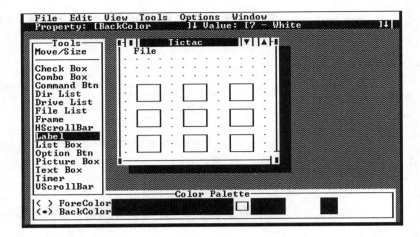

Figure 3-8 File Menu Open on Tic-Tac-Toe Template

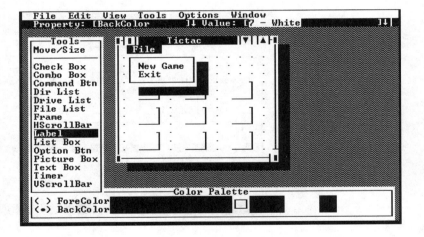

These two items are now simply controls, like buttons or text boxes. That is, we'll now find that NewItem and ExitItem are available in the Event Procedures... dialog box. Open the code window for NewItem_Click( ), like this:

```
Sub NewItem_Click( )

End Sub
```

When the user chooses this item, this is the Sub procedure that will be executed; in other words, we'll be using the Click event for menu items, just as we did for buttons. In our case, the user wants to start a new Tic Tac Toe game, so we'll have to reset the variable we've called XTurn like this (i.e., "o" will go first):

```
Sub NewItem_Click( )
    XTurn = 0              'Set XTurn False
        :
End Sub
```

In addition, we need to set the caption property of all the command buttons to "". As an added touch, we can set the focus (that is, the black, double outline that appears around a command button) to the top left button, although this is not necessary:

```
Sub NewItem_Click( )
    XTurn = 0
    For loop_index = 0 To 8
        TTT(loop_index).Caption = ""
    Next loop_index
    TTT(0).SetFocus
End Sub
```

Here, we're using the BASIC *for loop* to loop over the caption of each button. In general, the for loop works like this (we present *Basic* syntax like this throughout the book as a review only):

```
for loop_index = begin To end [, Step stepsize]
        :
    [body of for loop]
        :
Next loop_index
```

The variable we've called loop_index is originally set to the value begin, and tested against the value end; if it's less than end, the body of the loop is executed, and loop_index is incremented by 1—unless you include the Step keyword and a stepsize (which can be negative); in that case, stepsize is added to loop_index instead (if stepsize is negative, the loop ends when the value in loop_index is less than begin). In our case, we're simply setting the caption of buttons TTT(0) to TTT(8) to the empty string, "", in the body of the loop:

```
    Sub NewItem_Click( )
        XTurn = 0
—>      For loop_index = 0 To 8
—>          TTT(loop_index).Caption = ""
—>      Next loop_index
        TTT(0).SetFocus
    End Sub
```

Now the New Game option in the File menu is active—that's all there is to it. Making the Exit option active is even easier. Open the ExitItem_Click( ) Sub procedure template in the code window like this:

```
Sub ExitItem_Click( )

End Sub
```

All we want to do here is to end the application if the user selects this item, and we can do that with the Basic End statement like this:

```
Sub ExitItem_Click( )
—>      End
End Sub
```

When Visual Basic executes the End statement, it ends the program and removes the window from the screen, just like selecting Close in the system menu. And that's it for our Tic-Tac-Toe game; everything is ready to go—it was that quick. The full, operating version appears in Figure 3-9, and the code appears in Listing 3-1. Every time the user clicks a command button, an x or an o (in alternating sequence) appears. To start over, you can select the New Game item in the File menu; to stop completely, you can select Exit. Note that this is only a demonstration program; as mentioned, the program allows you to click a command button that's already been clicked, and doesn't stop even when someone wins—the idea here is to demonstrate menus, and we've already put them to work for us.

Listing 3-1 Tic-Tac-Toe Game

```
TicTac.Frm

Dim Shared XTurn As Integer

Sub TTT_Click(Index As Integer)
    If (Xturn) Then
        TTT(Index).Caption = "x"
        XTurn = False
```

```
            Else
                TTT(Index).Caption = "o"
                XTurn = True
            End If
        End Sub

        Sub NewItem_Click( )
            XTurn = 0
            For loop_index = 0 To 8
                TTT(loop_index).Caption = ""
            Next loop_index
            TTT(0).SetFocus
        End Sub

        Sub ExitItem_Click( )
            End
        End Sub
```

Figure 3-9 Tic-Tac-Toe Application

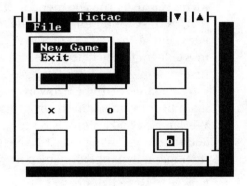

There are times when you should use command buttons for options, and there are times when you should use menus instead. Generally, you use command buttons when the options they represent are so frequently used that it's acceptable to have them continually presented to the user. On the other hand, commands such as the ones we've used in our notepad last chapter—i.e., Cut, Paste, and Clear All are usually part of a menu, and are not displayed as command buttons. In fact, let's modify our notepad so that it uses menus instead of command buttons; it will demonstrate how close command buttons and menus are from a VB programming point of view, and will get us started on the ability to handle files that we will complete when we discuss files later.

Developing Our Pad Example

The notepad we've developed is fine as far as it goes, but it is of limited use; in particular, the contents of the notepad disappear when you close the application. Instead, it would be much better if we could save our work on disk, and even read in preexisting files to modify them.

Towards that end, let's modify our Pad project to start working with menu selections; later, we'll be able to add the actual mechanics of Visual Basic file handling. To begin, then, let's design our Pad's menu system.

Again, just select the Menu Design Window from the Window menu in Visual Basic; the Menu Design Window opens. Since the leftmost menu is usually the File menu in Visual Basic applications, type File first, as the caption for that menu. Give this menu a CtlName of, say, FileMenu. After you've entered these two names, press the Enter key to move down to the first of the entries that will go in this menu. The first item might be Load File..., so type that as the caption, then indent it by clicking the right arrow in the group of four arrows above the main list box; in addition, give this Menu item the CtlName LoadItem. We can also make a provision to save files with a Save File... item, so add that next, giving it a CtlName of SaveItem. After that, we'll need a final menu item of Exit, which is expected in the File menu.

However, since Exit doesn't fit in with Load File... and Save File..., we can set it off as its own group by placing a menu separator in our menu. A separator is one of the horizontal lines that run across a menu (as shown in Figure 3-10—note that Exit is set off from the rest of the menu items with a separator in Visual Basic's File menu as well), and that divide menu items into groups. You specify that you want a menu separator simply by typing a hyphen (-). Type a hyphen as the caption now and separator as the CtlName. Finally, enter Exit as the last item in the File menu; at this point, the Menu Design Window should look like Figure 3-10. Close the Menu Design Window by clicking Done; the Pad should now look like Figure 3-11.

Figure 3-10 Menu Design Window for Pad, Stage 1

```
┌──────────────────────────────────────────────────────────────────┐
│                        Menu Design Window                          │
│                                                                    │
│  Caption: │File                   │        Tag: │              │   │
│                                                                    │
│  CtlName: │FileMenu               │      Index: │              │   │
│  [ ] Checked  [X] Enabled    Shortcut Key: [<none>          ]↓│   │
│  [X] Visible  [ ] Separator                                        │
│     ┌───┐ ┌───┐ ┌───┐ ┌───┐   ┌─────────┐ ┌────────┐ ┌────────┐   │
│     │ ◄ │ │ ► │ │ ▲ │ │ ▼ │   │  Next   │ │ Insert │ │ Delete │   │
│     └───┘ └───┘ └───┘ └───┘   └─────────┘ └────────┘ └────────┘   │
│  ┌──────────────────────────────────────────────────────────┐↑    │
│  │File                                                       │█    │
│  │..Load File...                                             │█    │
│  │..Save File...                                             │█    │
│  │..─                                                        │     │
│  │..Exit                                                     │     │
│  │                                                           │↓    │
│  └──────────────────────────────────────────────────────────┘     │
└──────────────────────────────────────────────────────────────────┘
```

Figure 3-11 Pad Template with File Menu

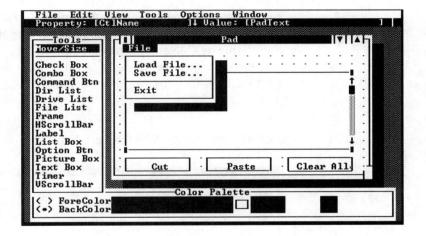

As you can see, the separator was inserted, setting the Exit option off from the others. It is often a good idea to group menu items this way, since it makes it simpler for the user to find commands connected with each other.

Unfortunately, the only File menu item that we can make active at this time is the Exit item, since we'll have to wait until we have expertise with files before handling Load File... and Save File.... Open the Exit item's Click event and this template appears:

```
Sub ExitItem_Click( )

End Sub
```

Just add the End statement here, so that we can quit the application if
the user chooses to:

```
   Sub ExitItem_Click( )
—> End
   End Sub
```

The menu following the File menu is usually the Edit menu in word
processors and editors. Let's add that now. Open the Menu Design
Window again, and click the blank line in the main list box below the
last entry (i.e., Exit) so that it's highlighted. Now move up to the
Caption box and type Edit; give this menu a CtlName of EditMenu.
Note that since we left the Menu Design Window and came back, the
automatic indentation was turned off (i.e., Edit is made a menu bar
item).

Since we'll be supplanting the notepad's command buttons with menu
items here, the three items in the Edit menu should be Cut, Paste, and
Clear All. Enter them one at a time, making sure they're indented and
giving them the CtlNames CutItem, PasteItem, and ClearItem respectively. At this point, the Menu Design Window should look like Figure 3-12. Close the window; now the Pad template should look like
Figure 3-13.

Figure 3-12 Menu Design Window with Edit Menu

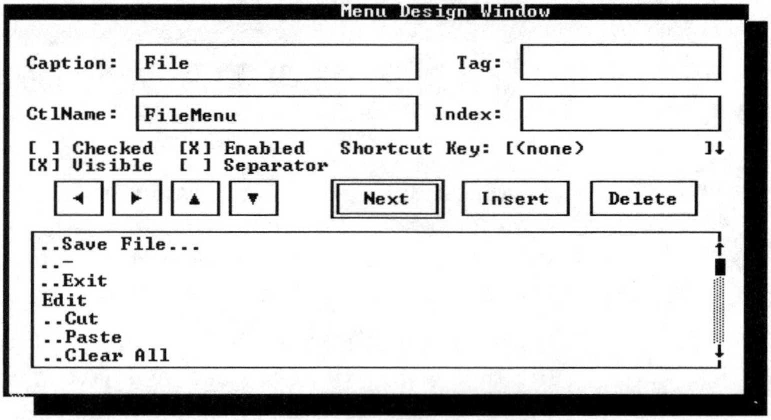

Figure 3-13 Pad Template with Edit Menu

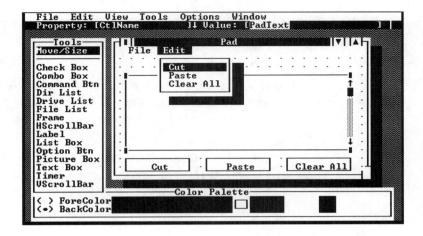

The only work remaining is to transfer the procedures from the command buttons Cut, Paste, and Clear All to the menu items. Each of them are click events, so they can be transfered whole. This is also easy to do in Visual Basic; just open the code window to display CutButton_Click( ), as in Figure 3-14.

Figure 3-14 CutButton_Click( ) Code Window

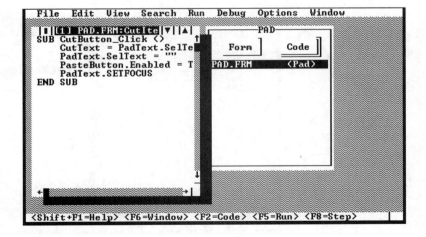

We've called this control CutButton, so the Sub procedure that appears looks like this:

```
Sub CutButton_Click( )
    CutText = PadText.SelText
    PadText.SelText = " "
    PasteButton.Enabled = True
    PadText.SetFocus
End Sub
```

Much of this will be the same under the menu system, so we can just change the name to CutItem_Click( ) (the name of the Cut item in the Edit menu) instead of CutButton_Click( ):

```
—>   Sub CutItem_Click( )
         CutText = PadText.SelText
         PadText.SelText = " "
         PasteButton.Enabled = True
         PadText.SetFocus
     End Sub
```

As soon as you make this change and switch to another line, Visual Basic checks the object list to see if this new name corresponds to an already existing object. In this case it does, so that Visual Basic assigns this procedure to the CutItem menu control. Note that this is indicated by the object box in the upper-left of the code window, which now reads CutItem, as shown in Figure 3-15.

Figure 3-15 CutItem_Click( ) Code Window

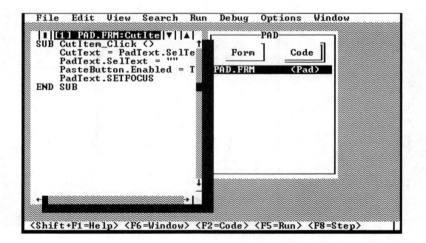

Peter Norton's Visual Basic for DOS

Next, we can do the same thing for the other buttons. The Paste button procedure, PasteButton_Click( ) looks like this now:

```
Sub PasteButton_Click( )
    PadText.SelText = CutText
End Sub
```

(You might recall that we saved the cut text in a form level string named CutText, and that here we are just pasting it back in.) We can change this to PasteItem_Click( ) easily enough; just edit the name of the Sub procedure until you have this:

```
—>Sub PasteItem_Click( )
    PadText.SelText = CutText
End Sub
```

That's it; we can handle the Clear All button the same way. Pop up this procedure in the code window:

```
Sub ClearButton_Click( )
    PadText.Text = ""
    PadText.SetFocus
End Sub
```

Next, change this to Sub ClearItem_Click( ) instead:

```
Sub ClearItem_Click( )
    PadText.Text = ""
    PadText.SetFocus
End Sub
```

Now we've made our menu items active and we can start making the changes to the code itself. We'll no longer need to set the focus to other objects, because, in the absence of buttons, the text box will always have it (menu items cannot keep the focus when the menu closes). For that reason, remove the PadText.SetFocus line in all the procedures, until they look like this:

```
Sub CutItem_Click( )
    CutText = PadText.SelText
    PadText.SelText = ""
    PasteButton.Enabled = True
End Sub

Sub PasteItem_Click( )
    PadText.SelText = CutText
End Sub
```

```
Sub ClearItem_Click( )
    PadText.Text = ""
End Sub
```

In addition, you may recall that we enabled the Cut and Clear All buttons only after the user typed something—that is, after there was a change in PadText, we executed these lines:

```
Sub PadText.Change( )
    CutButton.Enabled = True
    ClearButton.Enabled = True
End Sub
```

It turns out that menu items have an enabled property just as buttons do; in fact, you're probably more used to seeing menu items than button captions grayed out. All we have to do is to change our references to button Enabled properties into menu item Enabled properties; in other words, what was CutButton.Enabled will become CutItem.Enabled, and what was ClearButton.Enabled becomes ClearItem.Enabled:

```
    Sub PadText.Change( )
—>      CutItem.Enabled = True
—>      ClearItem.Enabled = True
    End Sub
```

Also, you might recall that we enabled the Paste button only after some text had been cut (i.e., in the procedure CutButton_Click( )). We can change that reference also from PasteButton.Enabled to PasteItem.Enabled like this:

```
    Sub CutItem_Click( )
        CutText = PadText.SelText
        PadText.SelText = ""
—>      PasteItem.Enabled = True
    End Sub

    Sub PasteItem_Click( )
        PadText.SelText = CutText
    End Sub

    Sub ClearItem_Click( )
        PadText.Text = ""
    End Sub
```

Now all the references to buttons in the code have been replaced by references to menu items, so that you can cut the buttons, removing them from the form. To do that, click them in the Form Designer and then select the Cut item in the Edit menu, readjusting the size of the form to absorb the space left by their absence.

At this point, we're almost through. The final step is to make sure that all the menu items in the Edit menu (Cut, Paste, Clear All) are grayed out when the application starts (i.e., before the user has started typing). As you might expect, we can do that at design time in the Menu Design Window. Open that window by selecting it in the Window menu, and move the highlight bar in the main list box until the Cut item is highlighted. Then click the Enabled check box—the middle check box in the row of three—turning it off (i.e., the x in the box disappears), as shown in Figure 3-16.

Figure 3-16 Menu Design Box with Enabled Option Off

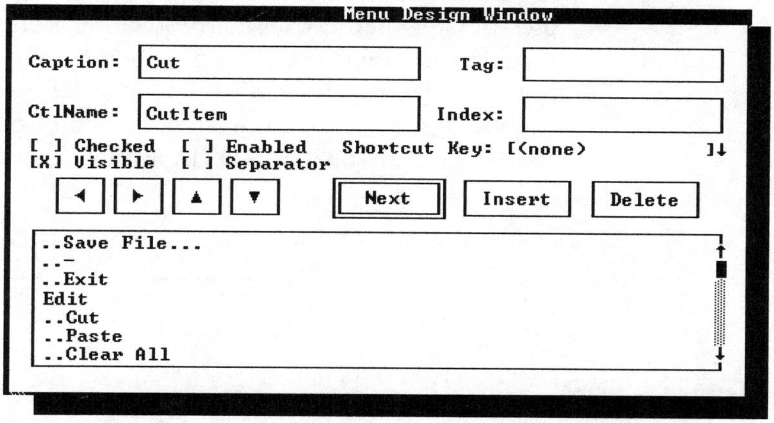

Do the same for Paste and Clear All, the other two menu items in the Edit menu, and click the Done button. Now, when you run the Pad application, the Edit menu items originally appear grayed out, as in Figure 3-17. When you start typing, however, the Cut and Clear All items are made active; when you actually do cut something, the Paste item is enabled as well.

That is the way to enable or disable menu items—with the Enabled property. Setting it to True enables the menu item; setting it to False disables it. This capability is often extremely valuable to ensure that the user doesn't choose an impossible option—for example, attempting to save a file before there is any text in the text window.

Figure 3-17 Pad with Edit Menu Grayed Out

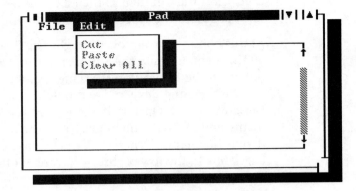

However, you must keep track of the items you've disabled, and you should also realize that it's unattractive and frustrating to the user to present large menus where almost all items are grayed out. If you have many grayed items, a better option might be to remove those items from your menus altogether, and replace them when they become enabled again (we'll see how to do this in Visual Basic later). All the code in our Pad so far appears in Listing 3-2, event by event.

Listing 3-2 Pad Application Code Version 1

Pad.Frm

```
Dim CutText As String

Sub ExitItem_Click()
    End
End Sub

Sub CutItem_Click()
    CutText = PadText.SelText
    PadText.SelText = ""
    PasteItem.Enabled = True
End Sub

Sub PasteItem_Click()
    PadText.SelText = CutText
End Sub

Sub ClearItem_Click()
    PadText.Text = ""
End Sub
```

```
Sub PadText.Change( )
    CutItem.Enabled = True
    Clear Item.Enabled = True
End Sub
```

However, there are still some ways to improve our pad.

Marking Menu Items with Dots

TIP: *If you want*
Spellchecking to be
dotted as soon as the
program starts, select
the Checked box for
that item in the Menu
Design Window.

I n Visual Basic for DOS, you can mark menu items with a dot to indicate that they are active (as with a check mark in Windows). For example, one common menu item that is treated like this is a spellchecking item. When dotted, it indicates that the spellchecking option is turned on.

Let's add a Spellchecking item to our notepad temporarily (i.e., we won't leave the item in our menus because we won't really have spellchecking), to show how to use dots in front of menu items. To add Spellchecking, open the Menu Design Window and add a new menu named Utilities (CtlName: UtilityMenu) and give it one item: Spellchecking (CtlName: SpellItem). Next, exit the form designer by selecting the Event Procedures... menu item in the Edit menu. Open the SpellItem_Click( ) event in the code window like this:

```
Sub SpellItem_Click( )

End Sub
```

The property of menu items that indicates whether or not they are checked is the Checked property. For example, to place a dot in front of Spellchecking, we would set SpellItem.Checked to True. Here, however, we should toggle it on and off: if it's off when the user selects it, we should turn it on; and if it's on, we should turn if off. We can do that by flipping the logical state of SpellItem.Checked with the BASIC operator Not:

```
Sub SpellItem_Click( )
—>    SpellItem.Checked = Not SpellItem.Checked
End Sub
```

And that's all there is to it; now when the user clicks this item over and over, it will toggle "Spellchecking" on and off. When dotted, Spellchecking appears as shown in Figure 3-18.

Figure 3-18 Our Dotted Spellchecking Item

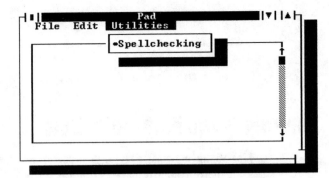

That's it for checking and unchecking menu items; the code appears in Listing 3-3.

Listing 3-3 Pad Application Code Version 2

```
Pad.Frm

Dim CutText As String

Sub ExitItem_Click( )
    End
End Sub

Sub CutItem_Click( )
    CutText = PadText.SelText
    PadText.SelText = ""
    PasteItem.Enabled = True
End Sub

Sub PasteItem_Click( )
    PadText.SelText = CutText
End Sub

Sub ClearItem_Click( )
    PadText.Text = ""
End Sub

Sub PadText.Change( )
    CutItem.Enabled = True
    ClearItem.Enabled = True
End Sub
```

```
Sub SpellItem( )
    SpellItem.Checked = Not SpellItem.Checked
End Sub
```

Now, however, we should remove the Spellchecking item before progressing (since we won't actually support spellchecking here). Open the Menu Design Window and delete both the menu itself, Utilities, and the single item in it, Spellchecking, using the Delete button. Visual Basic automatically removes the event procedure associated with SpellItem (SpellItem_Click( )).

Let's add some real utility to our notepad. In most complete Visual Basic applications which use menus, you can also use access keys (i.e., one letter of a menu name or item is underlined, indicating that typing that letter will select the corresponding option) and shortcut keys (e.g., like Ctrl+A). Naturally, we can add those options to our Visual Basic programs also.

Adding Access Keys to Menus

A dding an access key—the highlighted letter in a name or caption—to menus is as easy as it was with buttons; we just place an ampersand (&) in front of the letter that we want to use. For example, we can change Cut to &Cut in order to make C the access key for the Cut item in the Edit menu. Note again that the access keys should be unique on their level—that is, no two menu names in the menu bar should have the same access key. No two menu items in the same menu should have the same access key, either.

In fact, we'll use the first name of each item or menu name as its access key, with an exception: since Cut and Clear All appear in the Edit menu, we will use C for the Cut item's access key and A for Clear All. Finally, we give the access key x to the Exit option, even though it begins with E, which is unique in the File menu. The Visual Basic convention is that Exit be given x as an access key, and many users have become accustomed to using it that way (and few menu items are likely to begin with x). All the access keys we'll use for Pad are marked with an ampersand, and appear in Figure 3-19.

Figure 3-19 Pad Menu Design Window with Access Keys

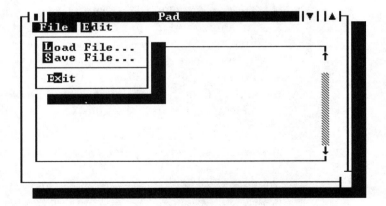

```
                         Menu Design Window
   Caption:  &File                      Tag:
   CtlName:  FileMenu                    Index:
   [ ] Checked  [X] Enabled    Shortcut Key: [<none>]        ↕
   [X] Visible  [ ] Separator
      ◄    ►    ▲    ▼        Next        Insert      Delete
   ..&Save File...                                          ↑
   ..–
   ..E&xit
   &Edit
   ..&Cut
   .. &Paste
   ..Clear &All                                             ↓
```

Now when you run the Pad, you'll see the access keys highlighted, as in Figure 3-20. Our pad is looking more professional, but there is one last change still to be made—adding short cut keys.

Figure 3-20 Pad Template Access Keys

```
   ▐█▌                        Pad                      ▐▼▌▐▲▌
   File  Edit
        ┌──────────────┐
        │Load File...  │─────────────────────────┐
        │Save File...  │                          │     ↑
        │──────────────│                          │
        │Exit          │                          │▨
        └──────────────┘                          │▨
                                                   │▨
                                                   │▨
                                                   │▨
                                                   │     ↓
```

Adding Shortcut Keys to Menus

You've probably seen shortcut keys in menus already—for example, Visual Basic's File Menu in Figure 3-1 has three shortcut keys for handling file operations. Ctrl+F12 is a short cut for adding a file,

Shift+F12 is a shortcut for saving a file, and F12 is a shortcut for the Save File As... menu item. We can add shortcuts like this to our Pad as well.

To do that, open the Menu Design Window again. You select shortcut keys with the shortcut key box which appears on the right-hand side. As in most cases, Visual Basic is capable of presenting you with all the options available here (that is, instead of having to look it up, the options are displayed on the screen for your immediate use); just click the arrow next to the shortcut key box. When you do, a list of the possible short cut keys appears, as shown in Figure 3-21.

Figure 3-21 Shortcut Keys in the Menu Design Window

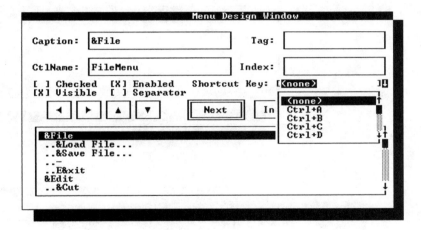

The first menu item we might give a shortcut key to is the Load File item in our File menu. Since we'll have no use for the Ctrl key combinations (like Ctrl+A or Ctrl+B) in our application, we can use them as shortcut keys—Ctrl+Letter key combinations are often easier for the user to remember than function key combinations (although those are available in the shortcut key drop-down list box as well, of course). To connect Ctrl+L with the Load File item, just highlight that item in the main list box and select Ctrl+L from the shorcut key list box. When you do, Ctrl+L appears in the main list box on the same line as Load File....

NOTE: *Keep in mind that, while you have to have a menu open to use the access keys in that menu, shortcut keys like Ctrl+X or Shift-F3 are valid even when the menu is closed, so they should be unique over all menus, not just the one they're defined in.*

In this way, we can keep going, choosing shortcut keys for most of the items, as shown in Figure 3-22. To make these shortcut keys active, just click the Done box in the Menu Design Window and run the Pad application. As you can see in Figure 3-23, our shortcut keys are now displayed in the menus themselves, next to the items they represent.

Figure 3-22 Shortcut Keys for the Pad Application

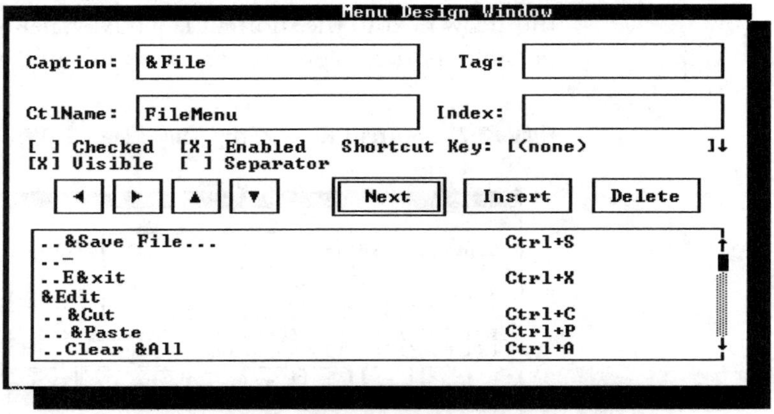

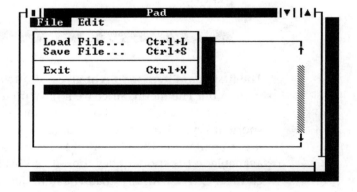

Figure 3-23 Pad with Short Cut Keys

That's it for developing the Pad for now; it's shown us a great deal about menu design, including how to gray items in a menu to show they're inactive, how to mark menu items with a dot, how to use access keys and separator bars, and how to use shortcut keys. Now, however, let's look into gaining more menu power.

Changing Menu Items at Run Time

As you may recall, the alarm clock program had two option buttons—Alarm Off and Alarm On. We can convert this application to use a menu, just as we did for the pad. In particular, our goal here will be to have one menu—Alarm—with one item in it. At first, that item will be Alarm Off, but when you select it at run time, it will change to Alarm On, and so on, toggling back and forth as required.

To do that, we can open the Alarm project and the Menu Design Window in that project. All we'll need here is a single menu named Alarm, with a CtlName of, say, AlarmMenu, and with one item in it: Alarm Off, which we can give the CtlName of OnOffItem to (i.e., the option buttons were named OnOffButton). Now open the code window and display this code:

```
Sub OnOffButton_Click (Index As Integer)
    If (Index = 1) Then
        AlarmOn = True
    Else
        AlarmOn = False
    End If
End Sub
```

As you may recall, the variable AlarmOn was a formlevel variable which determined whether or not the program would beep when the allotted time elapsed. We can change this Sub procedure code, rewriting it like this:

```
Sub OnOffItem_Click( )
    If (AlarmOn) Then
        AlarmOn = False          'Toggle alarm
        OnOffItem.Caption = "Alarm Off"
    Else
        AlarmOn = True           'Toggle alarm
        OnOffItem.Caption = "Alarm On"
    End If
End Sub
```

That's it; we can delete the option buttons now (using the Form Designer's Edit menu), since all reference to them in the code has been removed. By changing the Caption property of the single menu item, we're able to change that menu item at run time. When you run the clock now, you'll see the menu name Alarm in the menu bar; opening it will reveal the Alarm Off item. Clicking that item not only closes the menu but also changes it to Alarm On, as shown in Figure 3-24. In this way, we're able to toggle the caption of the Alarm On/Off item to match the alarm setting.

Figure 3-24 Alarm Clock with Menu

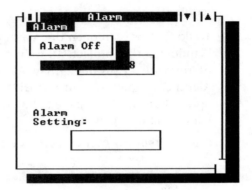

There is another way to do this as well—we could have used the Visible property of menu items instead. For example, if we had two menu items, AlarmOnItem (Alarm On) and AlarmOffItem (Alarm Off), setting the AlarmOnItem.Visible property to True would display the Alarm On menu item, and setting the AlarmOffItem.Visible property to False would hide it:

```
Sub OnOffItem_Click( )
    If (AlarmOn) Then
        AlarmOn = False          'Toggle alarm
—>      AlarmOnItem.Visible = False
—>      AlarmOffItem.Visible = True
    Else
        AlarmOn = True           'Toggle alarm
—>      AlarmOnItem.Visible = True
—>      AlarmOffItem.Visible = False
    End If
End Sub
```

This is the way you can hide options in your menus when necessary (for example, to avoid presenting too many grayed out options). That is, setting the Visible property this way can be an important part of menu design.

Or, if we prefer, we can make our alarm clock function with dots (i.e., menu dots are designed for cases where you toggle options on and off). To put a menu with dots into the alarm clock, we can open the Menu Design Window and again set up a menu with the Caption Alarm and CtlName AlarmMenu. Then we put one item into this menu—OnItem, with the caption Alarm On (i.e., when this item is dotted, the alarm will be on). Close the Menu Design Window and click the Alarm On menu item to open the code window with this Sub procedure template:

```
Sub OnItem_Click( )

End Sub
```

We can dot the Alarm On item and set AlarmOn appropriately like this:

```
Sub OnItem_Click( )
    If (AlarmOn) Then
        AlarmOn = False
        OnItem.Checked = False
    Else
        AlarmOn = True
        OnItem.Checked = True
    End If
End Sub
```

This way, the Alarm On item toggles between being dotted and undotted, corresponding to the state of the alarm, as in Figure 3-25 (alternatively, you can have two items: Alarm On and Alarm Off, placing a dot in front of the appropriate one).

As we've seen, then, it's possible to change a menu item's caption at run time, as well as to make it visible or invisible. However, this doesn't take care of all possibilities; what if you wanted to add or delete entirely new menu items at run time? We'll look into this possibility next.

Figure 3-25 Alarm Clock Application with Menu Dot

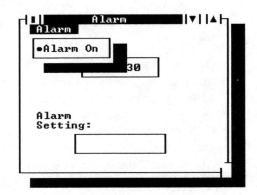

Adding and Deleting Menu Items

L et's say that you wanted to write a menu-driven phone book application; that is, you wanted a program which you could use to keep track of your friends' phone numbers. Such an application might have two text boxes in it: one holding a name, and the other one holding the matching phone number. If all the stored names appeared in a menu, it would be easy to select among them—when you choose a name, it would appear in the name text box, and the corrresponding phone number would appear in the phone number text box. However, we'll have to take into account that such a list of names (as displayed in our menu) can grow or shrink.

In Visual Basic, you can add menu items with the Load statement, and you can remove them with the Unload statement (as we'll see, Load and Unload can be used for many VB controls). However, to do this, the menu items must be part of a control array (i.e., they must use the same click procedure, although their indices will be different). The reason for this is that you cannot add entirely new code for a new click procedure at run time (i.e., when you want to add a new item to a menu); instead, Visual Basic must already have the code necessary to handle the new menu item.

Using Load and Unload is not difficult; for example, if we had a menu item named, say, the_item, and whose index was 0, we could add another item named the_item(1) like this:

```
Load the_item(1)
```

This adds another item right below the last item; to add a new item to the menu itself, we can load a string into the_item(1)'s Caption property like this:

```
Load the_item(1)
—>the_item(1).Caption = "Asparagus"
```

Similiarly, we can unload items using Unload. Let's say that we had added these vegetables to a menu like this:

```
Load the_item(1)
the_item(1).Caption = "Asparagus"
Load the_item(2)
the_item(2).Caption = "Potato"
Load the_item(3)
the_item(3).Caption = "Spinach"
Load the_item(4)
the_item(4).Caption = "Corn"
```

Now let's say that we wanted to remove the Asparagus item. Since Visual Basic only allows you to remove the last item in a control array with Unload, we'd have to do that by moving all the other items up and then deleting the last item like this:

```
Load the_item(1)
the_item(1).Caption = "Asparagus"
Load the_item(2)
the_item(2).Caption = "Potato"
Load the_item(3)
the_item(3).Caption = "Spinach"
Load the_item(4)
the_item(4).Caption = "Corn"

—>For loop_index = 1 To 3
—>    the_item(loop_index).Caption = the_item
      (loop_index + 1).Caption
—>Next loop_index

—>Unload the_item(4)
```

Note also that in this case, the indices of each surviving item is decremented by one, so that you would have to account for that in code. In addition, note that we did nothing with the first item in the array, the_item(0). This is the conventional defect of using Load and

Unload for menu items: you can't unload items created at design time—but you can't set up a control array unless you have at least one element in place at design time. In other words, no matter what we do, we'll always have to have one element of the control array in the menu—but since we don't know what items we want to place in our menu before run time (i.e., the names of our friends), what caption should we give it at design time?

The usual solution to this, when designing a menu, is to give the 0 item—the one that starts the control array—an invisible menu item as a caption. That way, all subsequent menu items that you add will come after this invisible 0 item. Let's see how this works in practice.

We can design a new form named, say, Phone.Frm. Add two text boxes and labels (Name: and Number:) as shown in Figure 3-26, then open the Menu Design Window. We can call the menu in our phone book application File, because it can conceivably be expanded to save phone directories on disk.

Figure 3-26 Phone Project Template

Give the first item in that menu the caption Add Current Name, and a CtlName of AddNameItem. Next, put in a separator bar by typing a hyphen (-), give it the control name of, say, Separator. After that, add another item with any caption (except a null string, ""), even a space. Give this dummy item—the first item in our control array—a CtlName of, say, NNN. In addition, give it an Index of 0 (by putting 0 in the box marked Index), and make it invisible (by clicking the Visible box so that the X disappears). In other words, our control array will be named NNN( ), and we can refer to specific items in it as NNN(1),

NNN(2), and so on (note that because NNN(0) will always remain invisible, you can give it any name you like). Finally, add the last item of any File menu, Exit, with a CtlName of ExitItem.

If you run the program, you'll see a menu, as in Figure 3-26. The program works in this way: the user should be free to type a name in the name text box, and a phone number in the number text box. Then they can select the Add Current Name menu item, and the program should add that name to the menu; i.e., it should appear right below the separator bar. After the user has finished entering names this way, they can select a name from the menu. That name, along with the corresponding phone number, should appear in the text boxes.

We can start with the Add Current Name item in the menu; open the code window, displaying this Sub procedure template:

```
Sub AddNameItem_Click( )

End Sub
```

The first thing we'll want to keep track of is the number of menu items we have, so we can declare a variable named NumberNames as Static (i.e., its value won't change between successive calls):

```
      Sub AddNameItem_Click( )
—>        Static NumberNames
              :
      End Sub
```

Since we're adding a name in this procedure, our first action might be to simply increment NumberNames by one (static variables are initialized to 0) and Load a new menu item like this:

```
      Sub AddNameItem_Click( )
          Static NumberNames
—>        NumberNames = NumberNames + 1
—>        Load NNN(NumberNames)
              :
      End Sub
```

Next, we can load the name that is now in the name text box into the new menu item's Caption property this way (assuming we left the name text box's CtlName as Text1), and we can also set that item's Visible property to True (-1):

```
      Sub AddNameItem_Click( )
          Static NumberNames
          NumberNames = NumberNames + 1
          Load NNN(NumberNames)
  —>      NNN(NumberNames).Caption = Text1.Text
  —>      NNN(NumberNames).Visible = -1
                 :
      End Sub
```

Now we have to store the names and numbers themselves. To do that,
we can set up two string arrays, named, say, Names( ) and Numbers( ).
These arrays will have to have broader scope than just our current
procedure, because when the user clicks a name in the menu to
retrieve data, we'll have to read from these arrays in the corresponding
Click procedure to fill the name and number text boxes. For that
reason, we can declare Names( ) and Numbers( ) to be form-level
arrays. To do that, click the Code button and add the following
declaration to PHONE.FRM:

```
Dim Shared Names(1 To 10) As String
Dim Shared Numbers(1 To 10) As String
```

Making these arrays form-level arrays makes them accessible to all
procedures in the form. Now we can go back to AddNameItem_Click( )
and complete it as follows in order to store the current name and
number:

```
      Sub AddNameItem_Click( )
      Static NumberNames
      NumberNames = NumberNames + 1
      Load NNN(NumberNames)
      NNN(NumberNames).Caption = Text1.Text NNN(NumberNames).Visible -1
  —>Names(NumberNames) = Text1.Text      'Data from name text box
  —>Numbers(NumberNames) = Text2.Text    'Data from number text box
      End Sub
```

Now AddNameItem_Click( ) is complete, so that we're able to add our
friends' names to the File menu at run time. The next step after adding
names is retrieving them on demand, and we do that when the user
clicks a name in the menu. When that happens, an NNN_Click( )
event occurs (i.e., NNN( ) is the name we've given to our menu item

array). Note that the first item, NNN(0), is simply the place-holding dummy item, but the next item, NNN(1), corresponds to the first name in the menu under that bar; NNN(2) corresponds to the next name, and so on. To write the NNN_Click( ) Sub procedure, find and click NNN in the Objects box of the Event Procedure window, and double click the Click event in the Events box. This Sub procedure appears:

```
Sub NNN_Click(Index As Integer)

End Sub
```

When the user clicks a name in the menu, this procedure is called with an index number that corresponds to the item chosen. Since we've stored the names and numbers with the same index as the menu items themselves, we can display the requested name and number on the screen like this:

```
Sub NNN_Click(Index As Integer)
    Text1.Text = Names(Index)
    Text2.Text = Numbers(Index)
End Sub
```

That's all there is to it. If we add an End statement to make the Exit item active, we're done. The complete code appears in Listing 3-4.

Listing 3-4 Phone Book Application

```
Phone.Frm
  Dim Shared Names(1 To 10) As String 'Form-level array
  Dim Shared Numbers(1 To 10) As String 'Form-level array

Sub AddNameItem_Click ( )
    Static NumberNames
    NumberNames = NumberNames + 1
    Load NNN(NumberNames)
    NNN(NumberNames).Caption = Text1.Text
    NNN(NumberNames).Visible = -1
    Names(NumberNames) = Text1.Text
    Numbers(NumberNames) = Text2.Text
End Sub
```

continues

109

Listing 3-4 continued

```
Sub ExitItem_Click ( )
    End
End Sub

Sub NNN_Click (Index As Integer)
    Text1.Text = Names(Index)
    Text2.Text = Numbers(Index)
End Sub
```

Run the phone application; you can store names and numbers by typing them in the text boxes and selecting the Add Current Name item. Each time you do, another name is added to the menu, as shown in Figure 3-27; to retrieve the number for any name, just select that menu item.

Figure 3-27 Functioning Phone Book Application

We've come far in our work with menus in this chapter; however, there is one significant thing that we didn't do: we didn't make items like Load File... and Save File... active. Usually, a menu item with an ellipsis like this pops open a dialog box when selected—and for that reason, we'll cover dialog boxes next (and in the following chapter, we'll add file handling as well to make these items fully active).

Using Dialog Boxes

So far, all our programs have involved a single window; that is, a single form. However, it's common for applications to use many windows—dialog boxes, message boxes, warning boxes, help windows, and all sorts of other windows. Probably the most common types of such windows are dialog boxes. However, we'll learn a lot about other types of multiple form applications in this chapter.

In fact, Visual Basic provides some built-in windows that we can use for just this purpose: MsgBox( ) and InputBox$( ). These two Visual Basic statements display a message and get string input from the user, respectively. Using them is easy, and we'll start with them first. Next, we'll see how to work with multiple forms in general—how to create a second form when designing our application, how to display it, how to address the properties of other forms, and how to hide them again.

After that, we'll see how to create and use dialog boxes in general. Dialog boxes play an integral part in getting information from the user in Visual Basic; so far, we've handled tasks like numeric input, string input, and option selection by using buttons and menus. In real applications, however, these same tasks are often handled with dialog boxes. We'll also spend a good deal of time in this chapter with some of the controls that are often associated with dialog boxes: scroll bars and list boxes. With all that in mind, then, let's start with MsgBox( ) and InputBox$( ), the two simplest types of dialog boxes available.

Displaying a Message Box with MsgBox( )

The first function we'll cover, MsgBox( ), really only allows a restricted dialog: you place a message on the screen in a window, and the user is restricted to communicating back through buttons. You use MsgBox( ) as follows:

```
RetVal% = MsgBox (message$ [,type [,title$]])
```

where "message$" indicates the message you want to display (e.g., "Error Number 5" or "That button is already selected."), "type" indicates what buttons you want in the message box, and "title$" is the string you want placed in the message box window's caption (this string is truncated after the 255th character).

The type argument lets you select from a number of options, such as displaying OK buttons, Abort, Retry, or Ignore buttons, or Cancel buttons, as indicated in Table 4-1. The values in that table can be added together; for example, to display Yes, No, OK, and Cancel buttons, you'd use a type value of 4 + 1 = 5. Note that even if you don't specify a value for type, Visual Basic still places an OK button in the message box so that the user can close it. The return values for this function (allowing you to determine what button the user pushed) appear in Table 4-2.

Table 4-1 Type Argument for MsgBox( ) Function

Value	Means
0	OK button only
1	OK button and Cancel button
2	Abort, Retry, Ignore buttons
3	Yes, No, Cancel buttons
4	Yes, No buttons
5	Retry, Cancel buttons

Value	Means
0	First button has default focus
256	Second button has default focus
512	Third button has default focus

Table 4-2 MsgBox( ) Return Values

Value	Means
1	OK button was pressed
2	Cancel button was pressed
3	Abort button was pressed
4	Retry button was pressed
5	Ignore button was pressed
6	Yes button was pressed
7	No button was pressed

Let's put all this to use. Some common uses for message boxes are: help messages, About boxes (describing the application and the application's authors), and error messages. Let's begin with a help message. Start Visual Basic and put a command button into the middle of a form with the caption Help, and open its Click event in the code window. The following Sub procedure template appears:

```
Sub Command1_Click ()

End Sub
```

We can use MsgBox to display a simple help message: "This button displays Help.", as well as an OK button and a Cancel button (type = 1) like this:

```
Sub Command1_Click ()
    MsgBox "This button displays Help.", 1, "Help"
End Sub
```

(Notice that we can also use MsgBox( ) as a statement, not a function, which we do here since we're not interested in its return value). When clicked, the Help button puts our message box on the screen, as shown in Figure 4-1. That's all; we're using elementary dialog boxes already.

Figure 4-1 A Trial Help Message Box

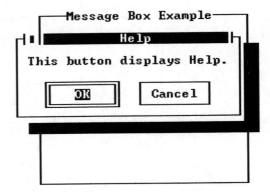

We can see an example of an error message box if we modify our Tic-Tac-Toe game; you may recall that the user could click any button, changing it to an x or an o whether or not something was already there. We can fix that by checking the clicked button's caption and displaying an error message if the button had already been clicked. We called the control array that handles the button clicks TTT, and this was the corresponding event procedure:

```
Sub TTT_Click (Index As Integer)

    If (Xturn) Then
        TTT(Index).Caption = "x"
        Xturn = False
    Else
        TTT(Index).Caption = "o"
        Xturn = True
    End If

End Sub
```

We can add an error message and leave the Sub procedure if the button was already clicked like this:

```
Sub TTT_Click (Index As Integer)
—>  If(TTT(Index).Caption <> "") Then
—>      MsgBox "That button was already clicked.", 1, "Error"
—>      Exit Sub
—>  End If

    If (Xturn) Then
        TTT(Index).Caption = "x"
        Xturn = False
    Else
        TTT(Index).Caption = "o" Xturn = True
    End If

End Sub
```

This way, if the user clicks a button that already had an x or an o displayed, an error box is displayed as in Figure 4-2, and the button is not changed. Now the user can simply click the OK button and click another button in the game instead.

Figure 4-2 An Error Message Box

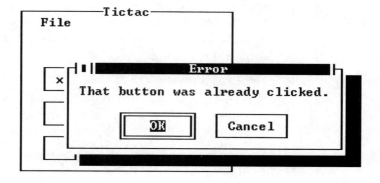

Because the general appearance of such message boxes is similar to standard message boxes in normal Visual Basic applications, using MsgBox( ) in your programs can make them seem more professional. And, as indicated, you can receive a limited amount of information back from MsgBox—which button a user clicked. However, that limits the user's input options to: Yes, No, Cancel, Abort, Retry, Ignore, and OK. On the other hand, the next function that we'll explore, InputBox$( ), has no such restriction.

An InputBox$( ) Application—A DOS Shell

We can see how InputBox$( ) functions by creating an application that uses it; in this case, we'll use Visual Basic's Shell statement, with which you can start DOS applications. The way you use Shell is like this:

```
RetVal = Shell command$
```

Here, command$ is the command string, just as you might type after the DOS prompt. That is, command$ must be the name of a file that ends in .EXE, .BAT, or .COM. We can create our own application called, say, DOS Shell, which will start applications on request. To get the name and path of the application to start, we can use the InputBox$( ) function. That function looks like this in general:

```
RetString$ = InputBox$(prompt$ [,title$ [,default$ [,x% [,y%]]]])
```

Here, RetString$ is the string that the user typed (i.e., the input from the input box), prompt$ is the prompt we display to indicate what type of input is desired, title$ is the caption we want to give the input box, default$ is the default string that first appears in the input box's text box (i.e., if the user types no other response, default$ is returned), and the optional x% and y% arguments indicate the position of the input box as measured from the upper left corner of the screen (in rows and columns).

Let's see all this in action. Create a new form called DOS Shell and open the Menu Design Window. We can create one menu named File, with two items in it: Run... and Exit, giving them the CtlNames RunItem and ExitItem as shown in Figure 4-3.

Now open the code window displaying the template for RunItem_Click( ) like this:

```
Sub RunItem_Click()

End Sub
```

We want to get a string for input here, so we can use InputBox$( ). In fact, because the menu item here has an ellipsis (Run...), the user is expecting a dialog box to appear. When we get a string back from InputBox$( ), we can just pass it on to Shell( ) like this:

```
Sub RunItem_Click()
    Shell InputBox$("Application to run:", "Run...")
End Sub
```

Figure 4-3 File Menu for DOS Shell Application

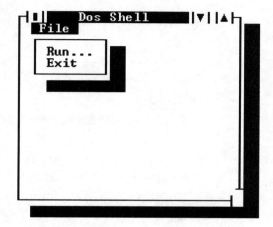

In this case, we're asking for an input box that has the prompt "Application to run:" and the caption "Run..." in the title bar. We can then pass the string that was typed back to the Shell( ) procedure. In addition, we should make the Exit item in our File menu active as well by placing the End statement in the ExitItem_Click( ) Sub procedure like this:

```
Sub ExitItem_Click()
    End
End Sub
```

At this point, we're set; when you run the DOS Shell application, you'll see a simple window on the screen with a File menu; when you open that menu, there are two items available: Run... and Exit. When you click Run..., a dialog box opens up—as it should—as shown in Figure 4-4. We can then type the name of a DOS application to run; the application is started, and functions normally.

Figure 4-4 DOS Shell Application First Attempt

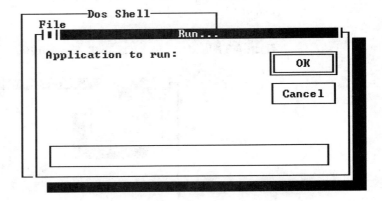

However, the appearance of the dialog box is less than optimal, which can always be a problem unless we can design our windows explicitly ourselves. As you can see, the prompt appears in the top of the dialog box, and the text box itself is some distance away, at the bottom. In other words, although InputBox$ works, you may be surprised at the results. A better option is for you to design the dialog box you want to use. Let's look into that next.

Creating Applications with Multiple Windows

As you might expect, it's not difficult to create multiple form programs under Visual Basic. Let's revise the DOS Shell program to use a dialog box of our own creation. To do that, we'll need a new form, which is easily created: just select the New Form... item in the File menu, and give our new form the name, say, Form2.Frm. The new form appears on the screen in the Form Designer.

The name of a form, like Form2, is not a CtlName property (because a form is not a control); instead, it is a form name, held in the FormName property. Until now, we haven't paid much attention to FormNames, but now that we're using multiple forms, they will become important. For example, now you'll be able to switch between forms using the project window—just click the name of the form you want to work on.

The First Form

TIP: *If you want to specifically indicate which of a number of windows to place on the screen first, you can use the Set Startup Form... item in Visual Basic's Run menu.*

When there are multiple forms involved, a natural question is: which one does Visual Basic start first when the application starts? It would be awkward if it decided to place our dialog box on the screen by itself. It turns out that, as you might expect, the default here is that the first form created when you're creating an application is the first form started when the application runs.

When the first form is started, a Form_Load event is generated for that form. This is a special event which occurs when a form is about to appear, so you can often do initialization of your entire application here. In particular, if your application depends on a number of windows being on the screen at the same time, you can use the Form_Load event of the first window (i.e., the one Visual Basic displays first) to display the others. (We'll see a great deal about the Form_Load event later.)

The question now is: how do we do just that—display other windows? After we've designed our dialog box, how will we be able to place it on the screen when we want it? Visual Basic has several ways of handling this task. For example, two statements, Load and Unload, load and unload forms into and out of memory. In this way, Load and Unload work much the same way as they did with menu items in the last chapter. Here, however, we can load and unload forms by using their FormName properties as follows:

```
Load Form2
UnLoad Form2
```

However, we should note that simply loading a form does not display it; that is handled by the Show *method*. As we've seen before (with the SetFocus method), a method is like a procedure, except that it's tied to an object (a control or form), just as a property is. In other words, a property is made up of data attached to the object; a method is a procedure attached to the object.

To show a form named Form2, then, we'd just have to execute this statement: Form2.Show [modal%], where the optional argument modal% can take on two values: 0 or 1. If it's 0, the user is free to use other forms even when this form (Form2 here) is on the screen; if it's 1, all other forms in our application become inactive, and the user cannot switch to them. In the latter case, the form is said to be modal

119

(i.e., the user's course of action is restricted). Dialog boxes are mostly modal—for example, InputBox$( ) places a modal dialog box on the screen. Note that if you omit the form name, the reference is assumed to be to the current form.

One more point is important about Show—you must have loaded a form before you can display it, but if a form is not loaded, Show loads it before displaying it. (For that reason, we'll be able to use the Show method alone to display forms, not Load followed by Show.)

Besides the Show method, there is the *Hide* method, which, predictably, hides the form from the screen once again. Together, Show, and Hide are the two methods that handle dialog box appearances and disappearances. For example, we can change the FormName of our dialog box's form from Form2 to, say, RunDialog. To load and display this form, we'll only have to execute the RunDialog.Show 1 statement (where we're making this dialog box modal by passing an argument of 1 to the Show method).

When there are a number of forms on the screen, you may wonder how to refer to the controls and properties of a specific one. The solution to that is simply to use the form as part of that control or property's name, like this: Form1.ExitItem or Form2.Text2. Until now, when we've been dealing with only one form, we didn't need to specify the form name when referring to a control—Visual Basic simply assumed that the current form was the one we wanted. However, with multiple forms, all we'll need to do is to specify the form name along with the property or method we want to access.

In other words, formerly referred to a control's set of properties like this: control.property. Now, however, we might have a number of forms to choose among, and can specify the same thing like this: form.control.property. In addition, now that we know a little about methods, we can refer to them by form as well, like this: form.method. Let's see some of this in action.

Creating Custom Dialog Boxes

The first step is to design our dialog box the way we want it. That is, we can start working on the second form, RunDialog, in the Visual Basic environment. To begin, change its form name property from Form2 to RunDialog using the FormName property in the properties bar. Also, give it the caption Run..., just as we labeled the InputBox$( ) dialog box before.

The job of this dialog box is to accept a string (i.e., the name of a Visual Basic application to run), so we'll need a text box in it. For that reason, place a text box in the upper half of the form, as shown in Figure 4-5, and remove the default text in it so that it appears blank. Also, we won't need minimizing or maximizing buttons here, since this is a modal dialog box (i.e., users can't do anything else in our application until they deal with this box), so find the MinButton and MaxButton properties of the Run... dialog box and set them to False. When you do, the buttons will disappear from the form.

Figure 4-5 Text Box Position in Run... Dialog Box

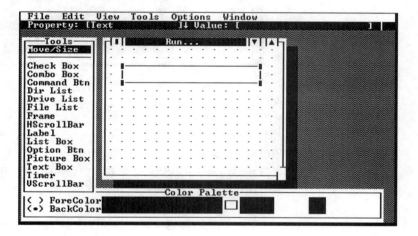

In addition, just like most other dialog boxes, this dialog box need not be resized, so change its BorderStyle property to Fixed Single—that is, a fixed-size, single-width border (when you select a fixed-border type, Visual Basic also removes the Size option in that form's system menu). We'll also want two buttons here: OK and Cancel. In particular, you should note that most dialog boxes should have Cancel options in them (especially if the dialog box is modal). This gives users a way out if the choices they've made until now have been in error or were unintentional. For that reason, double-click the command button tool twice, once for each new button, and position buttons below the text

121

box, labeling one OK and the other Cancel. We can give CtlNames to these buttons of, say, OKButton and CancelButton. The dialog box now appears as in Figure 4-6.

Figure 4-6 Our DOS Shell Dialog Template

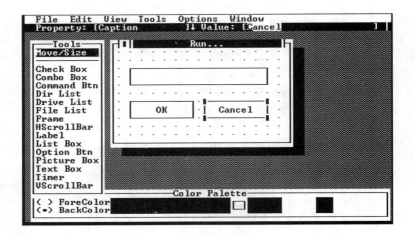

Now that we've designed the dialog box's appearance, let's go back and start working on the code that will make this box active. In particular, the event that should make the dialog box appear is the RunItem_Click( ) event (where RunItem is the CtlName of the Run... item in the application's File menu). Open up that procedure, which currently looks like this:

```
Sub RunItem_Click()
    Shell InputBox$("Application to run:", "Run...")
End Sub
```

This is the actual Shell statement that we put in earlier, but which is now going to be used only if the user presses the OK button in our dialog box. In other words, this procedure should be changed as shown below to simply display the dialog box:

```
Sub RunItem_Click()
    RunDialog.Show 1
End Sub
```

Recall that even if the RunDialog form is not in memory when the Show method is executed, Visual basic will automatically load it. In

fact, you can run the program right now; when you click the Run...
item in the File menu, our Run... dialog box will appear. On the other
hand, there's no way to get rid of it now, since it is modal (which
means that if you try to switch to other windows in the same application, you'll get a beep).

Let's start modifying the second form now. The real action in
RunDialog takes place in the click procedures associated with the
buttons. When the user clicks the OK button, the program is supposed
to execute the DOS application whose path and name were typed in
the text box.

Bring up RunDialog's OK button in the code window. To do that,
switch from our first form's file, Dosshell.Frm to the second form
(which is named Form2.Frm) in the Event Procedure's Files box. Next,
click OKButton in the Event Procedure's Objects box, and the Click
event in the Events box. The following Sub procedure template
appears:

```
Sub OKButton_Click()

End Sub
```

Since this is the procedure connected with the OK button, we are
supposed to run the application here; the path and name of that
application are presumably in the dialog box's text box, which is still
named Text1. For that reason, we can simply put this line in the
procedure:

```
Sub OKButton_Click()
    Shell Text1.Text
End Sub
```

However, before doing so, we should hide the dialog box. That way,
when the Visual Basic application finishes, we'll return to the original
Visual Basic Shell application, not to the dialog box:

```
Sub OKButton_Click()
—>     RunDialog.Hide
       Shell Text1.Text
End Sub
```

Now, immediately after the user clicks the OK button, the dialog box
disappears, and the desired application begins (if you leave the text
box blank and click OK, Command.Com will start). In addition, while

we're here, we should make the OK button the default (i.e., display it with a double black border). As a result, the user only has to type the name of the desired application and press the Enter key, since pressing the Enter key clicks the default button. To do that, set the button's Default property to True in the properties bar.

The other button in our dialog box is the Cancel button; if it's clicked, we should just hide the dialog box and return to the original form, the DOS Shell application. That procedure can look like this:

```
Sub CancelButton_Click()
    RunDialog.Hide
End Sub
```

This returns us to the original form and restores the focus to it—nothing else is required. That's all there is to it; the complete code for the whole program appears in Listing 4-1.

TIP: *You can check to see if a form is hidden with the Visible property: if Form.Visible is True, the form is visible; if False, invisible.*

Listing 4-1 Visual Basic Shell Application

```
Shell.Frm ————————————————————

Sub RunItem_Click ()
    RunDialog.Show 1
End Sub

Sub ExitItem_Click ()
    End
End Sub

Form2.Frm ————————————————————

Sub OKButton_Click ()
    RunDialog.Hide
    Shell Text1.Text
End Sub

Sub CancelButton_Click ()
    RunDialog.Hide
End Sub
```

As you can see, the program is quite short—only five lines of actual code, each line tied to its own event. In this way, event-driven programming can save us a good deal of work when it comes to I/O handling. (So far, we've mostly been dealing with I/O, but in the next chapter, when we start working with files, we'll start adding more code to our programs for internal processing of data behind the scenes.) Earlier in this chapter, we saw how to use InputBox$( ) as a dialog box of sorts, but now we've seen that it's almost as easy to create our own dialog boxes. The result is usually worth the trouble in Visual Basic.

In fact, there are many types of controls that you can find in dialog boxes—and buttons and text boxes are only two of them. For example, our next application will include a control panel, which will let us set various aspects of the main window with various controls including scroll bars (control panels are very popular in large scale Visual Basic applications). Let's look into that next.

Adding a Control Panel to Our Applications

We can start a new application to demonstrate how control panels work in Visual Basic applications. As you might know, a control panel is used to customize certain aspects of an application; in our case, we'll use it to set some properties of the main window: the background color, the height and width of the window, and the main window's caption. Let's call this application Panel.Mak; this program will give us experience with changing the properties of another window from the current one, as well as a new type of control —scroll bars.

We can make the form name of the main window App (standing for the application that will use the control panel). Start a new project, create a new form (i.e., select the New Form item in the File menu), and give it a name (i.e., FormName) App. Save that form and create a new form named ControlPanel, with a caption of Control Panel, and save it as Panel.Frm. We should also save the project as, say, Panel.Mak so that our project doesn't inadvertantly write over earlier files. Let's put a text box—which we might name NewCaption—into the control panel, with the label "Application Caption:", as shown in Figure 4-7.

Figure 4-7 Starting the Control Panel Application

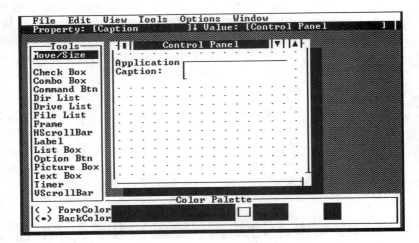

TIP: *If the text you want to put into a label is too long for the label's width, don't worry: like multi-line text boxes, labels have automatic word wrap.*

Delete the text now in the text box (i.e., "Text1"); this will be where users can change the name of the main window if they want to. These kinds of changes will go into effect when the user clicks the OK button, which we can give the CtlName OKButton to. Let's add that now at the bottom of the control panel, along with a Cancel button which we can call CancelButton. As an added touch, we can give the OK button the focus (which is usually the case in control panels) by setting its Default property to true in the properties bar.

As you might expect, the code for CancelButton does nothing more than hide the control panel as follows:

```
Sub CancelButton_Click ()
    ControlPanel.Hide
End Sub
```

On the other hand, we'll do more work in the OKButton procedure because of the way our control panel will work: rather than keep track of the changes made by the user, we'll just set the relevant properties of the main window, App, after they press the OK button. For example, here's how to set the main window's new caption in OKButton_Click( ):

```
Sub OKButton_Click ()
—>      App.Caption = NewCaption.Text
        ControlPanel.Hide
    End Sub
```

Notice the first line here: App.Caption = NewCaption.Text. In general, that's the way we refer to the properties of another form: by using the form name first. If we had wanted to change the properties of one of App's controls, we could have referred to it as App.Control.Property.

Note that we should also load the current settings of the main window's properties into the control panel's controls when the user opens it (e.g., when the user starts the control panel the first time, the text box should say: "App", which is the current caption of the main window), because that's the way a control panel usually works. Let's manipulate the size of the main window next.

Using Scroll Bars

The default measuring system in Visual Basic for DOS uses rows and columns, which means that the two properties we are interested in changing—the main window's height and width— are measured in rows and columns. We could, of course, just use a text window in the control panel and have the user set new sizes in terms of rows and columns, which means that we could read in the values using Val( ) and set the two appropriate App properties, App.Height and App.Width, directly. However, it's not so easy to get a feel for rows and columns; instead, we can use a popular Visual Basic control for converting a numerical value into a smooth range that's easily manipulated visually — scroll bars.

You've seen scroll bars already in Visual Basic. In fact, we've used them ourselves already, when we developed our multiline text box for the Pad application. However, Visual Basic took care of all the details there; now it's up to us. There are five primary properties of scroll bars that we'll be interested in here: Min, Max, Value, LargeChange, and SmallChange.

Min is the numerical value that you assign to the top or left of a scroll bar (all of these properties can go from 0 to 32,767), Max is the value you assign to the right or bottom, and Value is the current value corresponding to the position of the thumb—the box that moves inside the scroll bar, also called the scroll box. You set Min and Max yourself; the scroll bar then indicates the position of the thumb by placing a value in its Value property, which we can read directly

127

Chapter 4: Using Dialog Boxes

(Min <= Value <= Max). For example, if the thumb was all the way to the left in a horizontal scroll bar, the scroll bar's Value property would be equal to the value you put in the Min property.

The LargeChange property indicates the amount that Value should change each time the user clicks the bar above or below the thumb in the scroll bar—i.e., how far the thumb moves. SmallChange is the amount that Value should change when the user clicks one of the arrows at the top and bottom of the scroll bar. With the exception of Value, we can set all these properties at design time.

The main event with scroll bars is the Change event, which occurs every time the thumb is moved. However, since we don't want our changes to take effect unless the user clicks the OK button, we won't read the value of our scroll bars until then. Let's see how this works in practice. Click the vertical scroll bar tool in the Visual Basic toolbox (i.e., VScrollBar), and a scroll bar appears in our control panel. Because we'll be using a total of three scroll bars in the control panel (corresponding to the height and width of the main window, and the color to use for its background color), so place this first scroll bar over to the left in the control panel.

Next, we have to determine the Min and Max values for this scroll bar. Since there are 25 lines in the standard screen height, we can range from 4 (the minimum for a window in Visual Basic for DOS) to 25. This first scroll bar can set the main window's height, and we might call it NewHeight—which means that the properties we should set at design time are: NewHeight.Min = 4 and NewHeight.Max = 25 (similiarly, when we design a scroll bar to change the main window's width, we can call it NewWidth; NewWidth.Min will be 5, and NewWidth.Max will be 80).

To set those properties, click the Min property in the property bar; the default value is 0—set it to 4. Next, click the Max property—its default value is 32767; set it to 25. In addition, we'll have to specify values for LargeChange (when the user clicks the scroll bar above or below the thumb) and SmallChange (when the user clicks the arrows at the end of the scroll bar). For the purposes of this demonstration, we can use NewHeight.LargeChange = 4, and NewHeight.SmallChange = 1. Now the scroll bar will be active when we run the program (that is, we'll be able to read its setting simply by reading NewHeight.Value). For this reason, we should label the scroll bar. Put a label above it that says "New Height", as in Figure 4-8.

Figure 4-8 Our First Scroll Bar

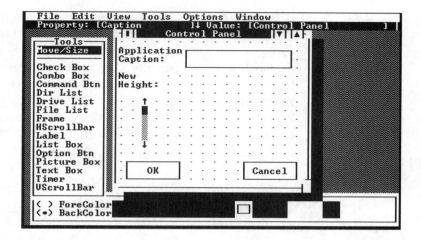

Next, create a new vertical scroll bar, giving it the CtlName NewWidth and a label above it that says "New Width". Place it next to the first scroll bar, and give it the Min and Max properties of 5 and 80 respectively. For the LargeChange and SmallChange values, we can use 1 and 4 again. Now let's add the necessary code to the OK button. When users click the OK button, they want the main window properties Height and Width set to NewHeight.Value and NewWidth.Value, respectively, so we can just add these lines to OKButton_Click ( ):

```
Sub OKButton_Click ()
        App.Caption = NewCaption.Text
—>     App.Height = NewHeight.Value
—>     App.Width = NewWidth.Value
        ControlPanel.Hide
End Sub
```

Let's see this in action. To do so, we'll have to add code to the main window to pop up the control panel in the first place. Go back to the main window, App, and open the Menu Design Window. In this case, we can create a single menu, named File (menu name: FileMenu), which has two items in it: Control Panel... (CtlName: ControlPanelItem) and Exit (CtlName: ExitItem). After creating the menu, close the Menu Design Window and open the ControlPanelItem_Click( ) in the code window, like this:

```
Sub ControlPanelItem_Click()

End Sub
```

When the user selects this item, we should load the control panel's
controls with the current settings of the main window and then
display the control panel on the screen. In other words, we want
to load ControlPanel.NewCaption.Text (recall that we gave
the control panel the form name of ControlPanel) with
App.Caption, ControlPanel.NewHeight.Value with App.Height, and
ControlPanel.NewWidth.Value with App.Width, like this (the thumb
in the scroll bars will move, matching the number we place in their
Value property):

```
Sub ControlPanelItem_Click()
    ControlPanel.NewCaption.Text = App.Caption
    ControlPanel.NewHeight.Value = App.Height
    ControlPanel.NewWidth.Value = App.Width
        :
End Sub
```

Then, after loading the defaults, we want to show the control panel,
which we can do like this (note that the control panel does not have
to be on the screen for us to change its properties):

```
    Sub ControlPanelItem_Click()
        ControlPanel.NewCaption.Text = App.Caption
        ControlPanel.NewHeight.Value = App.Height
        ControlPanel.NewWidth.Value = App.Width
—>      ControlPanel.Show
    End Sub
```

Again, that's the way to refer to the properties of another form—by
referring to the properties' full name, including form. In addition,
before starting the application, we should make the Exit item in the
File menu active, which we can do with the End statement, like this:

```
Sub ExitItem_Click()
    End
End Sub
```

Now start the application and click the Control Panel... item in the
File menu. When you do, the control panel opens and displays the
current defaults for both the main window's caption and size. You
might try changing the size to see if the program works; if you change

the text in the text box and then click the OK button, the control panel disappears and the caption in the main window will be changed to match your new caption. Or, if you use the scroll bars, you can reset the size of the window (which is really no great savings, because the main window can be resized as easily by dragging its edges—but as an example it's still impressive to see).

Now let's work on changing the color of the main window. The background color—that is, the color behind the text—is kept in the BackColor property, and that's the one we want to manipulate (the foreground color—the color of the text itself—is kept in the ForeColor property). We should notice, however, that background colors in Visual Basic for DOS can only range from 0 to 15, as shown in Table 4-3.

Table 4-3 Colors in Visual Basic for DOS

Value	Color
0	Black
1	Blue
2	Green
3	Cyan
4	Red
5	Magenta
6	Brown
7	White
8	Gray
9	Bright Blue
10	Bright Green
11	Bright Cyan
12	Bright Red
13	Pink
14	Yellow
15	Bright White

We can actually provide the user with some direct visual feedback, indicating the color they're selecting—and doing so will introduce us to the scroll bar change event at the same time. Create a label named, say, NewColor, and place it in the space between the OK and Cancel buttons at the bottom of the control panel, giving it a fixed single border by changing its BorderStyle property (by default, labels don't have a border), as shown in Figure 4-9. This is where we'll display the color as selected with the scroll bars.

Figure 4-9 Complete Control Panel Template

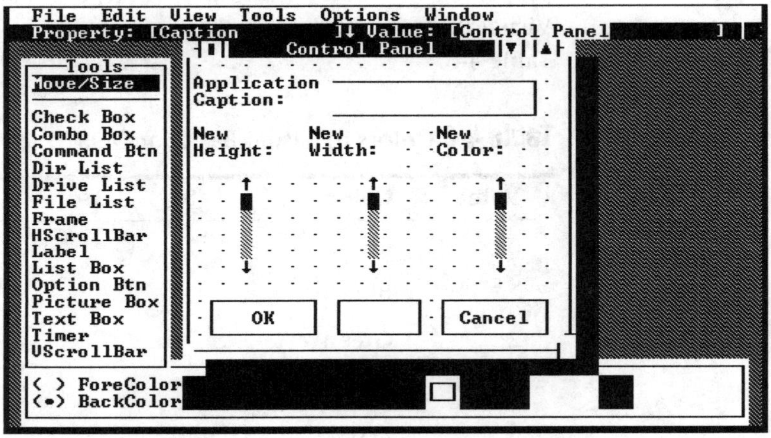

Setting a Form's BackColor

L et's add a new scroll bar to our control panel, which we can give the CtlName ColorScroll. Place it to the right of the other two scroll bars, as shown in Figure 4-9. Next, we can give it a Min value of 0 and a Max value of 15. We can also use SmallChange and LargeChange values of, say, 1 and 2. After setting these values in the scroll bar itself, open the following Sub procedure template in the code window:

```
Sub ColorScroll_Change()

End Sub
```

This is the event procedure that is called whenever ColorScroll.Value is changed. Although we could simply read this value when the OK button is clicked and change App.BackColor accordingly, we can use this event to keep track of the currently selected color and display it in the NewColor label, which we do simply like this:

```
Sub ColorScroll_Change()
    NewColor.BackColor = ColorScroll.Value
End Sub
```

Whenever the user changes the setting of the New Color scroll bar, the color in the NewColor label changes to match. Now run the program. When you do, you'll find that you can manipulate the color in the NewColor label simply by moving the scroll bar's thumb around. In addition, we'll need to change the color we've designed this way into the background color of the main window when the user clicks the OK button. We can do so by adding a line to the OK_Button_Click event as follows:

```
Sub OKButton_Click ()
    App.Caption = NewCaption.Text
    App.Height = NewHeight.Value
    App.Width = NewWidth.Value
—>    App.BackColor = ColorScroll.Value
    ControlPanel.Hide
End Sub
```

Now the user is able to select the color of the main window and see that color at the same time. When the user presses the OK button, the change is made instantly to the main window's BackColor property, turning it to whatever color is choosen. That's almost all for our control panel application; at this point, most of it is functional. The last step is to load the original background color from the main window into the control panel when it first starts— that is, to load the default color into the control panel. To do that, we can take the original color, App.BackColor, and load it into ControlPanel.NewColor.BackColor, as well as ControlPanel.ColorScroll.Value. Because the control panel pops up when the Control Panel... item is selected in the File menu, we can do that as follows:

```
Sub ControlPanelItem_Click()
    ControlPanel.NewCaption.Text = App.Caption
    ControlPanel.NewHeight.Value = App.Height
    ControlPanel.NewWidth.Value = App.Width
—>    ControlPanel.ColorScroll.Value = App.BackColor
—>    ControlPanel.NewColor.BackColor = App.BackColor
```

133

```
        ControlPanel.Show
End Sub
```

And that's all; we've completed the control panel application, which let us customize our main window through the use of scroll bars. Its code appears in Listing 4-2.

Listing 4-2 The Control Panel Application

```
App  - - - - - - - - - - - - - - - - - - - - - - - - - - - - - - - - - - - - - - - - - - - -

Sub ControlPanelItem_Click()
    ControlPanel.NewCaption.Text = App.Caption
    ControlPanel.NewHeight.Value = App.Height
    ControlPanel.NewWidth.Value = App.Width
    ControlPanel.ColorScroll.Value = App.BackColor
    ControlPanel.NewColor.BackColor = App.BackColor
    ControlPanel.Show
End Sub

Sub ExitItem_Click()
    End
End Sub

ControlPanel  - - - - - - - - - - - - - - - - - - - - - - - - - - - - - - - - - - - - - -

Sub ColorScroll_Change()
    NewColor.BackColor = ColorScroll.Value
End Sub

Sub OKButton_Click ()
    App.Caption = NewCaption.Text
    App.Height = NewHeight.Value
    App.Width = NewWidth.Value
    App.BackColor = ColorScroll.Value
    ControlPanel.Hide
End Sub

Sub CancelButton ()
    ControlPanel.Hide
End Sub
```

Scroll bars are not the only controls you find in dialog boxes, of course; other common controls include list boxes, and we'll take a look at them next.

Creating List Boxes

You use list boxes when you have a number of choices to present to the user, and you want to limit the choices to what you present (by contrast, a combo box is used more for suggested choices—that is, users can enter their own choices in the combo box's text box if they want to). For example, you might have a list of customized DOS applications that your program is capable of starting, so that you can present the choices in a list box. Or you might want to present the various file attribute options (plain file, read-only, hidden and so on) when writing to a file. In general, list boxes can be useful anywhere there are a number of choices to choose from. And, because list boxes can have scroll bars, the number of such choices can be significantly greater than you can present in a menu (which makes them popular in dialog boxes).

As an example, let's put together a mini-database program. Databases usually sort their data records according to some key, and we'll find we can do that here with a list box. Let's say that this database program is meant to keep track of stock inventory; for that reason, we might want to keep track of these things:

```
Name of the product
Number of the product
Additional space for comments
```

For example, if we had seven apples that had to be sold before they spoil next Thursday, our data might look like this:

```
Name of the product: "Apples"
Number of the product: "7"
Additional space for comments: "Sell by Thursday."
```

Each of these data items: "Apples", "7", and "Sell by Thursday." is called a *field* in a database. Together, they make up a *record*. To set up our application, we can add a menu to our main window with an item named Find Record...; when selected, a dialog box will open with a list box that lists the names associated with each record—e.g., Apples, Bananas, Cantaloupe, and so on:

```
┌─────────────────────────────────────────────┐
│                                               │
│              Find Record...                   │
│                                               │
├───────────────────────────────────────────────┤
│                                               │
│        ┌──────────────────────────┐           │
│        │                          │           │
│        │   Apples                 │           │
│        │   Bananas                │           │
│        │   Cantaloupe             │           │
│        │                          │           │
│        │                          │           │
│        │                          │           │
│        └──────────────────────────┘           │
│                                               │
│                                               │
│                                               │
│                                               │
└───────────────────────────────────────────────┘
```

By double-clicking one of these names, the user can bring up the corresponding record (i.e., the dialog box will disappear and the record's data will be placed into text boxes in the main window). One of the properties of list boxes that will help us here is the Sorted property; if True, Visual Basic keeps all the items in the list box sorted alphabetically—in other words, VB will handle the sorting of our products automatically.

To design this application, start Visual Basic, call this project Database.Mak and give the main form the caption "Database". Next, give it the FormName Form1 (to keep it separate from the pop-up database window, which will be called Form2). We'll need three text boxes on this main form, which we can label Name:, Number:, and Comment:, and to which we can give the CtlNames NameField, NumberField, and CommentField. In fact, we can make the comment box a multiline text box so that a considerable amount of text can be stored there. Next, we can add a menu named File with several items in it: Add Item, Find Item..., Save File..., Load File..., and Exit. At this point, the main window should look like the one in Figure 4-10.

Figure 4-10 Database Template Window

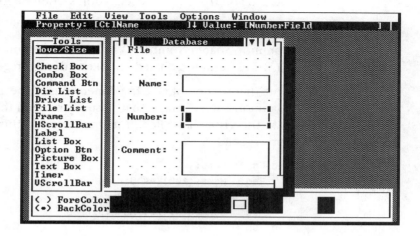

For the first menu choice, Add Item, let's use the CtlName AddAnItem (AddItem is a reserved word, as we're about to see); this item is available so that the user can fill the database with data. After editing the three text boxes, the user can select Add Item to add this data to a new record in our database. We use the CtlName FindItem for the next menu choice, Find Item...; this item is the one that will open the dialog box (the dialog box will contain the list box which holds the product names of each record, sorted alphabetically). When the user double clicks an item in the list, the dialog box will disappear and the correct record will appear in the main window. We'll be able to add the code for the next two menu items, Save File... and Load File..., in our chapter about files; in the meantime, give them the CtlNames SaveItem and LoadItem.

Let's write the AddAnItem_Click( ) procedure first. Open the code window, displaying this for the Add Item menu choice:

```
Sub AddAnItem_Click()

End Sub
```

When the user clicks Add Item, the current contents of the text boxes are to be stored in the data base. We can do that by setting up some global variables (note that they should be global, not form-level, variables, since our dialog box—an entirely separate form—will have to reach them as well) like this in Form1's declaration module (we'll have to add them to the declaration section of Form2 also):

```
Common Shared Names() As String
```

Common Shared Numbers( ) As String Common Shared Comments( ) As String Common Shared TotalRecords As Integer

Note that we do not give the dimensions of the arrays here; with Common Shared arrays, that's usually done in the form load event with the Visual Basic Redim statment, so add this code to Form1_Load( ):

```
Sub Form1_Load()
    Redim Names(100) As String
    Redim Numbers(100) As String
    Redim Comments(100) As String
End Sub
```

Now we've set aside enough space to hold records for 100 products. Also note that we're keeping track of the total number of records in a global integer named TotalRecords. Now we're free to fill those arrays with data (because the user has placed the data we'll need in the main window's text boxes before clicking Add Item). That is, we can store data in our database arrays this way in AddAnItem_Click( ) (note we increment TotalRecords first, because we're adding a new record):

```
Sub AddAnItem_Click()
    TotalRecords = TotalRecords + 1
    Names(TotalRecords) = NameField.Text
    Numbers(TotalRecords) = NumberField.Text
    Comments(TotalRecords) = CommentField.Text
        :
End Sub
```

For example, if we were about to create the first record, and this was the data in the main window's text boxes:

```
Name of the product: "Apples"
Number of the product: "7"
Additional space for comments: "Sell by Thursday."
```

then Names(1) would be set to "Apples", Numbers(1) to "7", and Comments(1) to "Sell by Thursday." Now that we've stored the data, we have to add the name of this product—Apples—to our (automatically alphabetized) list box so that the user can select records easily.

We do that with the *AddItem* method. Note that this is a method, which means that we have to attach it to the name of the list box we want to change. For example, we can call the list box that holds all the product's names, NameList, which means that we'd include a new line in AddAnItem_Click( ), as shown below:

```
Sub AddAnItem_Click()
    TotalRecords = TotalRecords + 1
    Names(TotalRecords) = NameField.Text
    Numbers(TotalRecords) = NumberField.Text
    Comments(TotalRecords) = CommentField.Text
—>  Form2.NameList.AddItem NameField.Text
End Sub
```

Where Form2 is the name of the second form, which will appear when the user wants to select a record. In general, you use AddItem in Visual Basic as follows:

```
form.listbox.AddItem string$ [, index]
```

The optional argument named index specifies the new entry's position in the list box—0 (at the top of the list box) is the first position, the next down is 1 and so on. Since our list box will be automatically sorted, we won't specify an index for our entries. Correspondingly, to remove an item, you can use the RemoveItem method:

```
form.listbox.RemoveItem index
```

Here, index is not optional — you must use it to specify which item in the list you want to remove. That's all you need to add an item; the next step is to find items on demand. Click on the Find Item... menu choice to bring up this template:

```
Sub FindItem_Click()

End Sub
```

The actual work of finding a record will be done by the second form, Form2, so we can pop that up on the screen now:

```
Sub FindItem_Click()
    Form2.Show
End Sub
```

And that's it for FindItem_Click( ). Let's design the dialog box named Form2 now. Create Form2 by clicking the New Form item in VB's File menu, saving it as Db2.frm, and give it a caption of Find Item.... Also, we should remove the Min and Max buttons, and give the box a fixed border by selecting the BorderStyle property. Next, create a list box by clicking the list box tool in the toolbox. Give this list box the CtlName that we've already used, NameList, and set the Sorted property to True so that the entries in it will appear in alphabetical order. (Note that the CtlName, NameList, appears in the list box; it will be gone at run time.)

Now add the two normal control buttons for a dialog box—OK and Cancel, as shown in Figure 4-11, with the CtlNames OKButton and CancelButton. It's a good idea to make the OK button the default (i.e., set its default property to True) as well. As before, it's easy to write the Cancel Button procedure—all we have to do is to hide Form2 like this:

```
Sub CancelButton_Click()
—>    Form2.Hide
End Sub
```

Figure 4-11 Find Item... Dialog Box Template

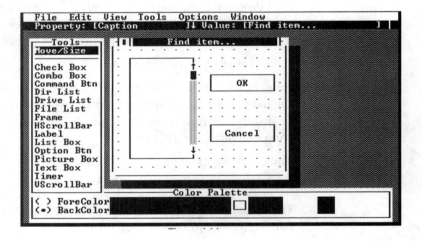

In addition, place these declarations in Form2's declarations section (i.e., click the Code button in the Project Window and then DB2.FRM):

```
Common Shared Names(100) As String
Common Shared Numbers(100) As String
Common Shared Comments(100) As String
Common Shared TotalRecords As Integer
```

Finally, we'll want to work with the list box in Form2 before it's on the screen, so that we can load it into memory before displaying it with Form2.Show. To load it into memory, we use the Load statement like this:

```
Sub Form1_Load()
    Redim Names(100) As String
    Redim Numbers(100) As String
    Redim Comments(100) As String
—>    Load Form2
End Sub
```

Now let's work on the dialog box's OKButton_Click( ) procedure:

```
OKButton_Click()

End Sub
```

When the user clicks the OK button—or double-clicks an item in the list box—is selected an item in the list box, and should display the corresponding record. For example, if this was our dialog box:

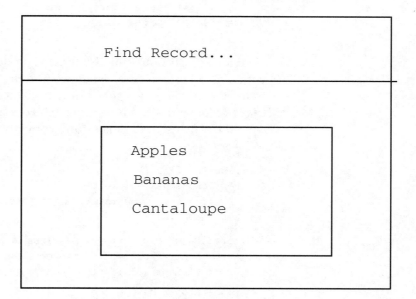

then clicking Apples should fill the text boxes in the main window with the data we've already stored by using Add Item:

```
Name of the product: "Apples"
```

```
Number of the product: "7"
Additional space for comments: "Sell by Thursday."
```

In general, we can determine what item is selected in a list box (one item is always selected in list boxes) by using these list box properties:

Text	The currently selected item
List	Array of String containing all the items
ListIndex	The index of the selected item (0 based)
ListCount	Total number of items in the list

The most commonly used property is Text—a string that holds the currently selected item. However, the others are very useful too (and we might notice that Text = List(ListIndex). In our case we'll have to find the record corresponding to the selection and display it. We can find the correct record with a loop like this in OKButton_Click( ):

```
Sub OKButton_Click()
    For Loop_Index = 1 To 100
        If (Names(loop_index) = NameList.Text) Then Exit For
    Next loop_index
        :
```

Here, we're just comparing the selected product name with the product names of each record. When we find the one we want (it must be in the list, because the list box only displays these names), we leave the For loop with the Visual Basic Exit For statement. At this point, we can fill the fields on the main form correctly and hide Form2, as follows:

```
Sub OKButton_Click()
    For loop_Index = 1 To 100
        If (Names(loop_index) = NameList.Text) Then Exit For
    Next loop_index

->      Form1.NameField.Text = Names(loop_index)
->      Form1.NumberField.Text = Numbers(loop_index)
->      Form1.CommentField.Text = Comments(loop_index)

->      Form2.Hide
    End Sub
```

We should note that the important events for list boxes are Click—when the user makes a selection—and DblClick, when the user makes a choice. Since that means that double-clicking an item is the same as clicking the OK button, we can add the same code there:

```
Sub NameList_DblClick()
    For loop_Index = 1 To 100
        If (Names(loop_index) = NameList.Text) Then Exit For
    Next loop_index

    Form1.NameField.Text = Names(loop_index)
    Form1.NumberField.Text = Numbers(loop_index)
    Form1.CommentField.Text = Comments(loop_index)

    Form2.Hide
End Sub
```

The only remaining thing to do is to make the Exit item active in the main window's menu, which we do in the usual way, with the VB End statement:

```
Sub ExitItem ()
    End
End Sub
```

The completed program appears in Figure 4-12, ready to use. You use it by typing data into the text boxes in the main window. When you want to read a record back, you can select Find Item... in the File menu to pop our dialog box on the screen. Select the item in the list box there and click the OK button, or double-click the item in the list box, and that item's records appear in the main window. The database is a success.

Figure 4-12 Database Application

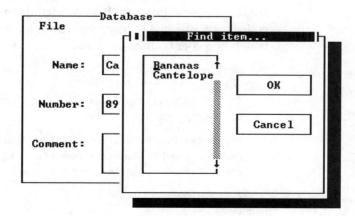

However, we might note here that we had to duplicate the same code in both NameList.DblClick( ) and OKButton_Click( ) (i.e., both display the selected product's records). One way of avoiding this is to place this code into a *module*, and call it from these two procedures. For example, if we created a Sub procedure called GetItem( ) that contained all this code, we could change both NameList.DblClick( ) and OKButton_Click( ) to this:

```
Sub NameList.DblClick()
    Call GetItem
End Sub

Sub OKButton_Click()
    Call GetItem
End Sub
```

That is, you use a *Call* statement to reference GetItem( ). Let's see how to add such modules now.

Creating a Module in Visual Basic

To create a module, select the New Module item in VB's File menu and call the new module, say, Db.Bas (you use the .Bas extension for module files). A code window opens up; the code we put here can be reached from anywhere in our entire application. We can place GetItem( ) in this module very simply: just type the code below into the code window (Visual Basic takes the name of this new procedure, GetItem, from the declaration in the first line: Sub GetItem( )). However, we should note that each time we refer to a control on some form, we have to include the form's name (since this code is not attached to any form), such as this reference to NameList, which becomes Form2.NameList:

```
Sub GetItem()
    For loop_Index = 1 To 100
—>      If (Names(loop_index) = Form2.NameList.Text) Then Exit For
    Next loop_index

    Form1.NameField.Text = Names(loop_index)
    Form1.NumberField.Text = Numbers(loop_index)
    Form1.CommentField.Text = Comments(loop_index)

    Form2.Hide
End Sub
```

When you enter this code, Visual Basic places it into the sub procedure GetItem( ). Next, place the usual declarations in the declaration area of Db.Bas (i.e., click the Code button in the project window and then DB.BAS; place the declarations in the code window that opens):

```
Common Shared Names(100) As String
Common Shared Numbers(100) As String
Common Shared Comments(100) As String
Common Shared TotalRecords As Integer
```

This module is just like any other file associated with the current project; that is, it is saved and loaded along with the others. That's all. The code for the entire database program, form by form (recall that we have not added any code for the Save File... or Load File... items yet), appears in Listing 4-3.

Listing 4-3 The Database Program

```
Common Shared Names(100) As String
Common Shared Numbers(100) As String
Common Shared Comments(100) As String
Common Shared TotalRecords As Integer

     Form1 ----------------------------------------------

Sub Form1_Load()
       Redim Names(100) As String
       Redim Numbers(100) As String
       Redim Comments(100) As String Load Form2
End Sub

Sub AddAnItem_Click ()
    TotalRecords = TotalRecords + 1
    Names(TotalRecords) = NameField.Text
    Numbers(TotalRecords) = NumberField.Text
    Comments(TotalRecords) = CommentField.Text
    Form2.NameList.AddItem NameField.Text
End Sub

Sub FindItem_Click ()
    Form2.Show
End Sub

Sub ExitItem_Click ()
    End
End Sub
```

continues

Listing 4-3 continued

```
Form2 - - - - - - - - - - - - - - - - - - - - - - - - - - - - -

Sub OKButton_Click ()
    Call GetItem
End Sub

Sub NameList_DblClick ()
    Call GetItem
End Sub

Sub CancelButton_Click ()
    Form2.Hide
End Sub

    Module1 - - - - - - - - - - - - - - - - - - - - - - - - - - - - - - - - -

Sub GetItem ()
    For loop_index = 1 To 100
        If (Names(loop_index) = Form2.NameList.Text) Then Exit For
    Next loop_index

    Form1.NameField.Text = Names(loop_index)
    Form1.NumberField.Text = Numbers(loop_index)
    Form1.CommentField.Text = Comments(loop_index)

    Form2.Hide
End Sub
```

However, there's one more important point here, and it has to do with data organization.

Creating Our Own Data Types

The way the database program is now, we're maintaining three arrays of data:

```
Common Shared Names(100) As String
Common Shared Numbers(100) As String
Common Shared Comments(100) As String
```

In fact, such fields like this are usually gathered together into their own *type*, and that introduces us to a powerful Visual Basic concept. In general, such a type declaration (always declared in the global module) looks like this:

NOTE: *Visual Basic notices that we're using form properties from other forms, like Form2.NameList.Text, in our module, and adds the declarations '$FORM Form1 and '$FORM Form2 to the module's declaration section automatically. This enables Visual Basic to share form-level variables with the module. In fact, Visual Basic adds the metacommand '$FORM form2name to any form's declaration area when you're also referring to another form, form2name here.*

```
Type typename
     elementname As variabletype
     [elementname As variabletype]
     [elementname As variabletype]
          :
End Type
```

For example, we can make a Record type for our database like this:

```
Type Record
     Name As String * 50
     Number As String * 20
     Comment As String * 200
End Type
```

This defines a new data type, Record, which contains the individual fields as shown above. Note that we are giving each string a definite size here—that's what * 50 or * 200 means; Name As String * 50 means that the string called Name will be exactly 50 characters long. We can declare an array of this type called, say, Database( ), like this (in the declaration section of Form1):

```
Type Record
     Name As String * 50
     Number As String * 20
     Comment As String * 200
End Type

Common Shared Database() As Record
```

Also, we can change Form1_Load( ) from:

```
Sub Form1_Load()
        Redim Names(100) As String
        Redim Numbers(100) As String
        Redim Comments(100) As String Load Form2
End Sub
```

To this:

```
Sub Form1_Load()
—>      Redim Database(100) As Record
        Load Form2
End Sub
```

Now we have an array, Database( ), of 100 such records:

NOTE: *Strings do not need to have a fixed length in a type declaration like this, except when they're used to set up records for random-access files, as we'll do in the next chapter.*

```
Name As String * 50          Database(1)
Number As String * 20
Comment As String * 200

Name As String * 50          Database(2)
Number As String * 20
Comment As String * 200

Name As String * 50          Database (3)
Name As String * 20
Comment As String * 200
```

                                :
                                :

and we can reach any one of them using the period (.) operator (just as we do to reach a Visual Basic property):

```
Database(3).Name = "Carrots"
Database(3).Number = "287"
Database(3).Comment = "Price too high?"
```

Let's use this new array in our database application to combine all three separate arrays (Names( ), Numbers( ), and Comments( )) together into one (Database( )). After setting up the new record type, Record, and the array of that type, Database( ), we've got to change the matching references in our program. For example, Names(TotalRecords) becomes Database(TotalRecords).Name. There are only two Sub procedures to change, as it turns out—the procedure in which we store the data, and the procedure in which we retrieve it. In Form1, the procedure for adding an item should be changed from this:

```
Sub AddAnItem_Click ()
    TotalRecords = TotalRecords + 1
    Names(TotalRecords) = NameField.Text
    Numbers(TotalRecords) = NumberField.Text
    Comments(TotalRecords) = CommentField.Text
    Form2.NameList.AddItem NameField.Text
End Sub
```

To this:

```
Sub AddAnItem_Click ()
     TotalRecords = TotalRecords + 1
—>    Database(TotalRecords).Name = NameField.Text
—>    Database(TotalRecords).Number = NumberField.Text
     Database(TotalRecords).Comment = CommentField.Text
     Form2.NameList.AddItem NameField.Text
End Sub
```

Here, we just change Names(TotalRecords) to
Database(TotalRecords).Name and so on. Also, in our module, we
should change the procedure for looking up an item, GetItem( ), from
this:

```
Sub GetItem ()
    For loop_index = 1 To 100
        If (Names(loop_index) = Form2.NameList.Text) Then Exit For
    Next loop_index

    Form1.NameField.Text = Names(loop_index)
    Form1.NumberField.Text = Numbers(loop_index)
    Form1.CommentField.Text = Comments(loop_index)

    Form2.Hide
End Sub
```

To this:

```
Sub GetItem ()
    For loop_index = 1 To 100
—>        If (Rtrim$(Database(loop_index).Name) =
                Rtrim$(Form2.NameList.Text)) Then Exit For
    Next loop_index

—>    Form1.NameField.Text = Database(loop_index).Name
—>    Form1.NumberField.Text = Database(loop_index).Number —>
    Form1.CommentField.Text = Database(loop_index).Comment

    Form2.Hide
End Sub
```

Note that we're using a fixed-length string for all fields, and since
Visual Basic pads such strings with spaces to the right, we had to
remove those spaces with the BASIC function Rtrim$( ) (which simply
trims any spaces off the right side of strings—its counterpart for

trimming spaces off the left is Ltrim$( )) before comparing to the item in the list box:

```
For loop_index = 1 To 100
—>     If (Rtrim$(Database(loop_index).Name) =
            Rtrim$(Form2.NameList.Text)) Then Exit For
   Next loop_index
```

That's all. The revised data base program, complete with its own data type (i.e., Record) appears in Listing 4-4.

Listing 4-4 Revised Database Program

```
Type Record
    Name As String * 50
    Number As String * 20
    Comment As String * 200
End Type

Common Shared Database() As Record
Common Shared TotalRecords As Integer

Form1 -----------------------------------------------

Sub Form1_Load()
    Redim Database(100) As Record
    Load Form2
End Sub

Sub AddAnItem_Click ()
    TotalRecords = TotalRecords + 1 Database(TotalRecords).Name =
    NameField.Text Database(TotalRecords).Number =
    NumberField.Text Database(TotalRecords).Comment =
    CommentField.Text Form2.NameList.AddItem NameField.Text
End Sub

Sub FindItem_Click ()
    Form2.Show
End Sub

Sub ExitItem_Click ()
    End
End Sub

Form2 -----------------------------
```

```
Sub OKButton_Click ()
    Call GetItem
End Sub

Sub NameList_DblClick ()
    Call GetItem
End Sub

Sub CancelButton_Click ()
    Form2.Hide
End Sub

Module1 --------------------------------------

Sub GetItem ()
    For loop_index = 1 To 100
        If (Rtrim$(Database(loop_index).Name) =
            Rtrim$(Form2.NameList.Text)) Then Exit For
    Next loop_index

    Form1.NameField.Text = Database(loop_index).Name
    Form1.NumberField.Text = Database(loop_index).Number
    Form1.CommentField.Text = Database(loop_index).Comment

    Form2.Hide
End Sub
```

That takes care of our database application—and with it, we finish this chapter on dialog boxes. We've come far; we've seen message boxes, input boxes, and then we've moved on to multiple forms in order to design our own dialog boxes. We also covered the typical kind of controls you find in dialog boxes: scroll bars and list boxes. There are, however, some other types of controls that you often find in dialog boxes — directory boxes and file list boxes. In the next chapter, we'll see how they work when we start working with files.

What About Files?

You may recall that our Pad program had two menu choices that we never supported: Load File... and Save File...; now, however, we'll be able to change that, because this is our chapter on file handling. Until now, all the data that our programs have handled has been very temporary—when the application ended, it was gone. Files, of course are the most common way to store data in the PC, so they are vitally important to most computer applications.

The file system in Visual Basic is very similar to the one in QuickBasic as far as the actual file manipulation statements go. If you're familiar with Open, Close, Input$ and Seek, you already have a considerable head start. As you might expect, however,the situation is very different when it comes to interacting with the user. For example, the user usually picks file names to load data from or save to from dialog boxes in Visual Basic applications (which is why we covered dialog boxes before covering files), and we'll see how to do that in this chapter as we set up our own file dialog boxes.

Two of these dialog boxes will be for the Save File...and Load File... items from our Pad application, and in this chapter we'll see how to make these items work. In addition, we'll see how to work with structured files, where the data is broken up into specific records, as it was in our database application in the last chapter. In fact, we'll be able to modify that application so that it can save its data to disk. With this and other topics coming up, let's get started immediately.

Saving Data in a File

If we wanted to add file support to our Pad application, we might start with the Save File... item (i.e, the user has to create files before reading them back in). When the user selects the Save File... item, we could pop a dialog box onto the screen with a list box and two buttons: OK and Cancel. The user could then type the name of the file he or she wanted to save their document to, and our program would then take that name, create the file (if necessary), and then store the document there. Let's put this into practice.

Start Visual basic and open the Pad project. If you take a look at the File menu, you'll see that the Save File... menu item already exists, so bring up the following template in the code window:

```
Sub SaveItem_Click ( )

End Sub
```

Users who click this menu item, want to save the current document, which means that our goal here is to place the Save File... dialog box on the screen. Let's name that dialog box (i.e., give it a FormName of) SaveForm; to display it, all we need to do is this:

```
Sub SaveItem_Click ( )
    SaveForm.Show
End Sub
```

Next, we should put together that dialog box, giving it a FormName of SaveForm, a caption that reads Save File..., and saving our work as, say, SaveForm.Frm. In addition, we should add a text box (which can call FilenameBox) to this new form, a label above the text box with the caption Save File As... (so the user knows that a file name is expected), an OK button (with the CtlName OKButton—and we should set its default property to True so that it has a black double border when the dialog box first appears), and a Cancel button (CtlName: CancelButton), as shown in Figure 5-1. Finally, because this is a dialog box, we can remove the Min and Max buttons, as well as making the BorderStyle fixed single.

Figure 5-1 Save File... Dialog Box

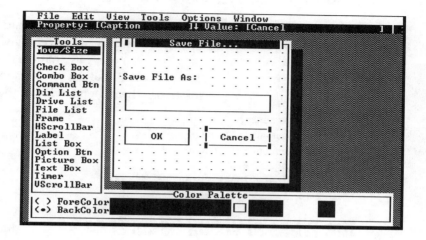

The Cancel button procedure is easy, so we can do that first since all we want to do—if the user decides to cancel—is to conceal the form again, we put this in CancelButton_Click( ):

```
Sub CancelButton_Click ()
    SaveForm.Hide
End Sub
```

The real work is done when the user clicks the OK button. Click on that button now to open the OK button's click procedure:

```
Sub OKButton_Click ()

End Sub
```

When we reach this point in the program, we can suppose that the text in FilenameBox holds a file name, and that we're supposed to save the current document—that is, the string named Pad.PadText.Text, where PadText is the name of the main multi-line text box that the document is stored in—to this file. There are three steps in this process: opening the file (or creating it if it does not exist), writing the data to the file, and closing it. We can take a look at each of these three steps in order as we build OKButton_Click( ), because each step tells us something about the Visual Basic file system.

Opening Files in Visual Basic

The way to open or create a file in Visual Basic is simply to use the Open statement; however, we have to give some consideration to the *way* we open or create that file. In particular, there are five ways of opening files in Visual Basic, corresponding to the five different ways we can use them; here's a list of the available *file modes*:

```
Sequential Input
Sequential Output
Sequential Append
Random Input/Output
Binary Input/Output
```

The Types of Visual Basic Files

The first three file modes all have to do with one type of file: sequential files. Sequential files are usually used for text files, where you write the file from beginning to end and read it the same way; that is, you don't jump around inside the file. Working with sequential files is like using cassette tapes; if you want to hear something at the end of the tape, you have to pass by everything in front of it first. In the same way, if you want some of the text at the end of a file opened for *sequential access*, you have to read all the text that comes before it first.

If sequential files are like cassette tapes, then random files—the next type—are like compact discs. Although you have to fast forward to the parts you want in a cassette tape, you can simply move around at will on a CD, without going through all the intervening tracks. In the same way, you can move around in a *random-access* file at will, taking data from whatever location you want. The price you pay is that the data in a random access file has to be carefully sectioned into *records*, so that you know exactly where to find the data that you want. For example, if the records we developed for our database application were all the same size, they would work perfectly in a random access file; when we wanted the twentieth record, we could simply skip over the first 19 and then start reading. However, text—such as the text we're storing in the Pad application—is not neatly sectioned into records of the same size. For that reason, we will place the text that we're about to save in a sequential file.

The third type of files are binary files, and here Visual Basic does not interpret the contents of the file at all. For example, executable (.Exe) files are binary files, and we treat them on a byte-by-byte basis in Visual Basic. To copy such a file, we would read in every byte of the original file (the source file), and then send them to the new file (the destination or target file). While we can set the amount of data we want to read under sequential or random access, binary files are always dealt with byte by byte.

Each of these three types of file access has its own set of Visual Basic statements, as we'll see in this chapter. Since that can get confusing, you'll find a collection of the most common VB file handling statements organized by file type in Table 5-1 for easy reference later.

Table 5-1 Visual Basic File Statements

Access	Common Visual Basic Statements
Sequential	Open, Line Input #, Print #, Write #, Input$, Close
Random	Type...End Type, Open, Put #, Len, Close, Get #
Binary	Open, Get #, Put #, Close, Seek, Input$

Our job here is to save the Pad's current document, and we'll do that by opening a sequential file (though it could actually be treated as a binary file, it is easier to write and read strings from sequential files). There are three ways of opening sequential files: for Input, for Output, and for Append. We open a file for input if we want to read from it, for output if we want to write to it, and for append if we want to add to the end of it. These three modes are consistent with the idea of opening the file and then working with the data from beginning to end (i.e., sequentially). For example, if we opened a file for sequential output, wrote a string to it, and then followed it with a second string, the second string would go directly after the first—and so on for any subsequent strings, one after the other. If you wanted to read them in again, you'd have to close the file and open it for input, and then you could read the data back from beginning to end.

Random files, where you can move around in the file at will, don't have any such restrictions—when you open a file for random access, it's for both input and output (on the other hand, recall that you have to section the data up into records in random files). In this case, where we're writing our Pad document to disk, we'll open our file for sequential output. In general, Visual Basic's file Open statement looks like this:

```
Open fff$ [For mmm] [Access aaa] [lll] As [#] nnn% [Len = rrr%]
```

This is what the file open statement means:

fff$	The filename (including an optional path)
mmm	Mode: can be Append, Binary, Input, Output, or Random
aaa	Access: can be Read, Write, or Read Write
lll	Lock: restricts access of other applications to this fileto: Shared, Lock Read, Lock Write, Lock Read Write
nnn%	Filenumber (1-255): The number we'll use to refer to this file from now on.
rrr%	Record length for random files, or size of the buffer you want Visual Basic to use for sequential files.

In our case, since the user wants to write to the file name now in FilenameBox.Text, we can use the following Open statement to open that file:

```
Open FilenameBox.Text For Output As # 1
```

In fact, this file might not even exist—the user might want us to create it. File creation is actually handled automatically by the Open statement: if the file does not exist and we're trying to open it for anything but input, Visual Basic will create the file for us. On the other hand, note that when we open an already existing file for output and then write to it, the original contents of the file are destroyed (if you want to add to the end of a sequential file while retaining what was there before, open the file for Append). Now we can start the Pad's Save File... dialog box with this line in the OK button's click procedure:

```
Sub OKButton_Click ( )
    Open FilenameBox.Text For Output As # 1       'Open file
        :
End Sub
```

NOTE: If we hadn't placed this statement in our code, we wouldn't have caught these errors—called trappable errors—in which case Visual Basic often notifies the user of the error directly, with a message box (undesirable in most applications).

From this point on, we'll be able to refer to this file as file # 1 when we want to write to it or close it, just as in standard BASIC. However, we should note that there is the possibility of error(s) when opening a file this way: the user may have specified an invalid path, for example, or misspelled the file name. To handle such errors, we can include an On Local Error GoTo statement, as follows:

```
    Sub OKButton_Click ( )
—>      On Local Error GoTo FileError
        Open FilenameBox.Text For Output As # 1       'Open file
            :
            :
```

This statement works in this way: if an error occurs, we'll automatically jump to the label FileError, where we can place a message box on the screen, and then execute a Resume statement, which passes control back to the line that caused the error, allowing the user to try again:

TIP: We'll go into greater depth about the specific kinds of errors that can occur in this and other situations in our chapter on error handling and debugging. In that chapter, we'll see a great deal more about the On Local Error GoTo and Resume statements.

```
    Sub OKButton_Click ( )
        On Local Error GoTo FileError
        Open FilenameBox.Text For Output As # 1       'Open file
            :
            :
        Exit Sub
—>  FileError:
—>      MsgBox "File Error", 0, "Pad"     'MsgBox for file error.
—>      Resume
    End Sub
```

In other words, if the file name was legal, and the corresponding file can be opened or created, we do so; if there was a problem, we indicate that fact and let the user change the file specification for another attempt. At this point, then, the file is open; the next step is to write our document to it.

Writing to Files in Visual Basic

The usual way of writing to a sequential file is by using either the Print # or Write # statements. Here's the way to use them:

```
Print # nnn%, expressionlist
Write # nnn%, expressionlist
```

Here, nnn% is the file number (1 for us here), and expressionlist is a list of the variables (including strings) that you want to write to the file. The two statements, Print # and Write #, are different; Write # inserts commas between the separate items in the expressionlist as it writes them to the file, places quotation marks around strings, and inserts a new (blank) line at the end of the file. Since we don't want any of these added characters, we'll use Print # instead. In fact, we'll only want to send a single string to the file: Pad.PadText.Text, so our Print # statement should look like this:

```
Sub OKButton_Click ( )
    On Local Error GoTo FileError
    Open FilenameBox.Text For Output As # 1       'Open file
—>  Print # 1, Pad.PadText.Text                   'Write document
        :
        :
    Exit Sub
FileError:
    MsgBox "File Error", 0, "Pad"      'MsgBox for file error.
    Resume
End Sub
```

That's all there is to writing the text into the file, now that it's been opened. In fact, closing the file isn't much harder; all we have to do is to use the Close statement, as follows:

```
Sub OKButton_Click ( )
    On Local Error GoTo FileError
    Open FilenameBox.Text For Output As # 1       'Open file
    Print # 1, Pad.PadText.Text                   'Write document
—>  Close # 1                                     'Close file
        :
    Exit Sub
FileError:
    MsgBox "File Error", 0, "Pad"      'MsgBox for file error.
End Sub
```

Here, Close # 1 closes file number 1, the file we're working on. After closing the file, we're through, and can exit the Sub procedure with an Exit Sub statement. At this point, the file has been successfully written to disk—or if not, we've alerted the user to that fact; that is, if the Print # statement generated an error (e.g., the disk was full), we jump to the FileError label and pop our message box on the screen as before.

The final step, if the file handling has gone smoothly, is to hide the Save File... dialog box (i.e., SaveForm) like this:

```
Sub OKButton_Click ( )
    On Local Error GoTo FileError
    Open FilenameBox.Text For Output As # 1        'Open file
    Print # 1, Pad.PadText.Text                    'Write document
    Close # 1                                       'Close file
—>  SaveForm.Hide
    Exit Sub
FileError:
    MsgBox "File Error", 0, "Pad"     'MsgBox for file error.
    Resume
End Sub
```

Let's see this in action. After making the above changes, you might try typing some lines of text into the Pad and then saving them, as shown in Figure 5-2. When you do, you'll find that the text is indeed saved to disk in the file you choose.

Figure 5-2 Saving a File with the Pad Application

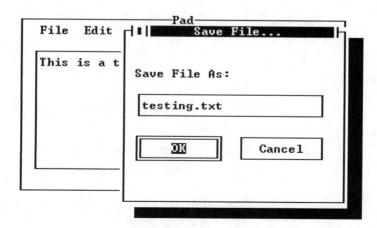

You might also note one more thing here; the text in the file is simply stored as one long string, without carriage returns—unless they were present in the original document—because the main text box itself stores it that way (and uses word wrap when it displays the text). That's all for our Save File... item; we've been able to write a sequential text file to disk, and our Pad application has become even more polished. However, the corresponding next step is to read files back in—that is, to make the Pad's Load File... item work also. Let's look into that process next.

Using the Visual Basic File Controls

The first step in reading the contents of a file is to get the name of that file. However, that's not just a simple matter of asking the user to type the name in a text box—we have to be able to search the disk (as with other, similar windowed applications) and let the user select from what's already there. Visual Basic provides three special controls for doing exactly that, and they are: *disk list boxes*, *directory list boxes, and file list boxes*.

The tools for creating these file controls appear in the Visual Basic toolbox. It turns out that these controls will do much of the work for us—that is, they'll search the disks and directories automatically, and we'll be able to work with various properties associated with them, instead of doing all the programming ourselves. Let's start this process by designing a a dialog box for the Load File... option, which we can call LoadForm and save as, say, Loadform.Frm. First, let's connect it to the Load File... menu item:

```
Sub LoadItem_Click ( )

End Sub
```

To display the Load File... dialog box (LoadForm), we can simply show it as follows:

```
Sub LoadItem_Click ( )
    LoadForm.Show
End Sub
```

Now let's design LoadForm; use the New Form item in Visual Basic's File menu to create the form, save it as Loadform.Frm, give it a

FormName of LoadForm, give it a caption of Load File..., remove the Min and Max buttons, change the BorderStyle property to single fixed, and put two buttons on it—an OK button (OKButton), which should have its Default property set to True, and a Cancel Button.

Next, add a drive list box by double-clicking the Drive List tool in the toolbox. Notice that the Drive List box is a drop-down list box, which will save us some space. We'll also need a Directory List box and a File List box, so double click those tools too, and arrange them as you want them in the dialog box—something like Figure 5-3.

Figure 5-3 Load File... Dialog Box Template

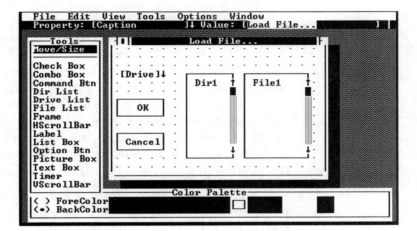

Users will be able to load any existing file this way, through the combination of the Drive, Directory, and File list boxes. They can use the Drive List box to specify the drive, the Directory List box to specify the directory in that drive, and the File List box to indicate the actual file they want to open. That file can be opened in two ways: by double-clicking the file name in the File List box, or by selecting (highlighting) it in the File List box and clicking the OK button.

And, as usual, making the Cancel button active is easy; we can just hide the dialog box when this button is clicked:

```
Sub CancelButton_Click( )
    LoadForm.Hide
End Sub
```

Now let's turn to the file controls. At this point, the three list boxes (drive, directory, and file) are not communicating with each other; that is, they would just show independent information for the current directory on disk. If we were to run this program and change the disk in the disk box list, the other two boxes wouldn't respond to the change. To get them to communicate, we have to know a little more about what the important events are for each of them, and we'll look into that next.

Drive List Boxes

The Drive List box is a drop down list box, as shown in Figure 5-3. The current drive is usually indicated in it; when the user clicks the attached arrow, the list box drops down, showing what other drives are available to choose from. When the user picks one, a Change event occurs in the list box. Since we haven't set the name of our Drive List box, it still has the default name of Drive1 (the default for drive list boxes), so the event procedure is Drive1_Change( ). The property of our Drive1 box that holds the drive is simply Drive1.Drive, and our next task is to pass this new drive on to the directory list box, which still has its default name of Dir1 (as is standard for directory list boxes). To do that, it turns out that we just need to pass the Drive1.Drive property on to the Dir1.Path property:

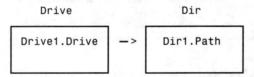

We can do that by bringing up the Drive1_Change( ) procedure:

```
Sub Drive1_Change ( )

End Sub
```

Just assign the Drive property of Drive1 to the Path property of Dir1 like this:

```
Sub Drive1_Change ( )
    Dir1.Path = Drive1.Drive
End Sub
```

That's all it takes to connect the drive and directory boxes together. In fact, we can run the program at this point; when we do, we can click the Load File... item of the Pad's File menu. The dialog box we've been designing, LoadForm, appears, displaying the current drive, directory, and files in that directory. If we click the drive box, the drop down list of all drives in the system appears. Clicking one of those changes us to that drive—and the change ripples through to the Directory List box, which also changes to list the directories on that new disk. The next step in our program now is to connect the Directory List box with the File List box, so that when the directory is changed, the files displayed will be the files in that directory.

Directory List Boxes

The Directory List box displays the directories available on a certain drive. It is a simple list box (that is, it is always displayed, not a drop-down list box like the Drive List box); the working drive is displayed in the top line (e.g., c:\), and the directories of that drive appear under-neath (e.g., DOS). If there are more directories than we've allowed space for, a vertical scroll bar appears on the right of the box. When the user changes the directory by clicking a new directory, a Dir1_Change event occurs, and the new path is placed in Dir1.Path. In addition, the way we've set things up, when the user changes drives, Drive1.Drive is loaded into Dir1.Path, which also generates a Dir1_Change event; in other words, the only event we need to be concerned about here is Dir1_Change, which now handles both drive and directory changes.

When such an event occurs, we need to communicate the news to the File List box, which we can do by passing on the Dir1.Path property to the Path property of the File List box, and since the File List box is still named File1 (the default for file list boxes), we can do that like this:

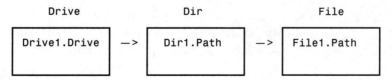

```
       Drive                    Dir                     File

┌────────────────┐      ┌────────────────┐      ┌────────────────┐
│                │      │                │      │                │
│  Drive1.Drive  │  ->  │   Dir1.Path    │  ->  │  File1.Path    │
│                │      │                │      │                │
└────────────────┘      └────────────────┘      └────────────────┘
```

To do this in code, bring up the directory list box's Sub procedure template in the code window:

NOTE: *We might also note that, while you can select a new drive with a single click, it takes two clicks to select a new directory in the Directory List box. This difference has to do with the difference between drop down and straight list boxes; the reason you need two clicks in the directory list box is so that users can move up and down through the list using the arrow keys without changing the working directory to each highlighted entry along the way; that is, the change is postponed until the users reach the directory they want.*

```
Sub Dir1_Change ( )

End Sub
```

Our goal here is to ripple any changes in the Dir1.Path property down to File1.Path, and we can do that simply like this:

```
Sub Dir1_Change ( )
    File1.Path = Dir1.Path
End Sub
```

In this way, every time there's a change in the working directory—or the working drive—the file list box will know about it. If we make this change and then start the program, we'll find that the list boxes are now all connected together. For example, we can click the Drive List box to change the drive, and the change will automatically be communicated to the Directory List box, which changes to display the new set of directories. That change in turn is also communicated to the File List box, which then displays the files in the new working directory.

On the other hand, if we change the working directory in the Directory List box, that change is also communicated to the File List box, which then displays the files in the new directory. In other words, the important events here were Drive1_Change and Dir1_Change, and the important properties that had to be transferred were Drive1.Drive —> Dir1.Path, and Dir1.Path —> File1.Path.

The way we actually read the filename that the user wants to load will be from the FileName property of File1—that is, File1.FileName—as follows:

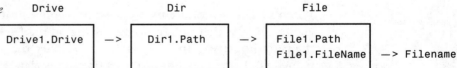

Our next task is to integrate the file list box into the program; when the user double clicks a file's name, we should open that file and load it into the Pad. Let's look at file list boxes next.

File List Boxes

The File List box shows the files in the current working directory. Like the Directory List box, it is a simple list box, with its list always displayed; if the list is too long for the box, a vertical scroll bar appears. The files shown in the list box correspond to two properties: the Path and Pattern properties. The Path property holds the path name of the directory whose files you want to display, and the Pattern property holds the file specification — "*.EXE", for example (the default pattern is "*.*").

File List boxes can respond to click or double click events. It's normal to let the user select a file from a File List box and close the current dialog box by double clicking a file's name; therefore, we should add code to the File1_DblClick( ) procedure. Note that this is the same as selecting a file and then clicking the OK button, which means that we should write one procedure that can be used by both events. We did that before by placing a procedure in a code module and then calling that general procedure from two event procedures, and we could do that again here. However, there's another way of doing the same thing, which we might demonstrate here; first, bring up File1_DblClick ( ) in the code window:

```
Sub File1_DblClick ( )

End Sub
```

We want to make this the same as the OKButton_Click ( ) procedure— but since that's also a procedure, we can simply call it like this:

```
Sub File1_DblClick ( )
    OKButton_Click
End Sub
```

(Note that if OKButton was part of a control array, we'd have to pass an index, like this: OKButton(3).) That's all there is to it; now let's write OKButton_Click( ), where all the action is going to be. Bring up this Sub procedure template in the code window:

```
Sub OKButton_Click ( )

End Sub
```

At this point, the user is trying to open a file; the correct drive is in Drive1.Drive, and the correct path is Dir1.Path. Now we need the actual file name from the file list box; as mentioned above, the currently selected file name is kept in the file list box's FileName property, so now we have the file's complete specification. We're ready to open the file.

One way of opening the required file is to actually change to the new drive (Drive1.Drive) with the Basic ChDrive statement, change to the new path with (Dir1.Path) with the Basic ChDir statement, and then open the file itself (File1.FileName). However, there is no need to change the default drive and directory at operating system level; instead, we can assemble the complete file specification ourselves.

The Path property of the Directory List Box, Dir1.Path, usually represents a complete path, including the drive letter (e.g., "C:\vb\bin\theprogs"), so we can add that to our file name, File1.FileName, if we add a backslash after the the path like this (using Basic's standard method of joining strings together with a + sign):

```
Filename$ = Dir1.Path + "\" + File1.FileName
```

Here, Filename$ is a local variable that we can use in our OKButton_Click( ) procedure. However, this is not quite good enough; if we happen to be in the root directory of a drive, such as d:\, then Dir1.Path would be "d:\"; if the current file were Novel.Txt, then Filename$—equal to Dir1.Path + "\" + File1.FileName—would be "d:\\Novel.Txt". In other words, we would have one backslash too many. To avoid this, we should check the last character of Dir1.Path; if it's a backslash already, we won't have to add one ourselves:

```
If (Right$(Dir1.Path, 1) = "\") Then
    Filename$ = Dir1.Path + File1.FileName
Else
    Filename$ = Dir1.Path + "\" + File1.FileName
End If
```

Now Filename$ holds the complete file specification of the file we're supposed to open, and we can open it with an Open statement. Since we're using sequential file access, and we want to read the file, we can open it for Input like this:

```
        If (Right$(Dir1.Path, 1) = "\") Then
            Filename$ = Dir1.Path + File1.FileName
        Else
            Filename$ = Dir1.Path + "\" + File1.FileName
        End If
—>      Open Filename$ For Input As # 1
```

Once again, there is the possibility of errors here (for example, the diskette with the file might have been inadvertantly removed), so we should put in some error handling code. That might look like this in the OKButton_Click ( ) Sub procedure:

```
Sub OKButton_Click ( )
—>      On Local Error GoTo FileError
            :
        Exit Sub
—>FileError:
—>      MsgBox "File Error", 0, "Pad"    'MsgBox for file error.
        Resume
    End Sub
```

Here, we simply display a message box if there was any kind of file error, allowing the user to try again after the problem has been fixed. Now we can add our file opening statements this way:

```
Sub OKButton_Click ( )
        On Local Error GoTo FileError
—>      If (Right$(Dir1.Path, 1) = "\") Then
—>          Filename$ = Dir1.Path + File1.FileName
—>      Else
—>          Filename$ = Dir1.Path + "\" + File1.FileName
—>      End If
—>      Open Filename$ For Input As # 1
            :
        Exit Sub

    FileError:
        MsgBox "File Error", 0, "Pad"    'MsgBox for file error.
        Resume
    End Sub
```

At this point, our use for the file controls is done; the file has been selected and opened. The next step is reading in the data, and we'll see how to do that now.

Reading from Files in Visual Basic

The standard ways to read a sequential file in Visual Basic (see Table 5-1) are Input #, Line Input # and Input$, and the way to use them is as follows:

```
Input # nnn%, expressionlist
Line Input # nnn%, stringvariable
Input$ (bbb%, [#] nnn%)
```

Here, nnn% is a file number (i.e., 1 for us), bbb% is the number of bytes to read, stringvariable is the name of a string variable to place data into, and expressionlist is a list of expressions that the data will be placed into.

For example, if we used Input # to fill Pad.PadText.Text, that move might look like this: Input # 1 Pad.PadText.Text. However, the problem with Input # is that it expects the items in the file to be separated by commas, spaces, or the ends of lines (i.e., a carriage return). For numbers, this means that when Input # encounters the first comma, space, or end of line, it assumes that the current number is finished; for strings, Input # terminates the string when it reaches a comma or end of line. But this is unacceptable to us, since the text of the document we're reading in may contain many commas. In fact, the user may have put in deliberate carriage returns into the document (although they are not required, since the Pad's mulitline text box has automatic word wrap), or may be trying to read in another application's document that has carriage returns in it.

Similarly, the Line Input # function reads strings from files—until it encounters a carriage return, when it quits. That means that we'd have to read in each line of the file (if it is divided into lines) separately. One way to do that would be as follows:

```
Do Until EOF(1)
    Line Input # 1, Dummy$
    Pad.PadText.Text = Pad.PadText.Text + Dummy$ + Chr$(13) +Chr$(10)
Loop
```

Here, we're using several capabilities of Visual Basic that we haven't used before, including the Do Until loop, EOF( ), and Chr$( ). These all function as in standard BASIC; the Do Until loop has this general form:

```
Do Until condition
    [statements]
Loop
```

The statements in this loop, if there are any, are repeatedly executed until *condition* becomes True, at which point execution stops (note that if the condition is True at the beginning, the statements in the body of the loop are not even executed once). In our case, we're using the EOF( ) function to make up the condition for our loop. This function takes a file number as its argument (for us, that would be EOF(1)), and returns a value of True when we've reached the end of the file. In the above loop, then, we keep reading lines from the file until we reach the end of that file. In addition, each time we read a line, we add carriage return and line feed characters to the end of the line, as follows:

```
   Do Until EOF(1)
       Line Input # 1, Dummy$
—>  Pad.PadText.Text = Pad.PadText.Text + Dummy$ + Chr$(13)+Chr$(10)
   Loop
```

Here, we're using the Chr$( ) function, which returns the ASCII character corresponding to the ASCII code passed to it; for example, Chr$(13) returns a carriage return. The reason we have to add a carriage-return line-feed pair at the end of each line is that Line Input # treats these two characters purely as delimiters between strings, and deletes them. Since they are actually part of the file, however, we can simply put them back.

NOTE: *The Input$( ) function is limited to reading files of 32,767 bytes if you open the file for sequential or binary access. However, if you want to use longer files, you can simply check the length of the file, LOF( ), and then read from the file several times in succession until you get all the data you need.*

A better option for us than either Input # or Line Input # is the Input$ function, which is specially made to read strings and doesn't supress carriage returns of line feeds. To use this function, however, we have to indicate the exact number of bytes we want to read; when we do, Input$ returns a string (which we can assign to Pad.PadText.Text). The number of bytes we want to read is simply the length of the file in bytes, and we can use another file function, LOF( ), to get that for us. Like EOF( ), LOF( ) takes a file number as an argument. LOF( ), however, returns the length of the indicated file in bytes (the file must be open for LOF( ) to work). Thus, we can read in the whole file in the following manner, with the Input$( ) statement:

```
Pad.PadText.Text = Input$(LOF(1), # 1)
```

In fact, because you specify the number of bytes to read, you can also use this statement to read data from binary files. We can add our Input$ statement to OKButton_Click( ) this way, where we place the string that's read in (i.e., the whole contents of the file) directly into the Pad's text box (Pad.PadText.Text):

```
Sub OKButton_Click ( )
    On Local Error GoTo FileError
    If (Right$(Dir1.Path, 1) = "\") Then
        Filename$ = Dir1.Path + File1.FileName
    Else
        Filename$ = Dir1.Path + "\" + File1.FileName
    End If
    Open Filename$ For Input As # 1
—>  Pad.PadText.Text = Input$(LOF(1), # 1)
        :
    Exit Sub
FileError:
    MsgBox "File Error", 0, "Pad"     'MsgBox for file error.
    Resume
End Sub
```

All that remains now is to close the file, and, of course, to hide the dialog box (LoadForm). We can do that as follows, ending OKButton_Click( ):

```
Sub OKButton_Click ( )
    On Local Error GoTo FileError
    If (Right$(Dir1.Path, 1) = "\") Then        'Get file name
        Filename$ = Dir1.Path + File1.FileName
    Else
        Filename$ = Dir1.Path + "\" + File1.FileName
    End If
    Open Filename$ For Input As # 1                'Open file
    Pad.PadText.Text = Input$(LOF(1), # 1)     'Read file in

—>  Close # 1                      'Close file
—>  LoadForm.Hide                  'Hide dialog box
    Exit Sub
FileError:
    MsgBox "File Error", 0, "Pad"     'MsgBox for file error.
    Resume
End Sub
```

Now the Load File... dialog box is complete; to use it, simply start the program and select the Load File... item in the File menu. The Load File... dialog box opens, as shown in Figure 5-4. As you can see, the File List box presents the file names in alphabetical order; to open one of them, just double-click it, or select it and click the OK button. When you do, the OKButton_Click( ) procedure is executed, the file is opened, and read into the Pad. At that point, you can edit it and then save it to the disk again with the Save File... option.

Figure 5-4 Pad with Load File... Dialog Box

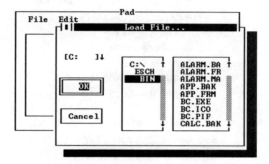

That's the end of the entire Pad application; we've made all the parts operational. All the code, form by form, appears in Listing 5-1.

Listing 5-1 Pad Application's Code

```
Pad  - - - - - - - - - - - - - - - - - - - - - - - - - - - - - - - - - - - -
Sub Command1_Click ( )
    PadText.SelText = CutText
    PadText.SetFocus
End Sub
Sub PadText_Change ( )
    CutItem.Enabled = True
    ClearItem.Enabled = True
End Sub
Sub CutItem_Click ( )
    CutText = PadText.SelText
    PadText.SelText = ""
    PasteItem.Enabled = True
```

continues

Listing 5-1 continued

```
        PadText.SetFocus
End Sub
Sub ExitItem_Click ()
        End
End Sub
Sub ClearItem_Click ()
        PadText.Text = ""
        PadText.SetFocus
End Sub
Sub PasteItem_Click ()
        PadText.SelText = CutText
End Sub
Sub SaveItem_Click ()
        SaveForm.Show
End Sub
Sub LoadItem_Click ()
        LoadForm.Show
End Sub
        SaveForm ------------------------------------
Sub CancelButton_Click ()
        SaveForm.Hide
End Sub
Sub OKButton_Click ()
        On Local Error GoTo FileError
        Open FileNameBox.Text For Output As #1
        Print #1, Pad.PadText.Text
        Close #1
        SaveForm.Hide
        Exit Sub
FileError:
        MsgBox "File Error", 0, "Pad"
        Resume
End Sub
        LoadForm ------------------------------------
Sub CancelButton_Click ()
        LoadForm.Hide
End Sub
Sub Drive1_Change ()
        Dir1.Path = Drive1.Drive
End Sub
```

```
Sub Dir1_Change ( )
    File1.Path = Dir1.Path
End Sub
Sub OKButton_Click ( )
    On Local Error GoTo FileError
    If (Right$(Dir1.Path, 1) = "\") Then
        Filename$ = Dir1.Path +      File1.Filename
    Else
        Filename$ = Dir1.Path + "\" + File1.Filename
    End If
    Open Filename$ For Input As #1
    Pad.PadText.Text = Input$(LOF(1), #1)
    Close #1
    LoadForm.Hide
    Exit Sub
FileError:
    MsgBox "File Error" + Str$(Err), 0, "Pad"
    Resume
End Sub
Sub File1_DblClick ( )
    OKButton_Click
End Sub
```

At this point, we've covered opening sequential files both for Input and for Output. And, as mentioned earlier, if you want to add to the end of a sequential file, you can open it for Append—in that case, everything you write to the file goes at the end of the preexisting file contents.

That's all for our coverage for sequential files; now let's move on to the next type: random files.

Using Random Files in Visual Basic

We're ready to move past sequential files to random-access files. These kinds of files usually break their data up into *records*, all of which have the same format, but (usually) different data. And, as you may remember, we set up the data in our database program in the last chapter into exactly those kinds of records, like this:

```
Type Record
    Name As String * 50
    Number As String * 20
    Comment As String * 200
End Type
Common Shared Database(100) As Record
```

In other words, each record, Database(n), looks like this:

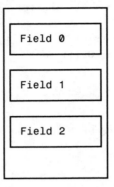

We can make well-organized files from such records, as follows:

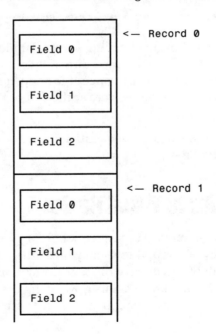

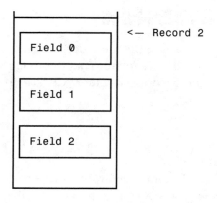

<- Record 2

As you may recall, the database application had five items in its menu, as shown in Figure 5-5: Add Item (added the current item to the database), Find Item... (opened the Find Item... dialog box), Save File..., Load File..., and Exit. Everything works in this menu except the two file items, which we have left until now to complete—but now we can complete them as well, because the database application is exactly where we should use random-access files.

Figure 5-5 Database Application with Menu Open

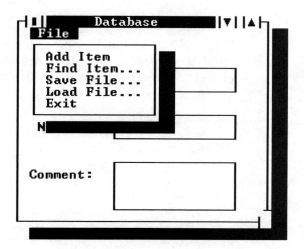

Writing Random-Access Files

We can start by saving the file, once the user selects the Save File... item in the File menu. That item's CtlName is SaveItem, and we open SaveItem_Click( ) in the code window as follows:

```
Sub SaveItem_Click ( )

End Sub
```

When users click this item, they want to save the database in a particular file. For this reason, we need to pop up a dialog box much like the one we designed earlier in this chapter for our Pad. In fact, we can use the *same* dialog box here. To load that form, just open Visual Basic's File menu, select the Add File... item, and then give the name of the Save File... form (we used Saveform.Frm above). That file is loaded automatically—in this way, you can swap forms such as dialog boxes between projects, saving you a great deal of design time, and making your applications more uniform. Now we can pop that dialog box onto the screen in SaveItem_Click( ), as follows:

```
    Sub SaveItem_Click ( )
—>      SaveForm.Show
    End Sub
```

Next, we'll have to make some changes to SaveForm's code, since it is set up to store sequential files. Just switch to that form using the project window, and open the main Sub procedure, OKButton_Click ( ), which currently looks like this:

```
Sub OKButton_Click ( )
    On Local Error GoTo FileError
    Open FilenameBox.Text For Output As # 1      'Open file
    Print # 1, Pad.PadText.Text                  'Write document
    Close # 1                                    'Close file
    SaveForm.Hide
    Exit Sub

FileError:
    MsgBox "File Error", 0, "Pad"    'MsgBox for file error.
    Resume
End Sub
```

We're using a random file of records this time, not a sequential file of text, so that we open the file as Random, instead:

```
Sub OKButton_Click ( )
    On Local Error GoTo FileError
->  Open FilenameBox.Text For Random As # 1 Len =
      Len(Database(1))
    Print # 1, Pad.PadText.Text              'Write document
    Close # 1                                 'Close file
    SaveForm.Hide
    Exit Sub

FileError:
    MsgBox "File Error", 0, "Pad"    'MsgBox for file error.
    Resume
End Sub
```

Here, we're indicating that the record length we'll be using is Len(Database(1)), which returns the length (in bytes) of our record size. Next, we want to write the entire array of records, Database( ), out to that file. For this reason, we should look into the options for writing random-access files.

The most common I/O statements for both binary and random-access files are Get # and Put #; these statements can get or put records from or to the file. In this case, we'll use Put #, whose syntax is as follows:

```
Put [#] nnn% , [rrr%], vvv%
```

Here, nnn% is a file number, rrr% is the record number you want to put into the file, and vvv% is the variable we want to put there. If we do not specify a record number, Visual Basic simply places one record after the last into the file. Since the total number of records is stored in the global integer TotalRecords, we can write that many records out in the following way (note that no records are written if TotalRecords is 0):

```
Sub OKButton_Click ( )
    On Local Error GoTo FileError
    Open FilenameBox.Text For Random As # 1 Len =
      Len(Database(1))
->  For loop_index = 1 To TotalRecords
->      Put # 1, , Database(loop_index)
->  Next loop_index
```

```
        Close # 1                                          'Close file
        SaveFormHide
        Exit Sub

FileError:
        MsgBox "File Error", 0, "Database"    'MsgBox for file
           error.
        Resume
End Sub
```

In addition, add our global variables to Saveform's declaration area as follows:

```
    '$FORM Form1
    Type Record
        Name As String * 50
        Number As String * 20
        Comment As String * 20
    End Type

—>  Common Shared Database( ) As Record
—>  Common Shared TotalRecords As Integer
```

That's all there is to it; now we can use the database's Save File... option as shown in Figure 5-6.

Figure 5-6 Database Application's Save File... Box

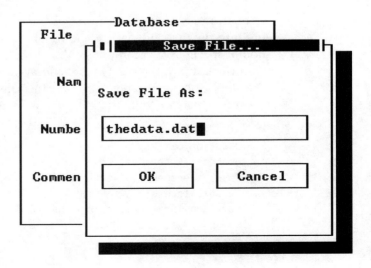

At this point, the file is written to disk (note that we also changed the error-message box in the FileError section of the code, giving it the title "Database" instead of "Pad"). If we had wanted to, we could have written any given record—instead of all of them—by specifying a particular record number as follows:

```
Put # 1, 5, Database(23)
```

This instruction writes record 5 in the file, filling it with the record Database(23); in this way, random access is truly random access—we have access to all records in the file. In other words, we can move around in the file at will, writing records in the order we want. This works in a similiar way with Get #, as we'll see next, when we read the file of records back in.

Reading Random-Access Files

We copied the Save File... dialog box from the Pad application to our database, and we can copy the Load File... dialog box as well (which is very useful, since all the file controls on that dialog box are already connected together). Once again, select the Add File... item in Visual Basic's File menu, and then add the .Frm file containing the Load File... dialog box (we named it Loadform.Frm above). Next, make the Load File... item in the Database's File menu active as follows:

```
   Sub LoadItem_Click( )
—>     LoadForm.Show
   End Sub
```

Then add the global variables to the declaration area:

```
      '$FORM Form1
          Type Record
          Name As String * 50
          Number As String * 20
          Comment As String * 20
      End Type

 —>  Common Shared Database( ) As Record
 —>  Common Shared TotalRecords As Integer
```

Now bring up the procedure OKButton_Click( ), which currently looks like this:

```
Sub OKButton_Click ( )
    On Local Error GoTo FileError

    If (Right$(Dir1.Path, 1) = "\") Then          'Get file name
        Filename$ = Dir1.Path + File1.FileName
    Else
        Filename$ = Dir1.Path + "\" + File1.FileName
    End If

    Open Filename$ For Input As # 1               'Open file
    Pad.PadText.Text = Input$(LOF(1), # 1)     'Read file in

    Close # 1                     'Close file
    LoadForm.Hide                 'Hide dialog box

    Exit Sub

FileError:
    MsgBox "File Error", 0, "Pad"    'MsgBox for file error.
    Resume
End Sub
```

Once again, we open the file as before, for random access:

```
Sub OKButton_Click ( )
    On Local Error GoTo FileError

    If (Right$(Dir1.Path, 1) = "\") Then          'Get file name
        Filename$ = Dir1.Path + File1.FileName
    Else
        Filename$ = Dir1.Path + "\" + File1.FileName
    End If

—>  Open Filename$ For Random As # 1 Len = Len(Database(1))
    Pad.PadText.Text = Input$(LOF(1), # 1)     'Read file in

    Close # 1                     'Close file
    LoadForm.Hide                 'Hide dialog box

    Exit Sub
```

```
FileError:
    MsgBox "File Error", 0, "Pad"     'MsgBox for file error.
    Resume
End Sub
```

Now we have to get records from the file using Get #, which you use to read from random and binary files, and whose syntax follows:

```
Get [#] nnn% , [rrr%], vvv%
```

As with Put #, nnn% is a file number, rrr% is the record number you want to get from the file, and vvv% is the variable we want to place the data in. If we do not specify a record number, Visual Basic simply gets the next record from the current position in the file. Our first job here is to find out how many records there are in the file, and we can do that simply by dividing the length of the file by the size of each record. After we do, we can read the data in, record by record, as follows:

```
Sub OKButton_Click ( )
    On Local Error GoTo FileError

    If (Right$(Dir1.Path, 1) = "\") Then          'Get file name
        Filename$ = Dir1.Path + File1.FileName    .
    Else
        Filename$ = Dir1.Path + "\" + File1.FileName
    End If

    Open Filename$ For Random As # 1 Len = Len(Database(1))
    NumberFileRecords = LOF(1) / Len(Database(1))
    For loop_index = 1 To NumberFileRecords
        Get # 1, , Database(loop_index)
    Next loop_index

    Close # 1                     'Close file
    LoadForm.Hide                 'Hide dialog box

    Exit Sub

FileError:
    MsgBox "File Error", 0, "Database"    'MsgBox for file
        error.
    Resume
End Sub
```

(Note that, once again, we changed the name of the error-box title in the FileError section of the code from "Pad" to "Database".) However, simply loading a file does not make the database active. In addition, we have to load the record names we've read into the database's sorted list box, where they can be selected by the user. That list box is maintained in the database's Find Item... dialog box; to load the record names into that list box, we must first erase all the current entries (using Visual Basic's RemoveItem method), and then we can reload them from Database(), using the AddItem method:

```
Sub OKButton_Click ( )
    On Local Error GoTo FileError

    If (Right$(Dir1.Path, 1) = "\") Then            'Get file name
        Filename$ = Dir1.Path + File1.FileName
    Else
        Filename$ = Dir1.Path + "\" + File1.FileName
    End If

    Open Filename$ For Random As # 1 Len = Len(Database(1))
    NumberFileRecords = LOF(1) / Len(Database(1))
    For loop_index = 1 To NumberFileRecords
        Get # 1, , Database(loop_index)
    Next loop_index

    Close # 1                        'Close file

—>     For loop_index = 1 To TotalRecords
—>         Form2.NameList.RemoveItem 0
—>     Next loop_index

—>     TotalRecords = NumberFileRecords          'After safely
         reading file

—>     For loop_index = 1 To TotalRecords
—>         Form2.NameList.AddItem Database(loop_index).Name
—>     Next loop_index

—>     Form1.NameField.Text = Database(1).Name
—>     Form1.NumberField.Text = Database(1).Number
—>     Form1.CommentField.Text = Database(1).Comment
```

```
        LoadForm.Hide                  'Hide dialog box
        Exit Sub

FileError:
        MsgBox "File Error", 0, "Database"    'MsgBox for file
            error.
        Resume
End Sub
```

That's all, then; we've read in the file and filled the program variables correctly. The database Load File... dialog box is now functional, as shown in Figure 5-7.

Figure 5-7 Database Load File Dialog Box

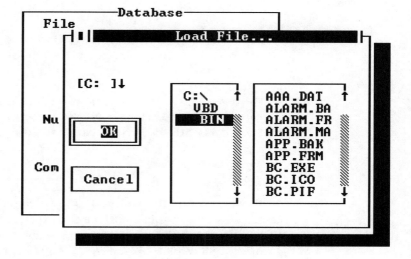

Note that we did not have to read in the whole array of records at once; in fact, we could have read in only one record at a time if we wanted to (saving a significant amount of memory). For example, if we always stored our data in a file named Db.Dat, we could change the Sub procedure that looks up records, GetItem( ), *from* the following (which retrieves the data from the array Database( )):

```
Sub GetItem ( )
    For loop_index = 1 To 100
        If (Rtrim$(Database(loop_index).Name) =
            Rtrim$(Form2.NameList.Text)) Then Exit For
```

```
            Next loop_index

            Form1.NameField.Text = Database(loop_index).Name
            Form1.NumberField.Text = Database(loop_index).Number
            Form1.CommentField.Text = Database(loop_index).Comment

            Form2.Hide
        End Sub
```

to the following (which retrieves the data from the Db.Dat file directly):

```
Sub GetItem ( )
    For loop_index = 1 To 100
        If (Rtrim$(Database(loop_index).Name) =
            Rtrim$(Form2.NameList.Text)) Then Exit For
    Next loop_index

—>      Open "Db.Dat" For Random As # 1 Len = Len(Database(1))
—>      Get # 1, loop_index, Database(loop_index)
—>      Close # 1

        Form1.NameField.Text = Database(loop_index).Name
        Form1.NumberField.Text = Database(loop_index).Number
        Form1.CommentField.Text = Database(loop_index).Comment

        Form2.Hide
End Sub
```

In this way, we can move around in the file, retrieving the specific records we want. At this point, our file expertise is almost complete. However, we should note that we don't have to specify the record number in the Get # statement if we don't want to; we can use *Seek* instead. Let's look at Seek as our last file topic.

Using the Seek Statement

This statement can be extremely useful, because it allows us to specify which record will be read from or written to next. Its syntax is like this:

```
Seek [#] nnn%, ppp&
```

Here, nnn% is the file number, and ppp& (a long integer) is the new position in the file; for sequential files, ppp& is measured in bytes, for random files, in record numbers. In other words, the following line:

```
Get # 1, loop_index, Database(loop_index)
```

is the same as:

```
Seek # 1, loop_index
Get # 1, , Database(loop_index)
```

Using Get, Put, and Seek together, we have a great deal of control over our files; in particular, we can work byte by byte in binary files, if we want to, with these statements.

That completes our coverage of files. We've seen VB's file handling statements, we've seen how they work in practice, and now we've added file handling capabilities to two of our major applications. As you can see, working with files in Visual BASIC is much like working with files in standard BASIC, except that in Visual Basic we have the added advantage of three new types of file controls to make selecting files easier. This is very much the way Visual Basic is, in general—just like standard BASIC, except when it comes to communicating with the user. In fact, while we're on the subject of communicating with the user, let's turn to the next chapter, where we'll start working with one of the most exciting ways of doing just that—graphics.

Visual Basic in Graphics Mode

So far, we've been working only with text in Visual Basic for DOS. However, Visual Basic also supports graphics modes—although not in the way you might think. In graphics mode, we can indeed draw graphics figures, such as circles, lines, and rectangles; but we cannot display any forms on the screen (i.e., we work with the whole screen at once), nor can we use any events such as Command1_Click or Form_KeyPress or even mouse events. This means that Visual Basic for DOS operates in quite a different way in graphics mode. Since graphics programming is highly popular, here we will see how to work with Visual Basic in graphics mode. In the following chapter, we will be able to use that knowledge when we write a complete mouse-driven paint program that will allow us to draw our own figures with a click of the mouse.

In this chapter, we'll start by seeing the type of graphics that Visual Basic supports in text mode: ASCII graphics, including how to print to a form and how to use picture boxes. Then we press on, seeing how to switch our program from text mode into graphics mode at the click of a button and how to get back again. After that, we'll see how to write dedicated graphics programs that don't need to switch in and out of text mode.

For the most part, we'll have to find a whole new way of accepting input (both keyboard input and mouse input) and of displaying results (on the screen instead of in a text box or label).

Text Mode Graphics

We won't have to switch away from forms and event-based programming if we can use text-based graphics. That is, if we can construct the graphics figures we want out of the ASCII character set, we're ready for action without worrying about graphics modes. The ASCII box-drawing characters are very popular for this purpose, and they appear in Figure 6-1. To draw one of these characters, you use the Visual Basic Chr$( ) function. For example, to draw a short horizontal bar, you would use Chr$(196).

Figure 6-1 The ASCII Box-Drawing Characters

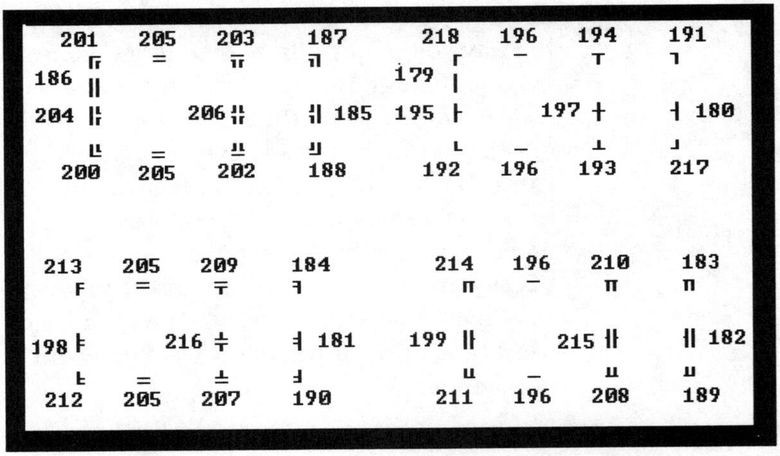

Let's see this in action. We can draw directly on the form with the Form.Print method. To print a short horizontal bar, use the following instructions:

```
Form1.Print Chr$(196)
```

In fact, if we omit the form name (Form1 here), Visual Basic assumes that we want to print on the current form, like this:

```
Print Chr$(196)
```

In this way, we'll be able to draw boxes using the box-drawing characters. In fact, in Visual Basic for DOS, if you set NumLock on, you can enter the ASCII code of the character you want (as shown in Figure 6-1) directly by holding down the Alt key and typing the number on the numeric keyboard. (To print Chr$(196), you would hold down the Alt key and type 196.) In this way, we can write the small program that appears in Figure 6-2, which we place in the Form_Load( ) procedure so that it's run as soon as the form is loaded (i.e., as soon as the program runs in this case).

In addition, you must set the form's *AutoRedraw* property to True before trying to print on the form from the Form_Load() procedure. The reason is that the Visual Basic AutoRedraw property makes sure that whatever was on the form is saved and is automatically restored after the form is uncovered or resized. After Form_Load() runs, the form is actually cleared in preparation for running the program; thus, if AutoRedraw is False, the form appears blank. This program results in the form you see in Figure 6-3.

Using Picture Boxes

Besides text-mode printing in forms, we can also print in a new control—*picture boxes*. In Visual Basic for Windows, picture boxes display graphics in graphics mode, but in Visual Basic for DOS, they display text-mode graphics. To use a picture box, double-click the Picture Box tool in the tool box and draw the (rectangular) picture box until it covers most of the form. The name of this picture box is Picture1. Set its AutoRedraw property to True so that we can draw in it from the Form_Load() procedure; then change the program we originally used in Figure 6-2, prefacing every Print statement with

Picture1 (i.e., Print becomes Picture1.Print) as shown in Figure 6-4. The result of this program appears in Figure 6-5.

Figure 6-2 Programming with the Box-Drawing Characters

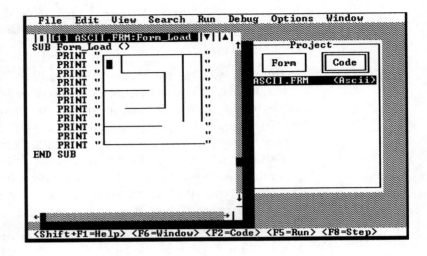

Figure 6-3 Using Box-Drawing Characters

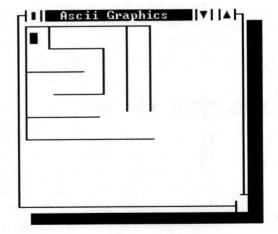

Figure 6-4 Programming with Picture Boxes

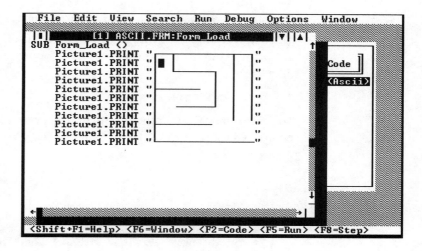

Figure 6-5 Box-Drawing Characters in Picture Boxes

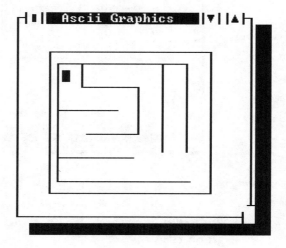

It turns out that we can use the Print method with more than just the form and picture boxes. We can use it to print on the printer as well.

Using the Printer in Visual Basic

Printing with the printer is easy in Visual Basic. All you need to do is to use the Print method of the Printer object. For example, to print text on the printer, you can use Printer.Print like this:

```
Printer.Print "This is a test."
```

To print our ASCII graphics figure on the printer, we'd only have to change Picture1.Print in our program to Printer.Print, as shown in Figure 6-6.

Figure 6-6 Programming the Printer

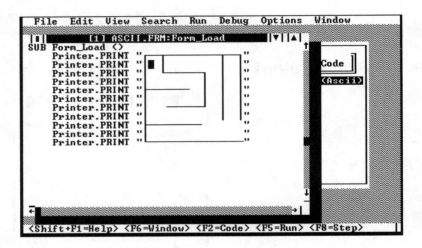

That's all there is to printing in Visual Basic; everything you can do with the Print method, you can do with the printer by using the Printer.Print method. It's that easy. Now let's turn to *real* graphics.

Graphics Modes

We'll start our discussion of graphics modes by seeing what's available. In Visual Basic, you switch into and out of graphics modes with the Screen statement. When you use a Screen statement, you specify what new screen mode you want (mode 0 = the normal text mode that Visual Basic for DOS usually operates in). You'll find a listing of these screen modes in Table 6-1; here, we'll usually use screen mode 8 (in which the screen is 640 dots wide by 200 dots high, and we have 16 colors to work with).

Table 6-1 Visual Basic Screen Modes

Adapter	Mode	Resolution	Text Format	Color/Attribute
AT&T	3	720x348	80x25	
	4	640x400	80x25	
CGA	0	Text Mode	40x25,43, or 50 80x25,43, or 50	16/16
	1	320x200	40x25	16 background
	2	640x200	80x25	
EGA	0	Text Mode	40x25,43, or 50	16/16 or 64/16
	1	320x200	40x25	16/4
	2	640x200	80x25	16/2
	7	320x200	40x25	16/16
	8	640x200	80x25	16/16
	9	640x350	80x25, 80x43	16/4 (64k) 64/16 (>64k)
Hercules	0	Text Mode	40x25,43, or 50	16/2
	3	720x348	80x25	
	4	640x400	80x25	
MCGA	0	Text Mode	40x25,43, or 50	16/2
	1	320x200	40x25	
	2	640x200	80x25	
	11	640x480	80x30, 80x60	256k/2
MDGA	0	Text Mode	40x25,43, or 50	16/2
VGA	0	Text Mode	40x25,43, or 50	64/16
	1	320x200	40x25	16/4
	2	640x200	80x25	16/2
	7	320x200	40x25	16/16
	8	640x200	80x25	16/16
	9	640x350	80x25, 80x43	16/4 (64k) 64/16 (>64k)
	10	640x350	80x25, 80x43	9 gray shades/4
	11	640x480	80x30, 80x60	256k/2
	12	640x480	80x30, 80x60	256k/16
	13	320x200	40x25	256k/256

For example, let's say that we were in a normal Visual Basic procedure, Command1_Click( ) for a command button named Command1:

```
Sub Command1_Click ()

End Sub
```

Now let's say that we wanted to switch into graphics mode to display a graph or picture of some kind. We cannot simply add this statement to switch into screen mode 8:

```
       Sub Command1_Click ()
—>         Screen 8              'Will not work.
                 :
       End Sub
```

Instead, since we cannot have forms on the screen when in graphics modes, we must first hide the standard Visual Basic for DOS screen with the Hide method of the Screen object, like this:

```
       Sub Command1_Click ()
—>         Screen.Hide
           Screen 8
                 :
       End Sub
```

Now we switch into graphics mode 8, and the entire screen is cleared (and becomes black). At this point, we are free to draw our graphics figures. For example, we can draw a line on the screen from position (10, 10) to (100, 200). All graphics positions are measured in pixels, not rows and columns: (x, y) (where (0, 0) is the top left of the screen). To do that, we would execute the following statement (we'll see a great deal about the Line statement in the next chapter):

```
       Sub Command1_Click ()
           Screen.Hide
           Screen 8
—>         Line (10, 10) - (100, 200)
                 :
       End Sub
```

Now a line appears on the screen, as in Figure 6-7. However, we've left ourselves with a problem: how do we return to text mode so that we can continue with our program? For example, we might want to switch back into text mode when the user presses a key. To see how to do this, we can explore receiving character input while in graphics modes next.

Figure 6-7 Our First Graphics Figure

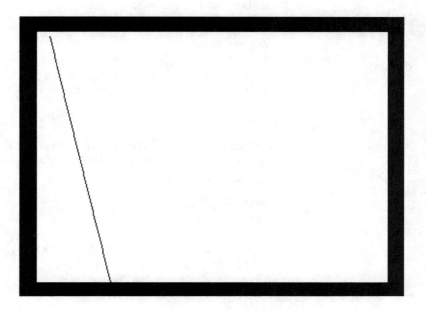

Keyboard Input in Graphics Mode

There are several ways of reading character input in graphics mode, including Input, Input$, Line Input, and Inkey$. We'll take a look at each of them in turn.

The Input Statement

The Print statement still works in graphics mode, so that we can use it for character output. For example, we might run a program in graphics mode that accepts three floating-point numbers, averages them, and prints out the result. To do that, we might start as follows:

```
Sub Command1_Click ()
    Screen.Hide
    Screen 8
    Print "This program takes the average of three numbers."
        :
End Sub
```

Now we need to read the three numbers, and we can do that with the Input statement as follows:

```
Sub Command1_Click ()
    Screen.Hide
    Screen 8
    Print "This program takes the average of three numbers."
—>  Input "The numbers"; A!, B!, C!
        :
End Sub
```

This prints the prompt "The numbers?" on the screen, and, when the user types them, places them in the variables A!, B!, and C!. Now we can display the result:

```
Sub Command1_Click ()
    Screen.Hide
    Screen 8
    Print "This program takes the average of three numbers."
    Input "The numbers"; A!, B!, C!
—>  Print "Thank You. The average is: ";(A! + B! + C!)/3.0
        :
End Sub
```

To make the program complete, we must restore the screen to mode 0 (text mode) and redisplay any forms as follows:

```
Sub Command1_Click ()
    Screen.Hide
    Screen 8
    Print "This program takes the average of three numbers."
    Input "The numbers"; A!, B!, C!
    Print "Thank You. The average is: ";(A! + B! + C!)/3.0
—>  Screen 0
—>  Screen.Show
End Sub
```

That's all there is to it. We have now written a program that switches us into graphics mode, reads input, displays a result, and switches us back into text mode. Unfortunately, the Input statement should be avoided by professional programmers. One problem is that it places a mandatory question mark after the prompt string. If our code had looked like this:

```
  —>      Input "Please type three numbers"; A!, B!, C!
          Print "Thank You. The average is: ";(A! + B! + C!)/3
```

the prompt on the screen would look like this:

```
Please type three numbers?
```

This looks more like a plea than a prompt. The real problem, however, is that Input produces a "Redo from start" error message if the values typed do not fit into the variable list provided, or if the values are not separated by valid delimiters such as commas. This doesn't exactly match the idea of user-friendliness, nor does it promote a professional image. Let's look into Input$ next.

The Input$ Function

Although the Input$() function is usually used to read strings from files, you can use it to read keys from the keyboard as well. In fact, one of its chief advantages is that it does not echo characters on the screen, providing an alternate method of input from the rest of the Basic statements and functions.

Unfortunately, you have to specify *exactly* how many characters to read. An example follows, in which we read (exactly) 10 characters and find the first occurrence of the letter 'e':

```
Sub Command1_Click ()
    Screen.Hide
    Screen 8
    Print "Please type a string of 10 characters."
—>  Instring$ = Input$(10)  'Note: no echoing on-screen.
    The_Value% = Instr(Instring$,"e")
    If The_Value% = 0 THEN
        Print "Thank you. There was no 'e' in that string."
    Else
        Print "Thank you. The first 'e' was character"; The_Value%
    End If
End Sub
```

First we print our prompt ("Please type a string of 10 characters."), and then read the input string:

```
        Print "Please type a string of 10 characters."
—>      Instring$ = Input$(10)  'Note: no echoing on-screen.
        :
```

Now we can search the string for the first 'e', if there was one, and print its location:

```
Print "Please type a string of 10 characters."
Instring$ = Input$(10)   'Note: no echoing on-screen.
—> The_Value% = INSTR(Instring$,"e")
If The_Value% = 0 THEN
     Print "Thank you. There was no 'e' in that string."
Else
     Print "Thank you. The first 'e' was character"; The_Value%
   End If
```

Note our use of Print here. Normally, after printing, Print skips to the next line. However, if we use a semicolon (;), it does not do so:

```
Print "Thank you. The first 'e' was character"; The_Value%
```

In fact, we can do even more with Print in graphics mode—we can use the Locate statement (not available in text mode) to indicate where on the screen we want to print. The Locate statement sets the position at which text will next be printed. We pass it a screen position as (text row, text column) not using pixel ranges, even though we're in graphics, because now we're printing text. For example, to display our prompt at row 5, column 7 on the screen, we could have done this:

```
Locate 5, 7
Print "Thank you. The first 'e' was character"; The_Value%
```

The Locate statement sets the new origin for text on the screen, and subsequent Print statements start printing at that location. Here, if we were to skip to the next line like this:

```
Locate 5, 7
Print "Line 1"
Print "Line 2"
```

Then "Line 2" would appear under location (5, 7) (= row, column), starting at (5, 8).

Our program works, and we can use Input$( ) for character input, but requiring a specific number of characters (carriage returns do not terminate input) is a big drawback. Let's look into Line Input next.

The Line Input Statement

The Line Input statement is a very useful one. All it does is read a string of characters from the keyboard. The string is terminated once you type a carriage return. Here's an example:

```
Sub Command1_Click ()
    Screen.Hide
    Screen 8
    Line Input "Please type a string: ";Instring$
    Print "Thank you. That string was";LEN(Instring$);"characters long."
    Screen 0
    Screen.Show
End Sub
```

In this case, we print out a prompt ("Please type a string: ")—note that no annoying question mark is added—and then we receive our input string. If you want to read strings, this is the statement for you. Still, Line Input doesn't give you character-by-character control. For that capability, we have to turn to Inkey$.

Inkey$

For real control, Inkey$ is the programmer's favorite. This function reads and returns one key from the keyboard. Here's an example:

```
Sub Command1_Click ()
    Screen.Hide
    Screen 8
    Print "Type a character."
    Do
—>        InChar$ = Inkey$
    Loop While InChar$ = ""
    Print "Thank you. That character was: "; InChar$
    Screen 0
    Screen.Show
End Sub
```

In this case, we're just waiting for a character to be typed. Because Inkey$ returns whatever is in the keyboard buffer immediately, we have to loop, calling it continuously until something is there:

```
        Print "Type a character."
—> Do
—>      InChar$ = Inkey$
—> Loop While InChar$ = ""
        Print "Thank you. That character was: ";InChar$
```

Inkey$ has three types of return values—strings of length zero (null strings, ""), length one, and length two (use the LEN( ) function to determine string length). If the return string is one character long, it's just a single character, such as "d" or "q".

If, however, the return string is two characters long, then it represents an *extended ASCII code*. The first character in this string is ASCII 0—CHR$(0). The second character is the key's *scan code*. There is a unique scan code for each key or legal key combination (such as Alt-k) on the keyboard, and you can look them up in the tables in your Visual Basic documentation. (Use the Visual Basic functions Right$( ), Left$( ), and Mid$( ) to separate out the first and second characters in the returned string.)

Although many programmers aren't familiar with scan codes, using them can add a lot of power to your programs; let's take a look at how to put them to work. In the following example, we set up a function that indicates which arrow key was pressed.

The GetArrowKey$ Example

In this example, let's write a function to read the arrow keys on the computer's numeric keyboard and return their values in an easy-to-interpret way. For example, if the right-arrow key was pressed, the return value might be "r." If the up-arrow key was pressed, we could return a value of "u." This lets us use the arrows keys easily in our programs, without having to memorize scan codes. Here are the possible return values from GetArrowKey$( ):

```
"r" —> Right-arrow key pressed
"l" —> Left-arrow key pressed
"u" —> Up-arrow key pressed
"d" —> Down-arrow key pressed
"h" —> Home key pressed
"e" —> End key pressed
```

GetArrowKey$() can be used like any other function, as long as we're in graphics mode. When you use it, it waits for an arrow key to be pressed and then returns the corresponding letter. Let's pass an argument called WarningBeep% to GetArrowKey$()—if you set WarningBeep% to a nonzero value, GetArrowKey$() will beep when you press any key but an arrow key.

We start setting up a new function by selecting the New Function... item in the Visual Basic Edit menu. A dialog box opens, asking for the name of the new function; type GetArrowKey$. A template like this opens:

```
Function GetArrowKey$ ()

End Function
```

Since we want to pass a single parameter named WarningBeep% to GetArrowKey$(), type that between the parentheses in the first line like this:

```
Function GetArrowKey$ (WarningBeep%)

End Function
```

Next we'll add a continuous loop, waiting for keys to be typed:

```
Function GetArrowKey$ (WarningBeep%)
        Do
         :
        Loop While 1
End Function
```

Now we can accept input from Inkey$:

```
Function GetArrowKey$ (WarningBeep%)
        Do
            Do
                InStr$ = Inkey$
            Loop While InStr$ = ""
                :
        Loop While 1
End Function
```

The outer loop, Do...Loop While 1, loops forever; the inner loop waits until a key has been pressed. After Inkey$ returns a key, we get its ASCII code with the Visual Basic Asc() function (the opposite of

Chr$()), and then check to make sure that the length of the incoming string is two; if not, and if WarningBeep% is non-zero, we beep:

```
Function GetArrowKey$ (WarningBeep%)
        Do
            Do
                InStr$ = Inkey$
            Loop While InStr$ = ""
—>          Code = Asc(Right$(InStr$, 1))
—>          If Len(InStr$) = 2 Then
                        :
                [check for arrow key]
                        :
—>          Else
—>                  If WarningBeep% Then Beep
—>          End If


        Loop While 1
End Function
```

Now we can check to see which arrow key, if any, has been pressed. That looks like this, using a Visual Basic Select Case statement (and getting the scan code values from our Visual Basic documentation):

```
Function GetArrowKey$ (WarningBeep%)
        Do
            Do
                InStr$ = Inkey$
            Loop While InStr$ = ""

            Code = Asc(RIGHT$(InStr$, 1))
            If Len(InStr$) = 2 Then
—>              Select Case Code
                    Case &H4D
                        GetArrowKey$ = "r"
                        Exit Function
                    Case &H4B
                        GetArrowKey$ = "l"
                        Exit Function
                    Case &H48
                        GetArrowKey$ = "u"
                        Exit Function
                    Case &H50
                        GetArrowKey$ = "d"
```

```
                          Exit Function
                    Case &H47
                        GetArrowKey$ = "h"
                        EXIT Function
                    Case &H4F
                        GetArrowKey$ = "e"
                        Exit Function
   —>         End Select
              If WarningBeep% Then Beep
          Else
              If WarningBeep% Then Beep
          End If
      Loop While 1
End Function
```

If an arrow key has been pressed, we return the correct character; if not, we loop back to the beginning and wait for another one (after beeping if we're supposed to). This is one way to use the scan codes you can read from Inkey$. As we can see, Inkey$ is a versatile function. For most purposes, we can put together a good input routine using Inkey$ in graphics modes. This completes our exploration or keyboard input in graphics modes. Now let's turn to mouse input.

Mouse Input in Graphics Mode

Normally, handling mouse input in Visual Basic is very easy. Most controls have Click events that have associated procedures that are automatically called when the control is clicked, like this:

```
Command1_Click ()

End Sub
```

In fact, even forms have a click event, which is called when the form itself is clicked:

```
Form1_Click ()

End Sub
```

However, sometimes just knowing a control or form was clicked wasn't enough—we want to know where it was clicked. And in text mode, we can do that with the mouse events, MouseDown, MouseMove, and MouseUp.

MouseDown Events

When the user positions the mouse cursor somewhere on a form and presses a mouse button, a *MouseDown* event is generated. This event is not the same as a Click event. In a Click event, the user must press and release the mouse button; a MouseDown event occurs when the user simply presses a mouse button. These kinds of events are recognized by forms, picture boxes, labels, and any control that includes a list (list boxes, combo boxes, directory list boxes, and so on). Note that controls such as buttons do not respond to MouseDown events, only to Click events.

In a MouseDown event, we get considerably more information than we did with the Click event. This is the Sub procedure template for a MouseDown event:

```
Sub Form_MouseDown (Button As Integer,Shift As Integer,X As
Single,Y As Single)

End Sub
```

As you can see, there are a number of arguments passed to this procedure that we haven't seen before: Button, Shift, X, and Y. The Button and Shift arguments pass mouse button and keyboard shift state information to us, and the X and Y arguments report the position of the mouse cursor using text-mode rows and columns. We can make use of that information by, for example, reporting the cursor's position when you press a mouse button. To do that, create two new text boxes, Text1 and Text2, and place them on the form. We can report the position, (X, Y), like this:

```
Sub Form_MouseDown (Button As Integer,Shift As Integer,X As
Single,Y As Single)
    Text1.Text = Str$(X)
    Text2.Text = Str$(Y)
End Sub
```

Now let's take a look at the two other arguments passed to us: Button and Shift, both integers. The Button argument describes which of the mouse buttons is pressed by encoding that information in its lowest three bits. That looks like this (an integer is two bytes, 16 bits, long):

Button

1 if middle button pressed, 0 otherwise
1 if right button pressed, 0 otherwise
1 if left button pressed, 0 otherwise

Note that we can only test for one button being pushed, not two or three at a time; that is, Button only reports which button was pushed first: right, left, or middle (not many mouse devices have middle buttons anymore, although some do). The event that we're going to examine next, the MouseMove event, does actually report when two or more buttons are pressed simultaneously; here, however, the Button argument can take only one of three values, as shown in Table 6-2.

Table 6-2 Values for the Button Argument (MouseDown, MouseUp)

Button Value	Binary	Means
1	0000000000000001	Left button was pushed
2	0000000000000010	Right button was pushed
4	0000000000000100	Middle button was pushed

Note in particular that Button cannot be 0, because at least one button must have been pushed to cause the MouseDown event. Let's make use of this information in our program; we can add another text box, Text3, to report which button caused the MouseDown event with a Select Case statement as follows:

```
Sub Form_MouseDown (Button As Integer,Shift As Integer,X As
Single,Y As Single)
    Text1.Text = Str$(X)
    Text2.Text = Str$(Y)
    Select Case Button
        Case 1
            Text3.Text = "Left Button"
```

```
        Case 2
            Text3.Text = "Right Button"
        Case 4
            Text3.Text = "Middle Button"
    End Select
End Sub
```

Now when you run the program, it reports not only the position of the mouse cursor when the MouseDown event occurred, but also which button caused it.

Besides X, Y, and Button, the Shift argument also returns some useful information. This integer indicates whether the Ctrl or Shift keys on the keyboard were pressed when the mouse button was clicked (i.e., some programs distinguish between Click and Shift-Click, and there is no "ShiftClick" event in Visual Basic). This information is encoded in the last two bits of Shift like this:

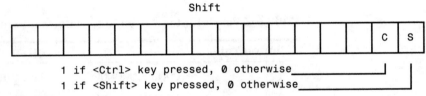

In other words, Shift can take on three values: 0 (i.e., neither key was pressed), 1, or 2 as shown in Table 6-3.

Table 6-3 Values for the Shift Argument

Shift Value	Binary	Means
0	0000000000000000	Neither Shift nor Ctrl were down
1	0000000000000001	Shift key was down
2	0000000000000010	Ctrl key was down

So far, we've seen that the MouseDown event reports four things: the X position of the mouse cursor, the Y position of the mouse cursor, which button was pushed, and which of the keyboard's shift or control keys (if either) were pushed.

MouseMove Events

Every time the mouse is moved across a form or selected controls (file list boxes, labels, list boxes, or picture boxes), a MouseMove event is generated. In addition, the Button argument in a MouseMove event reports the complete state of the mouse buttons—i.e., it can report if more than one button is being pressed (unlike MouseDown or the next event we'll examine, MouseUp). You'll find the values that it can report for Button in Table 6-4.

Table 6-4 Values for the Button Argument (MouseMove)

Button Value	Binary	Means
0	0000000000000000	No button is pushed
1	0000000000000001	Only left button is pushed
2	0000000000000010	Only right button is pushed
3	0000000000000011	Right and left buttons are pushed
4	0000000000000100	Only middle button is pushed
5	0000000000000101	Middle and left buttons are pushed
6	0000000000000110	Middle and right buttons are pushed
7	0000000000000111	All three buttons are pushed

MouseUp Events

The last type of mouse events, MouseUp events, look just like MouseDown events:

```
Sub Form_MouseUp (Button As Integer,Shift As Integer,X As
Single,Y As Single)

End Sub
```

Here, we can learn where the mouse cursor was when the mouse button went up—and also what button it was.

NOTE: *Because the Sub procedures and Functions that follow use the Interrupt() routine, you use the /L switch when you first start Visual Basic for DOS. This loads in the Quick Library (.Qlb) file that supports Interrupt().*

Using the MouseDown, MouseMove, and MouseUp events work well in text mode, but in graphics mode, we'll have to add our own support for the mouse. We can do that by using DOS interrupt &H33 (the mouse interrupt) to reach the mouse directly. This may sound difficult, but in fact it's very easy. We'll see how to initialize the mouse, read position and button information from it, and work with the mouse cursor. We'll also see examples, showing how to make use of mouse information.

There are two things you need to know before we start to use the mouse. First, under DOS, you must load the mouse driver software that came with your mouse before trying to use it. You can do that by running the .Com file that comes with the mouse (e.g., Mouse.Com for a Microsoft or a Logitech mouse, or Mousesys.Com for a Mouse Systems mouse). You must run this driver program before any program can use your mouse.

NOTE: *The mouse driver program loads the code to handle the mouse interrupt, interrupt &H33.*

Second, you have to initialize the mouse before using it. We'll start our mouse coverage by developing a function named MouseInitialize%() to do exactly that; before you can use the mouse, you must call MouseInitialize%(). After that, you can use any other mouse function or Sub procedure that we develop in whatever order you want, as demonstrated by the examples coming up.

Mouse Optional?

NOTE: *MouseInitialize%() initializes the mouse driver software that you loaded previously.*

In many programs, use of a mouse is optional and depends on whether or not a mouse and mouse driver are installed. You should know that, even if a mouse is optional, you can call and use the mouse Functions and Sub procedures we develop here without problem—if there is no mouse, you'll simply not see mouse "events" such as cursor movements or button presses. (And you should make sure that you don't loop forever, waiting to see such events.) In other words, using our mouse Sub procedures and Functions does no harm if there is no mouse. Now let's see how to use DOS interrupt &H33.

Using Interrupts

Each interrupt is a prewritten program already in memory, ready for us to use. The commands you use at the DOS level (e.g., Copy, Time, Ver, Xcopy, or Format) all make use of the built-in interrupts—and now we, as Visual Basic programmers, can too.

The way we pass and receive data to and from interrupt routines is by using the Visual Basic Interrupt() routine, and the 80x86's registers. The microprocessor handles data in 16-bit registers, which you can think of as the computer's built-in variables. The ones we'll see most, which are named ax, bx, cx, and dx, store data in the computer's CPU:

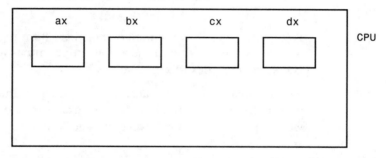

Each interrupt examines the way we've loaded some or all of these registers and takes action accordingly. Since each register is 16 bits long, it is exactly like a Basic Integer, and we can load integer values into them, such as 53, 3251, or –219:

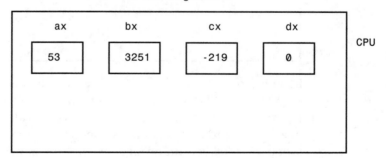

To the computer, however, each register can also be thought of as two bytes. Thus, you can also break up these registers into a high 8-bit register and a low 8-bit register. For example, the high 8-bit part of ax (bx, cx...) is called ah (bh, ch...), and the low 8-bit part of ax (bx, cx...) is called al (bl, cl...):

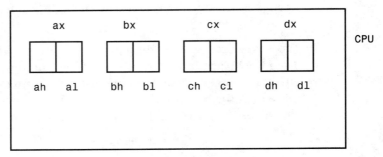

Frequently, we'll have to load one of these 8-bit registers, such as ah, with a particular value to use an interrupt, and as we work with registers, we'll use hexadecimal values.

Hexadecimal is handy because a 16-bit binary number—the size of each full register—makes up four hexadecimal digits. The values we can place in the 80x86's registers go from 0 to &HFFFF (65535):

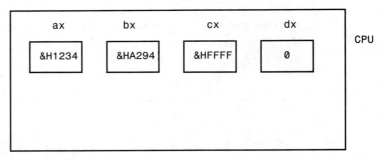

In addition, 8 bits (a byte) make up exactly two hex digits like this: &H12 or &H34. That is, a byte can hold values from 0 to &HFF (255). Because we can divide registers such as ax into ah and al, the top byte in a 16-bit word like ax is simply the first two hex digits, and the bottom byte is the bottom two. For example, if ax held &H1234, then ah contains &H12 and al contains &H34:

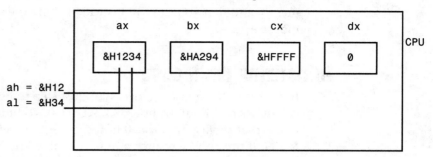

16-bit registers

To reach the 80x86's registers from Visual Basic, we first have to set up two data structures, InRegs and OutRegs, as type RegType. That type is defined this way:

```
Type RegType
      ax    As Integer
      bx    As Integer
      cx    As Integer
      dx    As Integer
      bp    As Integer
      si    As Integer
      di    As Integer
      flags As Integer
End Type
```

Now we'll be able to refer to registers such as ax as InRegs.ax, bx as InRegs.bx, and so on. Note that we had to set aside space for four new registers here—bp, si, di, and the flags register:

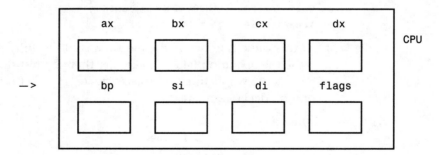

Now that we've defined our Type RegType, we're free to use Interrupt() in our mouse interface, and we'll do that soon. That interface will consist of several bite-sized functions that you can type into your program if you need them (using the Add Function... item in the Edit menu), and that you can call instead of using the standard text-mode mouse events.

Initializing the Mouse

Initializing the mouse is a necessary first step to using the mouse. We can do that with interrupt &H33, service 0. To indicate that we want to use that service, we place 0 in the ah register before calling interrupt &H33. If this service returns a nonzero value, the mouse is initialized; otherwise, the mouse cannot be used (because it's not installed in the computer, or the mouse driver is missing). In that case, and if your program depends on the use of a mouse, you should print an error message and quit.

After the mouse is initialized, we're all set until the computer is turned off—we don't have to initialize it again (although doing so does no harm). Note that initializing the mouse does not display the mouse cursor; to display the cursor, use the Sub procedure we'll develop later, MouseShowCursor( ).

The function we'll call MouseInitialize%( ) just uses interrupt &H33 service 0 (i.e., ah = 0) to initialize the mouse system. As mentioned, this is the necessary first step to using any other mouse function. Here's all we do: load ah with 0 and call interrupt &H33, then we set MouseInitialize% to the value returned in ax:

```
      Dim InRegs AS RegType, OutRegs AS RegType
—>    InRegs.ax = 0
—>    Call Interrupt(&H33, InRegs, OutRegs)
—>    MouseInitialize% = OutRegs.ax
```

If this value is nonzero, the mouse was successfully initialized; otherwise the operation failed. Make sure that you test this return value. Here's the whole function (place the RegType definition in the program's declaration area):

```
      Type RegType
              ax      As Integer
              bx      As Integer
              cx      As Integer
              dx      As Integer
              bp      As Integer
```

```
              si      As Integer
              di      As Integer
              flags   As Integer
End Type

Function MouseInitialize% ()

    Dim InRegs AS RegType, OutRegs AS RegType
    InRegs.ax = 0
    Call Interrupt(&H33, InRegs, OutRegs)
    MouseInitialize% = OutRegs.ax

End Function
```

Let's use MouseInitialize%( ) in graphics mode. Start a new project and type this in the code window:

```
Type RegType
              ax      As Integer
              bx      As Integer
              cx      As Integer
              dx      As Integer
              bp      As Integer
              si      As Integer
              di      As Integer
              flags   As Integer
End Type
              Screen.Hide
              Screen 8
              If MouseInitialize% Then
                  Print "Mouse Initialized."
              Else
                  Print "Mouse driver not installed."
                  While InKey$ = ""
                  Wend
                  End
              End If
              While InKey$ = ""
              Wend
              Screen 0
              Screen.Show
```

Note that we check the value returned by MouseInitialize%( )— if it's zero, we print out an error message ("Mouse driver not installed.") and quit. Otherwise, we print "Mouse Initialized." and then quit. Note also that we wait until a key is typed before exiting the graphics screen, allowing us to see the message that's printed:

```
Screen.Hide
Screen 8
If MouseInitialize% Then
    Print "Mouse Initialized."
Else
    Print "Mouse driver not installed."
    While InKey$ = ""
    Wend
    End
End If
While InKey$ = ""
Wend
Screen 0
Screen.Show
```

—> (pointing to `While InKey$ = ""`)
—> (pointing to `Wend`)

Next, add the definition of MouseInitialize%() with the Add Function... menu item and run the program. When you do, you should see "Mouse Initialized," as shown in Figure 6-8. However, the mouse cursor does not yet appear. When you save this program, give it a .Bas extension like this: Mouinit.Bas (i.e., our projects that operate independently of forms do not need .Frm and .Mak files).

Figure 6-8 Our Graphics Mouse Initialized

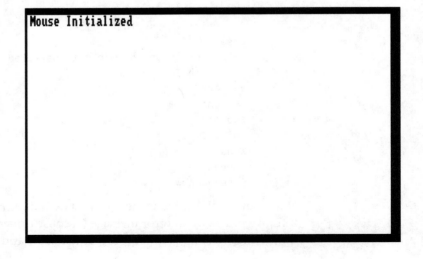

Now that we've set up the mouse system for use, let's start use of the mouse by displaying the mouse cursor.

Making the Mouse Cursor Visible

The next step in using the mouse is to show the mouse cursor on the screen. In graphics mode, the cursor appears as a large arrow. Let's write a small Sub procedure named MouseShowCursor( ) to do the work for us. Like all of the mouse Functions and Sub procedures we'll write, we just use another interrupt &H33 service here. In this case, we use service 1, which displays the mouse cursor:

```
        Dim InRegs AS RegType, OutRegs AS RegType
—>      InRegs.ax = 1
—>      Call Interrupt(&H33, InRegs, OutRegs)
```

When you use MouseShowCursor( ), the cursor appears on the screen. Here's the whole Sub procedure (as usual, place the RegType declaration in the program's declaration area):

```
Type RegType
        ax      As Integer
        bx      As Integer
        cx      As Integer
        dx      As Integer
        bp      As Integer
        si      As Integer
        di      As Integer
        flags   As Integer
End Type

Sub MouseShowCursor ()

Dim InRegs AS RegType, OutRegs AS RegType
    InRegs.ax = 1
    Call Interrupt(&H33, InRegs, OutRegs)

End Sub
```

To add this Sub procedure to your programs, just select the New Sub... item (i.e., it's a Sub, not a Function) in the Edit menu and type it in. Here's how to use MouseShowCursor( ):

```
Type RegType
        ax        As Integer
        bx        As Integer
        cx        As Integer
        dx        As Integer
        bp        As Integer
        si        As Integer
        di        As Integer
        flags     As Integer
End Type
        Screen.Hide
        Screen 8
        If MouseInitialize% Then
            Print "Mouse Initialized."
        Else
            Print "Mouse driver not installed."
            While InKey$ = ""
            Wend
            End
        End If
  —>    Call MouseShowCursor
        While InKey$ = ""
        Wend
        Screen 0
        Screen.Show
```

TIP: *If the mouse system is not initialized for some reason, calls to interrupt &H33 have no effect. We could have called MouseShowCursor( ) whether or not we were able to initialize the mouse system.*

Notice that we first initialize the mouse with the function MouseInitialize%( ), and, if that worked, we display the cursor with MouseShowCursor( ).

Now that we've displayed the mouse cursor on the screen, our next step will be to hide it.

Hiding the Mouse Cursor

TIP: *If the mouse cursor is already off, it stays off when we hide it.*

Now we'll hide the mouse cursor. There are times when the mouse cursor can be a distraction on the screen, and we'll fix that problem here.

Here we just make use of interrupt &H33 service 2, which hides the mouse cursor:

```
          Dim InRegs AS RegType, OutRegs AS RegType
—>        InRegs.ax = 2
—>        Call Interrupt(&H33, InRegs, OutRegs)
```

And here's what the whole Sub procedure looks like:

```
Type RegType
          ax        As Integer
          bx        As Integer
          cx        As Integer
          dx        As Integer
          bp        As Integer
          si        As Integer
          di        As Integer
          flags     As Integer
End Type

Sub MouseHideCursor ()

    Dim InRegs AS RegType, OutRegs AS RegType
    InRegs.ax = 2
    Call Interrupt(&H33, InRegs, OutRegs)

End Sub
```

This example program just displays the mouse cursor and then hides it after you press any key:

```
Type RegType
          ax        As Integer
          bx        As Integer
          cx        As Integer
          dx        As Integer
          bp        As Integer
          si        As Integer
          di        As Integer
          flags     As Integer
End Type

          Screen.Hide
          Screen 8
          If MouseInitialize% Then
              Print "Mouse Initialized."
          Else
              Print "Mouse driver not installed."
              While InKey$ = ""
```

```
                      Wend
                      End
              End If
              Call MouseShowCursor
              Print "Press any key to hide the mouse cursor."
              While InKey$ = ""
              Wend
     —>       Call MouseHideCursor
              While InKey$ = ""
              Wend
              Screen 0
              Screen.Show
```

Again, we initialize the mouse system, and, if successful, show the mouse cursor and print the prompt: "Press any key to hide the mouse cursor." When a key is pressed, we hide the mouse cursor with MouseHideCursor( ).

At this point, we've been able to set the mouse system up, show the cursor, and hide it at will. Those are good beginning steps—but now it's time to start reading information from the mouse.

For example, we may want to check the status of the mouse at some given time: Is there a button being pressed? And where is the mouse cursor? We'll work out the answer to these questions next.

Reading Immediate Mouse Information

There is one way of getting information from the mouse—interrupt &H33 service 3 returns the immediate status of the left and right buttons, as well as the row and column number (measured in screen pixels) of the mouse cursor's position. When you call it, it returns this information encoded in the bx, cx, and dx registers, providing us with a snapshot of what the mouse is doing now. Here's how the registers are set on return:

```
bx = 0   —>  No button down
     1   —>  Right button down
     2   —>  Left button down
     3   —>  Both buttons down

     cx = screen column of mouse cursor (using pixel ranges)

     dx = screen row of mouse cursor (using pixel ranges)
```

Let's write a Sub procedure to report these things to us. It would be ideal to have a Sub procedure we could call this way:

```
Call MouseInformation (Right%, Left%, X%, Y%)
```

The variables we pass could be set this way on return:

Right%	0 —> Right mouse button is up
	1 —> Right mouse button is down
Left%	0 —> Left mouse button is up
	1 —> Left mouse button is down
X%	Current x position of mouse cursor
Y%	Current y position of mouse cursor

This Sub procedure is designed to return a snapshot of the mouse's present state. As we saw, interrupt &H33 service 3 returns button information in OutRegs.bx; if this value is 1, the left button only is down. If it's 2, the right button only is down. If 3, both are down. (And if 0, neither are down). Here's how we can decode that information into the parameters Right% and Left%:

```
Sub MouseInformation (Right%, Left%, X%, Y%)

    Dim InRegs AS RegType, OutRegs AS RegType
    InRegs.ax = 3
    Call Interrupt(&H33, InRegs, OutRegs)

        Right% = 0
        Left% = 0

—>      Select Case OutRegs.bx
   :        Case 1
   :            Left% = 1
            Case 2
                Right% = 1
            Case 3
                Left% = 1
                Right% = 1
    End Select
                :
                :
```

Next, OutRegs.dx holds the present screen row in pixels, and OutRegs.cx holds the present screen column in pixels. We can place those values in X% and Y% like this:

```
Sub MouseInformation (Right%, Left%, X%, Y%)

    Dim InRegs AS RegType, OutRegs AS RegType
    InRegs.ax = 3
    Call Interrupt(&H33, InRegs, OutRegs)

        Right% = 0
        Left% = 0

        Select Case OutRegs.bx
            Case 1
                Left% = 1
            Case 2
                Right% = 1
            Case 3
                Left% = 1
                Right% = 1

    End Select

—>      X% = OutRegs.cx
—>      Y% = OutRegs.dx
```

Here's the whole Sub procedure:

```
Type RegType
        ax      As Integer
        bx      As Integer
        cx      As Integer
        dx      As Integer
        bp      As Integer
        si      As Integer
        di      As Integer
        flags   As Integer
End Type

Sub MouseInformation (Right%, Left%, X%, Y%)

  Dim InRegs AS RegType, OutRegs AS RegType
  InRegs.ax = 3
  Call Interrupt(&H33, InRegs, OutRegs)

      Right% = 0
      Left% = 0

      Select Case OutRegs.bx
          Case 1
                Left% = 1
```

```
            Case 2
                    Right% = 1
            Case 3
                    Left% = 1
                    Right% = 1
        End Select

        X% = OutRegs.cx
        Y% = OutRegs.dx

End Sub
```

This example program just reports the mouse state when you press a key:

```
Type RegType
        ax      As Integer
        bx      As Integer
        cx      As Integer
        dx      As Integer
        bp      As Integer
        si      As Integer
        di      As Integer
        flags   As Integer
End Type

        Screen.Hide
        Screen 8
        If MouseInitialize% Then
            Print "Mouse Initialized."
        Else
            Print "Mouse driver not installed."
            While InKey$ = ""
            Wend
            End
        End If

        Print "Position the mouse and press any key."
        While InKey$ = ""
        Wend

        Call MouseInformation (Right%, Left%, X%, Y%)
        IF Right% THEN
            Print "Right button down."
        ELSE
            Print "Right button up."
        End IF
```

```
IF Left% THEN
    Print "Left button down."
ELSE
    Print "Left button up."
End IF

Print "x value: ", X%, "y value: ", Y%

While InKey$ = ""
Wend
Screen 0
Screen.Show
```

Here you can see how we use MouseInformation( ) and then decode the returned values Right%, Left%, X%, and Y%. To use this program, make sure that you've loaded the mouse driver as outlined in the beginning of this chapter. When you press any key on the keyboard, this program will report the present mouse state.

The most severe limitation here is that MouseInformation( ) only provides an instant snapshot of what's going on with the mouse. If you want to use it for mouse input, you have to keep "polling" it—that is, looping over it until something happens. A better option is going to be using the Sub procedure we develop next that uses other, specialized interrupt &H33 services. There, button action is stored in a "queue," and it waits until you call for it. This way, you don't have to catch a button being pressed exactly as it is being pressed—you can find out about it when you're ready to deal with it.

Reading the Button-Pressed Queue

It would be useful to develop the mouse equivalent of Inkey$. We already have MouseInformation( ), but you must catch mouse events as they happen to use it. Instead, it would be much better if they could be stored and we could read them as we require them.

We can do that with service 5 (service 4 moves the mouse cursor, and we're going to skip that). This service lets us read the number of times a specific button has been pressed since we last checked. It also gives you the x and y screen position of the mouse cursor the last time the button was pressed. Pressing a mouse button is usually more significant than just moving the mouse cursor around the screen. For that reason, you can treat this service as the primary mouse input routine.

Let's write a Sub procedure called, for example, MouseTimes-Pressed(), to connect service 5 to Visual Basic. We should call MouseTimesPressed() once when we start accepting input to clear the mouse buffer, then loop over and call it periodically to see whether anything else has happened, much like Inkey$.

We need to query service 5 about the number of times a specific button—right or left—was pressed. The return values we expect are the number of times the button has been pressed and the mouse cursor's position the last time the button was pressed. In other words, we can set up MouseTimesPressed() like this:

```
Call MouseTimesPressed (Button%, NumberTimes%, X%, Y%)
```

We can use the same designation for the variable Button% as the interrupt &H33 services themselves use—a value of 0 for the left button and 1 for the right button. On return, we'll be able to read the other variables like this:

NumberTimes%	The number of times the specified button was pushed since the last time MouseTimesPressed() was called
X%	X coordinate of the mouse cursor the last time that button was pressed
Y%	Y coordinate of the mouse cursor the last time that button was pressed

Using interrupt &H33 service 5 makes this Sub procedure easy. We just place the button number (0 for the left button, 1 for the right) into InRegs.bx and call service 5:

```
Sub MouseTimesPressed (Button%, NumberTimes%, X%, Y%)

    Dim InRegs AS RegType, OutRegs AS RegType

—>  InRegs.bx = Button%
—>  InRegs.ax = 5
—>  Call Interrupt(&H33, InRegs, OutRegs)
        :
        :
```

The results come back in bx, cx, and dx. The bx register holds the number of times the specified button, left or right, was pressed since the last time service 5 was called. The dx register holds the screen (pixel) row where the button was last pushed, and cx holds the corresponding column:

```
Sub MouseTimesPressed (Button%, NumberTimes%, X%, Y%)

        Dim InRegs AS RegType, OutRegs AS RegType

        InRegs.bx = Button%
        InRegs.ax = 5
        Call Interrupt(&H33, InRegs, OutRegs)
—>      NumberTimes% = OutRegs.bx
—>      X% = OutRegs.cx
—>      Y% = OutRegs.dx
            :
```

That's it; here's the entire code for the Sub procedure MouseTimesPressed( ), ready to be put to work:

```
Rem Button% should be 0 to return left button info, 1 for right.

Type RegType
        ax      As Integer
        bx      As Integer
        cx      As Integer
        dx      As Integer
        bp      As Integer
        si      As Integer
        di      As Integer
        flags   As Integer
End Type

Sub MouseTimesPressed (Button%, NumberTimes%, X%, Y%)

    Dim InRegs AS RegType, OutRegs AS RegType

    InRegs.bx = Button%
    InRegs.ax = 5
    Call Interrupt(&H33, InRegs, OutRegs)

    NumberTimes% = OutRegs.bx
    X% = OutRegs.cx
    Y% = OutRegs.dx

End Sub
```

And now we can put it to work. This example program asks you to press the right mouse button a number of times and then press any key on the keyboard. When you do, the program reports the number of times you've clicked the button, and the last position at which you did so:

```
Type RegType
        ax      As Integer
        bx      As Integer
        cx      As Integer
        dx      As Integer
        bp      As Integer
        si      As Integer
        di      As Integer
        flags   As Integer
End Type

        Screen.Hide
        Screen 8
        If MouseInitialize% Then
            Print "Mouse Initialized."
        Else
            Print "Mouse driver not installed."
            While InKey$ = ""
            Wend
            End
        End If

        Print "Press the right button a number of times, then any
          key."
        While InKey$ = ""
        Wend
        Call MouseTimesPressed(1, NumberTimes%, X%, Y%)

        Print "You pressed it "; NumberTimes%; " times."
        Print "The last time was at ("; X%; ","; Y%; ")."

        While InKey$ = ""
        Wend
        Screen 0
        Screen.Show
```

Let's go through the steps: we initialize the mouse with MouseInitialize(), display the cursor with the Sub procedure MouseShowCursor(), and then read mouse information with MouseTimesPressed(). The limitation here is that MouseTimesPressed() only returns the location of the last time a specific button was pressed, and you still have to poll this Sub procedure periodically to find out what's going on with the mouse (but not as often as with

MouseInformation( ), where you have to catch the mouse event in the act).

In practice, this means that you should check MouseTimesPressed( ) frequently enough to make sure that mouse events don't get a chance to stack up in the mouse queue.

Another limitation here is that we're often more interested in when the mouse button was released, not pressed. For example, releasing the mouse button is important when you're dragging an object across the screen or making a menu selection. The next interrupt &H33 service, service 6, lets us handle that.

Reading the Button-Released Queue

We can use service 6 to write a Sub procedure that will give us button-release information; let's call this Sub procedure MouseTimesReleased( ). It should give us information about the number of times a particular button was released since we called it, and the screen position of the mouse cursor when it was last released. Here's how we might call MouseTimesReleased( ):

```
Call MouseTimesReleased (Button%, NumberTimes%, X%, Y%)
```

Again, we set Button% to 0 if we want right button information and to 1 for the left button. And, following MouseTimesPressed( ), this is how we can design the return values:

NumberTimes%	Integer—The number of times the specified button was released since the last time MouseTimesReleased( ) was called.
X%	Integer—The x coordinate of the mouse cursor the last time that button was released.
Y%	Integer—The y coordinate of the mouse cursor the last time that button was released.

This Sub procedure is very like MouseTimesPressed( ), except that we use interrupt &H33 service 6, not 5:

```
      Dim InRegs AS RegType, OutRegs AS RegType

      InRegs.bx = Button%
—>    InRegs.ax = 6
      Call Interrupt(&H33, InRegs, OutRegs)
                    :
                    :
```

After the call, we decode the information in exactly the same way as we did for MouseTimesPressed( ):

```
      Dim InRegs AS RegType, OutRegs AS RegType

      InRegs.bx = Button%
      InRegs.ax = 6
      Call Interrupt(&H33, InRegs, OutRegs)

—>    NumberTimes% = OutRegs.bx
—>    X% = OutRegs.cx
—>    Y% = OutRegs.dx
```

Here's the whole Sub procedure:

```
Rem Button should be 0 to return left button info, 1 for right.

Type RegType
        ax      As Integer
        bx      As Integer
        cx      As Integer
        dx      As Integer
        bp      As Integer
        si      As Integer
        di      As Integer
        flags   As Integer
End Type

Sub MouseTimesReleased (Button%, NumberTimes%, X%, Y%)

   Dim InRegs AS RegType, OutRegs AS RegType

   InRegs.bx = Button%
   InRegs.ax = 6
   Call Interrupt(&H33, InRegs, OutRegs)

   NumberTimes% = OutRegs.bx
   X% = OutRegs.cx
   Y% = OutRegs.dx

End Sub
```

This example program is just like the one for MouseTimesPressed(), except that it indicates the number of times the button was released, not the number of times it was pressed:

```
Type RegType
        ax      As Integer
        bx      As Integer
        cx      As Integer
        dx      As Integer
        bp      As Integer
        si      As Integer
        di      As Integer
        flags   As Integer
End Type

        Screen.Hide
        Screen 8
        If MouseInitialize% Then
            Print "Mouse Initialized."
        Else
            Print "Mouse driver not installed."
            While InKey$ = ""
            Wend
            End
        End If

        Print "Press the left button a number of times, then any
            key."
While InKey$ = ""
        Wend
        Call MouseTimesReleased(0, NumberTimes%, X%, Y%)

        Print "You released it "; NumberTimes%; " times."
        Print "The last time was at ("; X%; ","; Y%; ")."

        While InKey$ = "."
        Wend
        Screen 0
        Screen.Show
```

Again, we initialize the mouse, then show the mouse cursor, and after a key is pressed, read mouse information from MouseTimesReleased(). That's all we have to do; the results appear in Figure 6-9.

Figure 6-9 Our Graphics Mouse Released Program

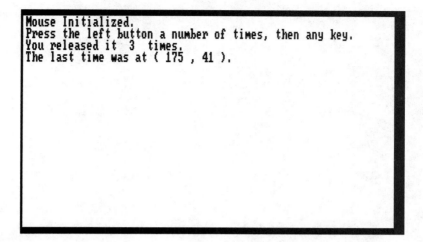

```
Mouse Initialized.
Press the left button a number of times, then any key.
You released it  3  times.
The last time was at ( 175 , 41 ).
```

That's it for our coverage of I/O in graphics mode—now we can put it to work when we write a mouse-driven paint program to operate in graphics mode in the next chapter.

A Mouse-Driven Paint Program

O ur full-scale graphics project is going to be a full-power mouse-driven paint program. We'll be able to draw lines, circles, boxes, and so on with our paint program—all using the mouse in Visual Basic's graphics mode. For example, to draw a line, we'll be able to press the mouse button while the cursor is at some location; then, when we move the cursor and release the mouse button, the line will be drawn automatically. As we work through this chapter, we'll see not only how to construct a paint program—we'll see what's avialable for us in Visual Basic for DOS's graphics mode: lines, rectangles, circles, and more. We'll even be able to save and retrieve our picture to and from disk.

Starting the Paint Program's Code

NOTE: *Because we use Interrupt( ) in this chapter, load Visual Basic for DOS with the /L switch.*

Since we're going to use the mouse, we have to start by defining the Type RegType, as well as InRegs and OutRegs as before. Just enter this—and the rest of the program—into the code window as a new Visual Basic for DOS project (at the end, save it as Paint.Bas):

```
Type RegType
        ax        As Integer
        bx        As Integer
        cx        As Integer
        dx        As Integer
        bp        As Integer
        si        As Integer
        di        As Integer
        flags     As Integer
End Type
        Dim InRegs As RegType, OutRegs As RegType
        :
        :
```

Our paint program has to handle many different types of actions—drawing pixels on the screen, drawing lines, boxes, and circles; and saving or loading images on disk. For that reason, organization is going to be important here, and we should make the main body of the program as simple as we can, breaking the rest of the code up into subroutines.

We can choose the subroutine structure (i.e., Gosub...Return) here so that all variables will be shared—there's no advantage to using Sub procedures or Functions in this case. We can start this way:

```
Type RegType
        ax        As Integer
        bx        As Integer
        cx        As Integer
        dx        As Integer
        bp        As Integer
        si        As Integer
        di        As Integer
        flags     As Integer
End Type
        Dim InRegs As RegType, OutRegs As RegType

   —>   Gosub Initialize
        :
```

In the Initialize subroutine, we can set the screen mode, print the menu bar, and initialize the mouse. When the program actually starts, the first thing we'll do is wait for the left mouse button to be pressed—we make all menu selections with the left mouse button or begin drawing with the left mouse button. That means that we can set up a perpetual loop, waiting for the left mouse button to be pressed:

```
Type RegType
        ax      As Integer
        bx      As Integer
        cx      As Integer
        dx      As Integer
        bp      As Integer
        si      As Integer
        di      As Integer
        flags   As Integer
End Type
        Dim InRegs As RegType, OutRegs As RegType
        Gosub Initialize
 —>     Do
 —>         Gosub GetLeftButtonPress
                :
                :
 —>     Loop While 1

        End
```

Next, we can set up the subroutine named GetLeftButtonPress to wait until the left button has been pressed. After that button has been pressed, we'll want to know whether a menu selection was made; let's design GetLeftButtonPress to set a variable named MenuSelectionMade% to 1 if the mousedown occurred in the menu bar, and 0 otherwise. This will allow us to check for a menu selection this way:

```
Type RegType
        ax      As Integer
        bx      As Integer
        cx      As Integer
        dx      As Integer
        bp      As Integer
        si      As Integer
        di      As Integer
        flags   As Integer
End Type
```

```
Dim InRegs As RegType, OutRegs As RegType
Gosub Initialize
Do
     Gosub GetLeftButtonPress
—>   If MenuSelectionMade% Then Gosub MenuChoice
                :
                :
Loop While 1
End
```

If a menu selection *was* made, we can handle it in a new subroutine
named MenuChoice. There, we'll have to toggle internal flags to turn
various drawing actions on or off. For example, if the user selected the
"Line" option, we can toggle a flag called LineFlag% to 1 in
MenuChoice. With that option selected, we'll be ready to draw lines
the next time the left mouse button goes down.

If the button *wasn't* pressed in text row 1—the menu bar row—
MenuSelectionMade% will not be set. In that case, maybe we're
supposed to start a drawing action, such as drawing lines or boxes. We
can see what we're supposed to do (if anything) by checking the flags
we set in MenuChoice, as follows:

```
Type RegType
          ax      As Integer
          bx      As Integer
          cx      As Integer
          dx      As Integer
          bp      As Integer
          si      As Integer
          di      As Integer
          flags   As Integer
End Type
          Dim InRegs As RegType, OutRegs As RegType
          Dim Storage(31266) As Integer
          Gosub Initialize
          Do
              Gosub GetLeftButtonPress
              If MenuSelectionMade% Then
                  Gosub MenuChoice
              Else
—>                If DrawFlag% Then Gosub DrawPixel
—>                If LineFlag% Then Gosub DrawLine
```

```
    —>            If BoxFlag% Then Gosub DrawBox
    —>            If CircleFlag% Then Gosub DrawCircle
    —>            If PaintFlag% Then Gosub DrawPaint
            End If
       Loop While 1
       End
```

The action goes like this: the user can start drawing lines by selecting
"Line" in the menu bar. When a menu selection like that is made, we
go to the subroutine MenuChoice and toggle the correct flag,
LineFlag%, to 1.

Then the user releases the mouse button. Internally, we return from
MenuChoice, loop back to the top of our main loop, and wait for the
next left button press in GetLeftButtonPress. The user moves the
mouse to the drawing area below the menu bar and presses the left
mouse button. Internally, we return from GetLeftButtonPress—with
MenuSelectionMade% not set this time. We check which flag is set
(LineFlag%) and enter the correct subroutine (DrawLine). We stay in
that subroutine, drawing the line, until the user releases the button.

From the users' point of view, the line appears with one end anchored
where they've pressed the mouse button. Users can move the mouse
cursor around the screen, pulling their end of the line as they require.
When they release the button, the line becomes fixed (and we return
from DrawLine to wait for the next left button press—which might be
either a new line or a new menu selection).

That's all there is to it, from a programming standpoint; the main
procedure in our program is complete (note that we've added an array
above called Storage( ) to hold the screen image for disk transfers). All
that remains is to write the subroutines.

Subroutine Initialize

In the initialization subroutine, we have to set the screen mode and
print the menu bar. We can do that like this:

```
Initialize:
       Screen 8
       Locate 1, 1
       Fore% = 1
       Back% = 2
       Color Fore%, Back%
```

```
Print "Exit    Color   Bkgrnd Draw    Line      " +
     "Box      Circle Paint   Save      Load";
     :
```

Note the use of the Color statement, which sets the foreground (drawing) and background colors, as defined in Table 4-3. The menu-bar options in our full-function paint program include

Exit   Exit the program

Color   Set the drawing (foreground color)

Bkgrnd   Set the background color

Draw   Draw pixel by pixel

Line   Draw a line

Box   Draw a box

Circle   Draw a circle

Paint   Fill a shape in with solid color

Save   Save image to disk

Load   Load image from disk

We also have to initialize the mouse and show the mouse cursor, which can be done as we've learned in the last chapter:

```
Initialize:
     Screen 8
     Locate 1, 1
     Fore% = 1
     Back% = 2
     Color Fore%, Back%
     Print "Exit    Color   Bkgrnd Draw    Line      " +
          "Box      Circle Paint   Save      Load";
—>   InRegs.ax = 0    'Initialize mouse
—>   Call Interrupt(&H33, InRegs, OutRegs)
—>   InRegs.ax = 1    'Show mouse cursor
—>   Call Interrupt(&H33, InRegs, OutRegs)
     :
     :
```

Finally, we can set all our drawing flags to 0 (False) as follows, and we're through:

```
Initialize:
     Screen 8
     Locate 1, 1
     Fore% = 1
     Back% = 2
     Color Fore%, Back%
     Print "Exit     Color    Bkgrnd  Draw     Line      " +
       "Box      Circle   Paint    Save     Load";
     InRegs.ax = 0    'Initialize mouse
     Call Interrupt(&H33, InRegs, OutRegs)
     InRegs.ax = 1    'Show mouse cursor
     Call Interrupt(&H33, InRegs, OutRegs)
—>   DrawFlag% = 0
  :   LineFlag% = 0
  :   BoxFlag% = 0
     CircleFlag% = 0
     PaintFlag% = 0
     Return
```

Now we're ready for GetLeftButtonPress.

Subroutine GetLeftButtonPress

This subroutine is easy; all we have to do is to wait for the left mouse button to be pressed, which we can check with interrupt &H33 service 5, as follows:

```
GetLeftButtonPress:
     Do
         InRegs.bx = 0              'Wait for left button press
         InRegs.ax = 5
         Call Interrupt(&H33, InRegs, OutRegs)
     Loop While OutRegs.bx = 0
         :
```

That's almost it; we still have to set the variable MenuSelectionMade% to report whether or not this was a menu-bar event. We can do that by simply checking whether the mouse cursor was in text row 1, the menu-bar row. We do that by dividing the mouse cursor's Y position by 8, since there are 8 pixels vertically in a character row in screen mode 8, as indicated in Table 6-1:

239

```
GetLeftButtonPress:
        Do
            InRegs.bx = 0              'Wait for left button press
            InRegs.ax = 5
            Call Interrupt(&H33, InRegs, OutRegs)
        Loop While OutRegs.bx = 0
  —>     Row% = OutRegs.dx \ 8 + 1
  :      If Row% = 1 Then
  :          MenuSelectionMade% = 1
        Else
            MenuSelectionMade% = 0
        End If
        Return
```

Now we know what action was taken by the mouse. We're ready to start handling menu selections.

Subroutine MenuChoice

In the MenuChoice subroutine (called if the user pressed the mouse button while the cursor was in the menu bar), we can keep track of which menu choice or drawing option was selected. The menu bar looks like this:

Exit	Color	Bkgrnd	Draw	Line	Box	Circle	Paint	Save	Load

Let's work through the options one by one. First, we have to reset all the drawing flags and figure out what choice was made; we can do that as shown below (the way we've printed things out, each menu choice takes up 8 screen columns, and each column is 8 pixels wide):

```
MenuChoice:
            DrawFlag% = 0
            LineFlag% = 0
            BoxFlag% = 0
            CircleFlag% = 0
            PaintFlag% = 0
            Choice% = OutRegs.cx \ 64 + 1
                :
```

Next, we can do what is required by the menu choice made with a Select Case statement. For example, for choice 1, "Exit," we just end the program:

```
MenuChoice:
        DrawFlag% = 0
        LineFlag% = 0
        BoxFlag% = 0
        CircleFlag% = 0
        PaintFlag% = 0
        Choice% = OutRegs.cx \ 64 + 1
  ->    Select Case Choice%
  ->        Case 1
  ->                End
                :
```

Choice 2 lets us set the foreground color; each time we click on this selection, we should increment the foreground color through the 16 options available in this mode (screen mode 8). We can indicate those colors by reprinting the word "Color" (which we are clicking) in the new foreground color:

```
MenuChoice:
        DrawFlag% = 0
        LineFlag% = 0
        BoxFlag% = 0
        CircleFlag% = 0
        PaintFlag% = 0
        Choice% = OutRegs.cx \ 64 + 1
        Select Case Choice%
            Case 1
                    End
  ->        Case 2
  :                 Fore% = Fore% + 1
  :                 If Fore% > 15 Then Fore% = 0
                    Color Fore%, Back%
                    InRegs.ax = 2    'Hide mouse cursor
                    Call Interrupt(&H33, InRegs, OutRegs)
                    Locate 1, 9
                    Print "Color    ";
                    InRegs.ax = 1    'Show mouse cursor
                    Call Interrupt(&H33, InRegs, OutRegs)
                    :
```

Note that we hide the mouse cursor before working with the screen (using interrupt &H33, service 2). It is best to do so whenever working with the screen, because if you change the screen pixels in the location of the mouse cursor and then move the mouse cursor, the mouse-driver software will replace the original screen pixels when the cursor moves on, not the ones you've just set. That is, the mouse-driver software reads the underlying screen pixels as you move the mouse cursor around the screen so that it can restore the screen as the cursor moves on. If you change those pixels without updating what the driver software has stored, you'll get the original pixels back. The way to avoid this is to hide the mouse cursor before undertaking a screen change and then to show it later.

The next option changes the background color, which we can do with the Basic Color statement; each time we change the background color, the background of the whole screen changes, so that users can easily select what they want:

```
MenuChoice:
            DrawFlag% = 0
            LineFlag% = 0
            BoxFlag% = 0
            CircleFlag% = 0
            PaintFlag% = 0
            Choice% = OutRegs.cx \ 64 + 1
            Select Case Choice%
                Case 1
                        End
                Case 2
                        Fore% = Fore% + 1
                        If Fore% > 15 Then Fore% = 0
                        Color Fore%, Back%
                        InRegs.ax = 2    'Hide mouse cursor
                        Call Interrupt(&H33, InRegs, OutRegs)
                        Locate 1, 9
                        Print "Color    ";
                        InRegs.ax = 1    'Show mouse cursor
                        Call Interrupt(&H33, InRegs, OutRegs)
                Case 3
      —>            Back% = Back% + 1
      —>            If Back% > 7 Then Back% = 0
      —>            Color Fore%, Back%
                        :
```

Now we come to the drawing options in the menu bar:

```
         |      |      |         |       |
         V      V      V         V       V
┌──────────────────────────────────────────────────────────────────┐
│ Exit    Color   Bkgrnd Draw    Line    Box     Circle  Paint   Save    Load│
└──────────────────────────────────────────────────────────────────┘
```

Each of these options is going to be handled in its own subroutine, but we have to toggle the appropriate flags here. That procedure looks like this:

```
MenuChoice:
            DrawFlag% = 0
            LineFlag% = 0
            BoxFlag% = 0
            CircleFlag% = 0
            PaintFlag% = 0
            Choice% = OutRegs.cx \ 64 + 1
            Select Case Choice%
                Case 1
                            End
                Case 2
                            Fore% = Fore% + 1
                            If Fore% > 15 Then Fore% = 0
                            Color Fore%, Back%
                            InRegs.ax = 2    'Hide mouse cursor
                            Call Interrupt(&H33, InRegs, OutRegs)
                            Locate 1, 9
                            Print "Color    ";
                            InRegs.ax = 1    'Show mouse cursor
                            Call Interrupt(&H33, InRegs, OutRegs)
                Case 3
                            Back% = Back% + 1
                            If Back% > 7 Then Back% = 0
                            Color Fore%, Back%
                Case 4
       —>               DrawFlag% = 1
                Case 5
       —>               LineFlag% = 1
                Case 6
       —>               BoxFlag% = 1
                Case 7
       —>               CircleFlag% = 1
```

243

```
                        Case 8
    —>                          PaintFlag% = 1
                                :
```

The next option, "Save," lets us save the image to the disk; in particular, we can save it as a file named Paint.Dat. Since we should save the
file when the option is selected, we should handle this option here, in
MenuChoice.

To save the screen image, we can use the Basic Get statement to load it
into an array. We'll need to set up an array, and we can use the array
of integers we've already named Storage( ). We want to save the
drawing area of the screen, whose top left corner will be (X1, Y1) = (0,
8) (omitting the menu bar) and whose bottom left corner is (X2, Y2) =
(639, 199). The number of bytes needed to store a screen image is
given by the formula:

```
Bytes = 4 + INT(((X2 X1+1)*(Bits/pixel/plane)+7)/8)*planes*((Y2-
    Y1)+1)
```

where Bits/pixel/plane is the number of bits per pixel per *plane* and
planes means the number of planes in the present screen mode. We
won't concern ourselves with screen planes here; to determine these
values for a specific screen mode, see the Visual Basic documentation.
For mode 8 and the size of the image we want to save, we'll need
62,532 bytes, or 31,266 integers. At this point, all we need to do is to
use Get, as follows:

```
Get (0, 8)-(639, 199), Storage
```

This will copy the screen image into the array Storage( ). (Note that we
should turn the mouse cursor off first to avoid saving it too.) Next, we
can dump the array Storage( ) directly to a file on disk using BSave,
Basic's binary save routine. To do so, we have to give BSave the address
of the data we want to save and the number of bytes to save.

Addresses in memory under DOS are made up of two words, a *segment*
address and an *offset* address. Briefly, a segment is a 64K section of
memory, and an offset is the location of a particular byte in that
segment, as measured from the beginning of the segment:

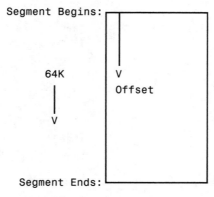

```
Segment Begins:

64K                    V
|                      Offset
V

Segment Ends:
```

All we have to know here is that we have to supply BSave with both the segment and offset address of the array Storage( ). To get the segment address, Visual Basic provides the Varseg( ) function; to get the offset in that segment, Visual Basic provides Varptr( ). We start by setting the segment address Visual Basic will use equal to the segment address of Storage( ) as follows:

```
Def Seg = Varseg(Storage(1))
```

Where Storage(1) is the first element in the array. Next, we just pass the name of the file we want to create on disk, Paint.Dat, followed by the offset address of the first byte to write, which is Varptr(Storage(1)), and the number of bytes to write, 62,532:

```
Def Seg = Varseg(Storage(1))
BSave "Paint.Dat", Varptr(Storage(1)), 62532
Def Seg
```

At the end, we reset the segment address Visual Basic will use for data back to its original value with Def Seg (no argument). Here's how it looks:

```
MenuChoice:
            DrawFlag% = 0
            LineFlag% = 0
            BoxFlag% = 0
            CircleFlag% = 0
            PaintFlag% = 0
            Choice% = OutRegs.cx \ 64 + 1
            Select Case Choice%
                Case 1
                        End
```

```
            Case 2
                    Fore% = Fore% + 1
                    If Fore% > 15 Then Fore% = 0
                    Color Fore%, Back%
                    InRegs.ax = 2    'Hide mouse cursor
                    Call Interrupt(&H33, InRegs, OutRegs)
                    Locate 1, 9
                    Print "Color    ";
                    InRegs.ax = 1    'Show mouse cursor
                    Call Interrupt(&H33, InRegs, OutRegs)
            Case 3
                    Back% = Back% + 1
                    If Back% > 7 Then Back% = 0
                    Color Fore%, Back%
            Case 4
                    DrawFlag% = 1
            Case 5
                    LineFlag% = 1
            Case 6
                    BoxFlag% = 1
            Case 7
                    CircleFlag% = 1
            Case 8
                    PaintFlag% = 1
            Case 9
                    InRegs.ax = 2    'Hide mouse cursor
                    Call Interrupt(&H33, InRegs, OutRegs)
                    Get (0, 8)-(639, 199), Storage
                    Def Seg = Varseg(Storage(1))
        —>          BSave "Paint.Dat", Varptr(Storage(1)),
                        62532
                    Def Seg
                    InRegs.ax = 1    'Show mouse cursor
                    Call Interrupt(&H33, InRegs, OutRegs)
```

And that's all there is to it. We've been able to use BSave to save a graphics image on the disk. The last option, "Load," lets us read the image from the file and place it on the screen again. We can do that with Bload, Visual Basic's binary load routine, and Put. Again, we have to supply Bload with the address of the beginning of Storage( ). We start by hiding the mouse cursor and loading Paint.Dat back into memory like this:

```
MenuChoice:
        DrawFlag% = 0
        LineFlag% = 0
        BoxFlag% = 0
        CircleFlag% = 0
        PaintFlag% = 0
        Choice% = OutRegs.cx \ 64 + 1
        Select Case Choice%
            Case 1
                    End
            Case 2
                    Fore% = Fore% + 1
                    If Fore% > 15 Then Fore% = 0
                    Color Fore%, Back%
                    InRegs.ax = 2    'Hide mouse cursor
                    Call Interrupt(&H33, InRegs, OutRegs)
                    Locate 1, 9
                    Print "Color    ";
                    InRegs.ax = 1    'Show mouse cursor
                    Call Interrupt(&H33, InRegs, OutRegs)
            Case 3
                    Back% = Back% + 1
                    If Back% > 7 Then Back% = 0
                    Color Fore%, Back%
            Case 4
                    DrawFlag% = 1
            Case 5
                    LineFlag% = 1
            Case 6
                    BoxFlag% = 1
            Case 7
                    CircleFlag% = 1
            Case 8
                    PaintFlag% = 1
            Case 9
                    InRegs.ax = 2    'Hide mouse cursor
                    Call Interrupt(&H33, InRegs, OutRegs)
                    Get (0, 8)-(639, 199), Storage
                    Def Seg = Varseg(Storage(1))
                    BSave "Paint.Dat", Varptr(Storage(1)),
                        62532
                    Def Seg
                    InRegs.ax = 1    'Show mouse cursor
```

```
                              Call Interrupt(&H33, InRegs, OutRegs)
                     Case 10
                              InRegs.ax = 2    'Hide mouse cursor
                              Call Interrupt(&H33, InRegs, OutRegs)
                              Def Seg = Varseg(Storage(1))
                   —>         Bload "Paint.Dat", Varptr(Storage(1))
                              :
```

Next, we can place the image back on the screen with the Visual Basic
Put statement, in this way: Put (0, 8), Storage, Pset. The Get and Put
statements transfer data to and from the screen rapidly, and both are
cornerstones of graphics routines in Visual Basic. The Pset option here
indicates that each bit we're putting on the screen should overwrite
what's already there. Finally, we just restore the mouse cursor, and
we've finished. The whole subroutine MenuChoice follows:

```
MenuChoice:
             DrawFlag% = 0
             LineFlag% = 0
             BoxFlag% = 0
             CircleFlag% = 0
             PaintFlag% = 0
             Choice% = OutRegs.cx \ 64 + 1
             Select Case Choice%
                  Case 1
                           End
                  Case 2
                           Fore% = Fore% + 1
                           If Fore% > 15 Then Fore% = 0
                           Color Fore%, Back%
                           InRegs.ax = 2    'Hide mouse cursor
                           Call Interrupt(&H33, InRegs, OutRegs)
                           Locate 1, 9
                           Print "Color    ";
                           InRegs.ax = 1    'Show mouse cursor
                           Call Interrupt(&H33, InRegs, OutRegs)
                  Case 3
                           Back% = Back% + 1
                           If Back% > 7 Then Back% = 0
                           Color Fore%, Back%
                  Case 4
                           DrawFlag% = 1
```

```
            Case 5
                    LineFlag% = 1
            Case 6
                    BoxFlag% = 1
            Case 7
                    CircleFlag% = 1
            Case 8
                    PaintFlag% = 1
            Case 9
                    InRegs.ax = 2    'Hide mouse cursor
                    Call Interrupt(&H33, InRegs, OutRegs)
                    Get (0, 8)-(639, 199), Storage
                    Def Seg = Varseg(Storage(1))
                    BSave "Paint.Dat", Varptr(Storage(1)),
                      62532
                    Def Seg
                    InRegs.ax = 1    'Show mouse cursor
                    Call Interrupt(&H33, InRegs, OutRegs)
            Case 10
                    InRegs.ax = 2    'Hide mouse cursor
                    Call Interrupt(&H33, InRegs, OutRegs)
                    Def Seg = Varseg(Storage(1))
                    Bload "Paint.Dat", Varptr(Storage(1))
                    Def Seg
                    Put (0, 8), Storage, Pset
          —>       InRegs.ax = 1    'Show mouse cursor
          —>       Call Interrupt(&H33, InRegs, OutRegs)
        End Select
      Return
```

Subroutine DrawPixel

So far, we've handled everything but the drawing subroutines in our
main procedure:

```
Type RegType
        ax      As Integer
        bx      As Integer
        cx      As Integer
        dx      As Integer
        bp      As Integer
        si      As Integer
```

```
            di      As Integer
            flags   As Integer
End Type
        Dim InRegs As RegType, OutRegs As RegType
        Dim Storage(31266) As Integer
        Gosub Initialize
        Do
            Gosub GetLeftButtonPress
            If MenuSelectionMade% Then
                Gosub MenuChoice
            Else
  ─>            If DrawFlag% Then Gosub DrawPixel
  ─>            If LineFlag% Then Gosub DrawLine
  ─>            If BoxFlag% Then Gosub DrawBox
  ─>            If CircleFlag% Then Gosub DrawCircle
  ─>            If PaintFlag% Then Gosub DrawPaint
            End If
        Loop While 1
        End
```

Let's handle the drawing subroutines now. The first one is DrawPixel;
when we enter this subroutine, we're supposed to keep setting the
pixel at the current mouse cursor position until the mouse button is
released. In this way, the user will be able to draw by pressing the left
mouse button and moving the mouse cursor around the screen.

We should start by clearing the mouse button release queue so that
we're not responding to a button release that occurred some time ago:

```
DrawPixel:
                InRegs.bx = 0   'Get left button releases to
                                    clear queue
                InRegs.ax = 6
                Call Interrupt(&H33, InRegs, OutRegs)
                :
```

Now, we should keep looping until the mouse button is released (by
checking interrupt &H33 service 6):

```
DrawPixel:
                InRegs.bx = 0   'Get left button releases to
                                    clear queue
                InRegs.ax = 6
                Call Interrupt(&H33, InRegs, OutRegs)
```

```
    —>        Do
                            :
                    [Set current pixel]
                            :
                 InRegs.bx = 0              'Left Button Releases
                 InRegs.ax = 6
                 Call Interrupt(&H33, InRegs, OutRegs)
    —>        Loop While OutRegs.bx = 0
        Return
```

Every time through this loop, while we're waiting for the mouse
button to be released we have to get the mouse cursor's current
position and set the pixel there to the foreground color. We get the
current position with interrupt &H33 service 3, hide the mouse cursor
with service 2, set the pixel with a Visual Basic Pset( ) statement, and
then show the mouse cursor again:

```
DrawPixel:
                 InRegs.bx = 0    'Get left button releases to
                                        clear queue
                 InRegs.ax = 6
                 Call Interrupt(&H33, InRegs, OutRegs)
                 Do
    —>              InRegs.ax = 3
     :              Call Interrupt(&H33, InRegs, OutRegs)
                    X% = OutRegs.cx
                    Y% = OutRegs.dx
                    InRegs.ax = 2    'Hide mouse cursor
                    Call Interrupt(&H33, InRegs, OutRegs)
                    Pset (X%, Y%)
     :              InRegs.ax = 1    'Show mouse cursor
    —>              Call Interrupt(&H33, InRegs, OutRegs)
                    InRegs.bx = 0              'Left Button Releases
                    InRegs.ax = 6
                    Call Interrupt(&H33, InRegs, OutRegs)
                 Loop While OutRegs.bx = 0
        Return
```

And that's all there is to it; the real work is done by Pset(X%, Y%),
which sets the pixel at the current location to the foreground color.
We've finished the first of the drawing subroutines, and now we can
set individual pixels, as shown in Figure 7-1.

Figure 7-1 Setting Pixels in Our Paint Program

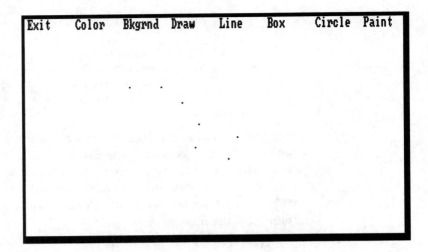

Subroutine DrawLine

The next subroutine is DrawLine:

```
Type RegType
        ax      As Integer
        bx      As Integer
        cx      As Integer
        dx      As Integer
        bp      As Integer
        si      As Integer
        di      As Integer
        flags   As Integer
End Type
        Dim InRegs As RegType, OutRegs As RegType
        Dim Storage(31266) As Integer
        Gosub Initialize
        Do
            Gosub GetLeftButtonPress
            If MenuSelectionMade% Then
                Gosub MenuChoice
            Else
                If DrawFlag% Then Gosub DrawPixel
    —>          If LineFlag% Then Gosub DrawLine
                If BoxFlag% Then Gosub DrawBox
```

```
                If CircleFlag% Then Gosub DrawCircle
                If PaintFlag% Then Gosub DrawPaint
            End If
        Loop While 1
        End
```

We can handle this task with the Visual Basic Line statement. You use it like this to draw a line from screen point (X1, Y1) to (X2, Y2):

```
Line (X1, Y1) - (X2, Y2), Color%
```

Here, Color% is an optional argument that specifies the line's color. We'll make use of this argument to both draw and erase lines. When we arrive in DrawLine, we have already clicked the mouse in the drawing area to establish the "anchor" point of one end of the line. Since all variables are global between our subroutines, we can read that location from OutRegs.cx and OutRegs.dx, which are still with the location the user clicked at (in GetLeftButtonPress):

```
DrawLine:
        X% = OutRegs.cx
        Y% = OutRegs.dx
                :
```

This provides us with the anchor point of the line, (X%, Y%). When we move the mouse cursor to a new location, (XNew%, YNew%), we'll draw a line from (X%, Y%) to (XNew%, YNew%):

```
    x━━━━━━━━━━━━━━━━━━━x
 (X%, Y%)          (XNew%, YNew%)
```

When we move to a new position after this, we'll set XNew% and YNew% to XOld% and YOld% and erase that line by drawing over it in the background color:

```
    x━━━━━━━━━━━━━━━━━x
 (X%, Y%)          (XOld%, YOld%)
```

And draw a new one to the new (XNew%, YNew%):

```
    x━━━━━━━━━━━━━━━━━━━━━━━x
 (X%, Y%)                (XNew%, YNew%)
```

In this way, one end of the line will always be anchored at the original click position, and the other end will follow the mouse cursor around. When we release the left button, we'll make the line permanent. To do this, we first clear the left mouse-button release queue and loop, waiting for the left button to be released:

```
DrawLine:
        X% = OutRegs.cx
        Y% = OutRegs.dx
        XOld% = X%
        YOld% = Y%

—>     InRegs.bx = 0    'Get left button releases to clear queue
:      InRegs.ax = 6
:      Call Interrupt(&H33, InRegs, OutRegs)

       Do
           :
           InRegs.bx = 0              'Left Button Releases
           InRegs.ax = 6
           Call Interrupt(&H33, InRegs, OutRegs)
       Loop While OutRegs.bx = 0
Return
```

Each time we loop, we have to check the new mouse cursor position, erasing the old line and drawing the new one (after hiding the mouse cursor). That procedure follows:

```
DrawLine:
        X% = OutRegs.cx
        Y% = OutRegs.dx
        XOld% = X%
        YOld% = Y%

        InRegs.bx = 0    'Get left button releases to clear queue
        InRegs.ax = 6
        Call Interrupt(&H33, InRegs, OutRegs)

        Do
—>      InRegs.ax = 3
:       Call Interrupt(&H33, InRegs, OutRegs)
:       YNew% = OutRegs.dx
:       XNew% = OutRegs.cx
:       InRegs.ax = 2    'Hide mouse cursor
:       Call Interrupt(&H33, InRegs, OutRegs)
:       Line (X%, Y%)-(XOld%, YOld%), Back%    'Erase old line
:       Line (X%, Y%)-(XNew%, YNew%), Fore%    'Draw new line
:       XOld% = XNew%
:       YOld% = YNew%
:       InRegs.ax = 1    'Show mouse cursor
```

```
    —>          Call Interrupt(&H33, InRegs, OutRegs)
             InRegs.bx = 0            'Left Button Releases
             InRegs.ax = 6
             Call Interrupt(&H33, InRegs, OutRegs)
        Loop While OutRegs.bx = 0
Return
```

When a user releases the left mouse button, the line becomes final. Now we're able to draw lines in our Paint program, as shown in Figure 7-2.

Figure 7-2 Drawing Lines in Our Paint Program

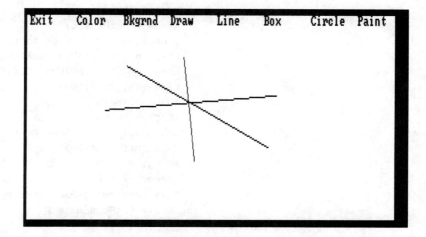

Subroutine DrawBox

The next subroutine is DrawBox. In fact, this subroutine is extremely simple, now that we've developed DrawLine. If we just add a "B" parameter to the end of the Line statement in Visual Basic:

```
Line (X1, Y1) - (X2, Y2), Color%, B <—
```

Then we'll get a box with its upper left corner at (X1, Y1) and lower-right corner at (X2, Y2). This is perfect for us; just copying over DrawLine and adding the B parameter means that the anchor point will now anchor one corner of the box, and the mouse cursor will drag the other corner around the screen. When the user releases the left mouse button, the box will become final:

```
DrawBox:
                    X% = OutRegs.cx
                    Y% = OutRegs.dx
                    XOld% = X%
                    YOld% = Y%

                    InRegs.bx = 0     'Get left button releases to
                                          clear queue
                    InRegs.ax = 6
                    Call Interrupt(&H33, InRegs, OutRegs)

                    Do
                        InRegs.ax = 3
                        Call Interrupt(&H33, InRegs, OutRegs)
                        YNew% = OutRegs.dx
                        XNew% = OutRegs.cx
                        InRegs.ax = 2    'Hide mouse cursor
                        Call Interrupt(&H33, InRegs, OutRegs)
                        Line (X%, Y%)-(XOld%, YOld%), Back%, B      <—
                        Line (X%, Y%)-(XNew%, YNew%), Fore%, B      <—
                        XOld% = XNew%
                        YOld% = YNew%
                        InRegs.ax = 1    'Show mouse cursor
                        Call Interrupt(&H33, InRegs, OutRegs)
                        InRegs.bx = 0              'Left Button Releases
                        InRegs.ax = 6
                        Call Interrupt(&H33, InRegs, OutRegs)
                    Loop While OutRegs.bx = 0
            Return
```

And that's all there is to it. The result appears in Figure 7-3.

Subroutine DrawCircle

We can also draw circles in Visual Basic with the Circle statement:

```
Circle (X%, Y%), Radius!, Color%
```

Here we are drawing a circle centered at (X%, Y%), with radius Radius!, and with a color specified by the value in Color%. We can adapt DrawLine here too; we'll make the anchor point the center of the circle and the mouse cursor location the edge of the circle —i.e., the radius will stretch from (X%, Y%) to (XNew%, YNew%). We can do that by changing the Line statements in DrawLine to Circle statements as follows:

```
DrawCircle:
            X% = OutRegs.cx
            Y% = OutRegs.dx
            XOld% = X%
            YOld% = Y%

            InRegs.bx = 0    'Get left button releases to
                                clear queue
            InRegs.ax = 6
            Call Interrupt(&H33, InRegs, OutRegs)

            Do
               InRegs.ax = 3
               Call Interrupt(&H33, InRegs, OutRegs)
               YNew% = OutRegs.dx
               XNew% = OutRegs.cx
               InRegs.ax = 2    'Hide mouse cursor
               Call Interrupt(&H33, InRegs, OutRegs)
        —>     Circle (X%, Y%), Sqr((X% - XOld%) ^ 2 + (Y% -
                  YOld%) ^ 2),
        —>        Back%
        —>     Circle (X%, Y%), Sqr((X% - XNew%) ^ 2 + (Y% -
                  YNew%) ^ 2)
               XOld% = XNew%
               YOld% = YNew%
               InRegs.ax = 1    'Show mouse cursor
               Call Interrupt(&H33, InRegs, OutRegs)
               InRegs.bx = 0              'Left Button Releases
               InRegs.ax = 6
               Call Interrupt(&H33, InRegs, OutRegs)
            Loop While OutRegs.bx = 0
Return
```

And that's all there is to drawing circles, as we can see in Figure 7-4.

Subroutine DrawPaint

The last subroutine we'll develop is DrawPaint. This subroutine will let us fill hollow figures with solid color. In this case, we can use the Visual Basic Paint statement, like this:

```
Paint (X%, Y%)
```

Figure 7-3 Drawing Boxes in Our Paint Program

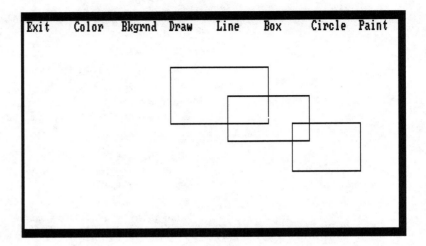

Figure 7-4 Drawing Circles in Our Paint Program

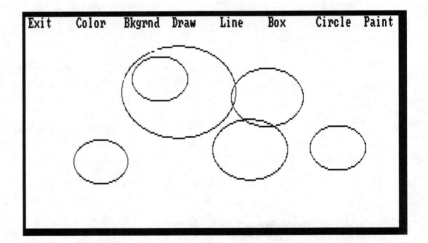

This statement fills an area in with the current foreground color. The problem is that this area must also be bounded by the current foreground color, or by another color, which we can specify like this:

```
Paint (X%, Y%), BorderColor%
```

This is a problem for us since our paint program is not sophisticated enough to figure out what the border color of the figure surrounding us at some given point is; instead, we'll have to settle for painting-in the current foreground color—which means that you can only paint figures that were drawn in the current foreground color (or you can set the foreground color to the color of the figure you want to fill in). With that restriction, we can fill figures with color as follows:

```
DrawPaint:
            X% = OutRegs.cx
            Y% = OutRegs.dx
            InRegs.ax = 2    'Hide mouse cursor
            Call Interrupt(&H33, InRegs, OutRegs)
      —>    Paint (X%, Y%)
            InRegs.ax = 1    'Show mouse cursor
            Call Interrupt(&H33, InRegs, OutRegs)
      Return
```

And we're done with the whole paint program. The whole thing, line by line, appears in Listing 7-1.

Listing 7-1 Paint.Bas

```
Type RegType
        ax      As Integer
        bx      As Integer
        cx      As Integer
        dx      As Integer
        bp      As Integer
        si      As Integer
        di      As Integer
        flags   As Integer
End Type

        Dim InRegs As RegType, OutRegs As RegType
        Dim Storage(31266) As Integer

        Gosub Initialize

        Do
            Gosub GetLeftButtonPress

            If MenuSelectionMade% Then
                Gosub MenuChoice
```

continues

Listing 7-1 continued

```
                    Else
                            If DrawFlag% Then Gosub DrawPixel
                            If LineFlag% Then Gosub DrawLine
                            If BoxFlag% Then Gosub DrawBox
                            If CircleFlag% Then Gosub DrawCircle
                            If PaintFlag% Then Gosub DrawPaint
                    End If

            Loop While 1

            End

Initialize:
            Screen 8
            Locate 1, 1
            Fore% = 1
            Back% = 2
            Color Fore%, Back%
            Print "Exit    Color   Bkgrnd  Draw    Line    " +
             "Box     Circle  Paint   Save    Load";

            InRegs.ax = 0    'Initialize mouse
            Call Interrupt(&H33, InRegs, OutRegs)
            InRegs.ax = 1    'Show mouse cursor
            Call Interrupt(&H33, InRegs, OutRegs)
            DrawFlag% = 0
            LineFlag% = 0
            BoxFlag% = 0
            CircleFlag% = 0
            PaintFlag% = 0
            Return

GetLeftButtonPress:
                    Do
                            InRegs.bx = 0    'Wait for left button press
                            InRegs.ax = 5
                            Call Interrupt(&H33, InRegs, OutRegs)
                    Loop While OutRegs.bx = 0
                    Row% = OutRegs.dx \ 8 + 1
                    If Row% = 1 Then
                            MenuSelectionMade% = 1
                    Else
```

```
                    MenuSelectionMade% = 0
          End If
          Return

MenuChoice:

          DrawFlag% = 0
          LineFlag% = 0
          BoxFlag% = 0
          CircleFlag% = 0
          PaintFlag% = 0
          Choice% = OutRegs.cx \ 64 + 1
          Select Case Choice%
              Case 1
                        End
              Case 2
                        Fore% = Fore% + 1
                        If Fore% > 15 Then Fore% = 0
                        Color Fore%, Back%
                        InRegs.ax = 2    'Hide mouse cursor
                        Call Interrupt(&H33, InRegs, OutRegs)
                        Locate 1, 9
                        Print "Color    ";
                        InRegs.ax = 1    'Show mouse cursor
                        Call Interrupt(&H33, InRegs, OutRegs)
              Case 3
                        Back% = Back% + 1
                        If Back% > 7 Then Back% = 0
                        Color Fore%, Back%
              Case 4
                        DrawFlag% = 1
              Case 5
                        LineFlag% = 1
              Case 6
                        BoxFlag% = 1
              Case 7
                        CircleFlag% = 1
              Case 8
                        PaintFlag% = 1
              Case 9
                        InRegs.ax = 2    'Hide mouse cursor
                        Call Interrupt(&H33, InRegs, OutRegs)
                        Get (0, 8)-(639, 199), Storage
                        Def Seg = Varseg(Storage(1))
```

continues

Listing 7-1 continued

```
                              BSave "Paint.Dat", Varptr(Storage(1)),
                                 62532
                              Def Seg
                              InRegs.ax = 1    'Show mouse cursor
                              Call Interrupt(&H33, InRegs, OutRegs)
                   Case 10
                              InRegs.ax = 2    'Hide mouse cursor
                              Call Interrupt(&H33, InRegs, OutRegs)
                              Def Seg = Varseg(Storage(1))
                              Bload "Paint.Dat", Varptr(Storage(1))
                              Def Seg
                              Put (0, 8), Storage, Pset
                              InRegs.ax = 1    'Show mouse cursor
                              Call Interrupt(&H33, InRegs, OutRegs)
             End Select
         Return

    DrawPixel:
                   InRegs.bx = 0    'Get left button releases to
                                       clear queue
                   InRegs.ax = 6
                   Call Interrupt(&H33, InRegs, OutRegs)

                   Do
                       InRegs.ax = 3
                       Call Interrupt(&H33, InRegs, OutRegs)
                       X% = OutRegs.cx
                       Y% = OutRegs.dx
                       InRegs.ax = 2    'Hide mouse cursor
                       Call Interrupt(&H33, InRegs, OutRegs)
                       Pset (X%, Y%)
                       InRegs.ax = 1    'Show mouse cursor
                       Call Interrupt(&H33, InRegs, OutRegs)
                       InRegs.bx = 0                'Left Button Releases
                       InRegs.ax = 6
                       Call Interrupt(&H33, InRegs, OutRegs)
                   Loop While OutRegs.bx = 0

         Return

    DrawLine:
                   X% = OutRegs.cx
                   Y% = OutRegs.dx
```

```
                        XOld% = X%
                        YOld% = Y%

                        InRegs.bx = 0  'Get left button releases to
                                           clear queue
                        InRegs.ax = 6
                        Call Interrupt(&H33, InRegs, OutRegs)

                        Do
                            InRegs.ax = 3
                            Call Interrupt(&H33, InRegs, OutRegs)
                            YNew% = OutRegs.dx
                            XNew% = OutRegs.cx
                            InRegs.ax = 2   'Hide mouse cursor
                            Call Interrupt(&H33, InRegs, OutRegs)
                            Line (X%, Y%)-(XOld%, YOld%), Back%
                            Line (X%, Y%)-(XNew%, YNew%), Fore%
                            XOld% = XNew%
                            YOld% = YNew%
                            InRegs.ax = 1    'Show mouse cursor
                            Call Interrupt(&H33, InRegs, OutRegs)
                            InRegs.bx = 0             'Left Button Releases
                            InRegs.ax = 6
                            Call Interrupt(&H33, InRegs, OutRegs)
                        Loop While OutRegs.bx = 0
                Return

    DrawBox:

                        X% = OutRegs.cx
                        Y% = OutRegs.dx
                        XOld% = X%
                        YOld% = Y%

                        InRegs.bx = 0  'Get left button releases to
                                           clear queue
                        InRegs.ax = 6
                        Call Interrupt(&H33, InRegs, OutRegs)

                        Do
                            InRegs.ax = 3
                            Call Interrupt(&H33, InRegs, OutRegs)
                            YNew% = OutRegs.dx
                            XNew% = OutRegs.cx
                            InRegs.ax = 2    'Hide mouse cursor
```

continues

Listing 7-1 continued

```
                            Call Interrupt(&H33, InRegs, OutRegs)
                            Line (X%, Y%)-(XOld%, YOld%), Back%, B
                            Line (X%, Y%)-(XNew%, YNew%), Fore%, B
                            XOld% = XNew%
                            YOld% = YNew%
                            InRegs.ax = 1     'Show mouse cursor
                            Call Interrupt(&H33, InRegs, OutRegs)
                            InRegs.bx = 0              'Left Button Releases
                            InRegs.ax = 6
                            Call Interrupt(&H33, InRegs, OutRegs)
                    Loop While OutRegs.bx = 0
            Return

     DrawCircle:

                    X% = OutRegs.cx
                    Y% = OutRegs.dx
                    XOld% = X%
                    YOld% = Y%

                    InRegs.bx = 0   'Get left button releases to
                                       clear queue
                    InRegs.ax = 6
                    Call Interrupt(&H33, InRegs, OutRegs)

                    Do
                        InRegs.ax = 3
                        Call Interrupt(&H33, InRegs, OutRegs)
                        YNew% = OutRegs.dx
                        XNew% = OutRegs.cx
                        InRegs.ax = 2   'Hide mouse cursor
                        Call Interrupt(&H33, InRegs, OutRegs)
                        Circle (X%, Y%), Sqr((X% - XOld%) ^ 2 + (Y% -
                            YOld%) ^ 2),
                               Back%
                        Circle (X%, Y%), Sqr((X% - XNew%) ^ 2 + (Y% -
                            YNew%) ^ 2)
                        XOld% = XNew%
                        YOld% = YNew%
                        InRegs.ax = 1    'Show mouse cursor
                        Call Interrupt(&H33, InRegs, OutRegs)
                        InRegs.bx = 0             'Left Button Releases
                        InRegs.ax = 6
                        Call Interrupt(&H33, InRegs, OutRegs)
```

```
                        Loop While OutRegs.bx = 0
            Return

DrawPaint:
                    X% = OutRegs.cx
                    Y% = OutRegs.dx
                    InRegs.ax = 2    'Hide mouse cursor
                    Call Interrupt(&H33, InRegs, OutRegs)
                    Paint (X%, Y%)
                    InRegs.ax = 1    'Show mouse cursor
                    Call Interrupt(&H33, InRegs, OutRegs)
            Return
```

Give it a try; it works well, and creating your own figures on the screen can be a lot of fun. You can even save the graphics you create on disk. Now, however, we're going to press on with our exploration of graphics with a popular way of drawing on the screen—the Draw statement.

Drawing a Graphics Clock

You can use the Visual Basic Draw statement to produce "vector" graphics—that is, line graphics—on the screen. Draw takes a *string* as its argument. For example, this statement draws a hexagon on the screen:

```
Draw "BU50 NL25 F12 D20 G12 L50 H12 U20 E12 R25 BD22"
```

Each letter is a directive to Draw, and each number is a length in pixels. Here's what the letters mean:

U	Up
D	Down
L	Left
R	Right
E	Up and right
F	Down and right
G	Down and left
H	Up and left
B	Pen up (don't draw)
N	Pen down (draw)

265

This table allows us to decipher our Draw statement. When we first use Draw, its "pen" is at the center of the screen. Here, we pick up the pen and move up 50 pixels and then put the pen down and move to the left 25 pixels:

```
Draw "BU50 NL25..."
```

Next, we move diagonally down and to the right by 12 pixels and then straight down by 20:

```
Draw "BU50 NL25 F12 D20..."
```

Then diagonally left and down by 12, to the left 20 units, and so on, until our hexagon is finished:

```
Draw "BU50 NL25 F12 D20 G12 L50 H12 U20 E12 R25 BD22"
```

As it turns out, we can draw at angles other than just 0, 45, and 90 degrees. We can use the "TA=" (Tilt Angle) argument to *rotate* the drawing actions that follow. For example, this draws a line of 50 pixels straight up—that is, at 90 degrees:

```
Draw "NU50"
```

However, we might want to draw this line at 95 degrees instead. To do that, we tilt our axes by 5 degrees counterclockwise:

```
ANG = 5
Draw "TA="+Varptr$(ANG)+" NU50"
```

This strange form, in which we pass a string pointer to a variable holding the tilt angle, is required when you want to use the "TA=" argument. In this case, we tilt the vertical 5 degrees counterclockwise, so a line that was formerly straight up is now at 95 degrees. A negative angle would have tilted the axes clockwise. Keep in mind that the tilt remains in effect until you change it.

Let's put this to work by drawing a clock that displays the current time. We start by drawing our hexagon and then moving the pen back to its center:

```
Screen 8
Draw "BU50 NL25 F12 D20 G12 L50 H12 U20 E12 R25 BD22"
:
```

Now we calculate the angle from the vertical of both the minute and hour hands using the Visual Basic Timer function (notice that we make the angles negative, because we want to treat them as clockwise angles):

```
Screen 8
Draw "BU50 NL25 F12 D20 G12 L50 H12 U20 E12 R25 BD22"
TimeMark! = Timer
Hours! = Int(TimeMark! / 3600)
Remainder! = TimeMark! - 3600 * Hours!
If Hours! > 12 Then Hours! = Hours! - 12
```
—> `HourAngle! = -Hours! / 12 * 360`
```
Minutes! = Int(Remainder! / 60)
```
—> `MinuteAngle! = -Minutes! / 60 * 360`
```
    :
```

Finally, we can just draw the hour and minute hands like this:

```
Screen 8
Draw "BU50 NL25 F12 D20 G12 L50 H12 U20 E12 R25 BD22"
TimeMark! = Timer
Hours! = Int(TimeMark! / 3600)
Remainder! = TimeMark! - 3600 * Hours!
If Hours! > 12 Then Hours! = Hours! - 12
HourAngle! = -Hours! / 12 * 360
Minutes! = Int(Remainder! / 60)
MinuteAngle! = -Minutes! / 60 * 360
```
—> `Draw "TA=" + Varptr$(HourAngle!) + " NU8"`
—> `Draw "TA=" + Varptr$(MinuteAngle!) + " NU12"`
```
       :
```

Then we wait for a key to be struck before leaving graphics mode, and we're done:

```
Screen 8
Draw "BU50 NL25 F12 D20 G12 L50 H12 U20 E12 R25 BD22"
TimeMark! = Timer
Hours! = Int(TimeMark! / 3600)
Remainder! = TimeMark! - 3600 * Hours!
If Hours! > 12 Then Hours! = Hours! - 12
HourAngle! = -Hours! / 12 * 360
Minutes! = Int(Remainder! / 60)
MinuteAngle! = -Minutes! / 60 * 360
Draw "TA=" + Varptr$(HourAngle!) + " NU8"
Draw "TA=" + Varptr$(MinuteAngle!) + " NU12"
```
—> `While Inkey$ = ""`
—> `Wend`
—> `Screen 0`

We can revise this program so that it keeps updating the figure on the screen—as it stands, it only draws the clock once, reflecting the current time, as shown in Figure 7-5.

Figure 7-5 Our Graphics Clock

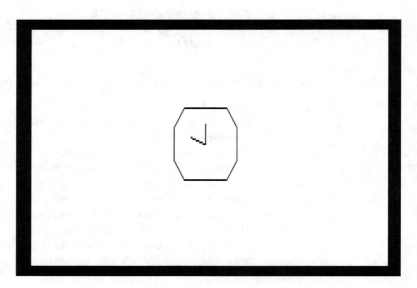

Presentation Graphics in Visual Basic

If you have the Visual Basic Professional Edition, there's another type of graphics you should be aware of, especially if you do any business programming—Presentation Graphics. This package of routines can present data in a variety of chart formats. For example, let's say that we wanted to track peanut butter consumption by region, where these were our figures:

Region	Peanut Butter Consumption (tons)
North	219
East	19
South	119
West	319

Using the Professional Edition Presentation Graphics packages, we could display our data in a pie chart, a bar chart, or a line chart—and we'll take a look at all three here.

Pie Charts

To start, we should note that you'll need to load the special Presentation Graphics Quick library named Chart.Qlb using the /L switch like this /L Chart. Let's call our pie chart program Pie.Bas. We have to include two .Bi files that come with the Professional Edition first:

```
' $Include: 'Font.Bi'
' $Include: 'Chart.Bi'
        :
```

Next, we'll need to load the name of each of our four regions into an array (which we'll name Regions( )), the peanut butter consumption in each region into another array (named Consumption( )), and create one last array named Exploded( ).

```
' $Include: 'Font.Bi'
' $Include: 'Chart.Bi'

        Dim Regions(4) As String
        Dim Consumption(4) As Single
        Dim Exploded(4) As Integer
                :
```

This final array is only necessary for pie charts—if the value in Exploded( ) corresponding to a particular section of the pie is nonzero, that section is treated as "exploded"—meaning that it is drawn as though it were being separated from the rest of the pie. We'll leave the values in Exploded( ) at 0, meaning that none of our pie slices will be exploded from the rest of the pie. Let's fill the other arrays now:

```
' $Include: 'Font.Bi'
' $Include: 'Chart.Bi'

        Dim Regions(4) As String
        Dim Consumption(4) As Single
        Dim Exploded(4) As Integer

        Regions(1) = "North"
        Regions(2) = "East"
```

```
        Regions(3) = "South"
        Regions(4) = "West"

        Consumption(1) = 219
        Consumption(2) = 19
        Consumption(3) = 119
        Consumption(4) = 319
        :
        :
```

Now we have to select a graphics mode—but we can't just use
Screen( ). Instead, we have to use the new Professional Edition statement ChartScreen( ). The argument we pass to ChartScreen( ) has to be
a valid Visual Basic screen mode; in this case, let's use (VGA-only)
mode 12:

```
' $Include: 'Font.Bi'
' $Include: 'Chart.Bi'

        Dim Regions(4) As String
        Dim Consumption(4) As Single
        Dim Exploded(4) As Integer

        Regions(1) = "North"
        Regions(2) = "East"
        Regions(3) = "South"
        Regions(4) = "West"

        Consumption(1) = 219
        Consumption(2) = 19
        Consumption(3) = 119
        Consumption(4) = 319

        Call ChartScreen(12)        <—
        :
        :
```

Now we're ready to specify what type of graph we want. We do that by
setting up a variable of type ChartEnvironment, which is defined in
Chart.Bi as follows:

```
Type ChartEnvironment
    ChartType     As Integer     ' 1=Bar, 2=Column, 3=Line,
                                 '   4=Scatter, 5=Pie
    ChartStyle    As Integer     ' Depends on type
    DataFont      As Integer     ' Font to use for plot characters
    ChartWindow   As RegionType  ' Overall chart window
    DataWindow    As RegionType  ' Data portion of chart
```

```
    MainTitle    As TitleType    ' Main title options
    SubTitle     As TitleType    ' Second line title options
    XAxis        As AxisType     ' X-axis options
    YAxis        As AxisType     ' Y-axis options
    Legend       As LegendType   ' Legend options
End Type
```

We have to pass a variable of this type to the Professional Edition graphing tools, and setting the fields in this data structure allows us to specify the titles we want in our chart. Let's call our ChartEnvironment variable OurChart:

```
' $Include: 'Font.Bi'
' $Include: 'Chart.Bi'

        Dim OurChart As ChartEnvironment      <—
        Dim Regions(4) As String
        Dim Consumption(4) As Single
        Dim Exploded(4) As Integer

        Regions(1) = "North"
        Regions(2) = "East"
        Regions(3) = "South"
        Regions(4) = "West"

        Consumption(1) = 219
        Consumption(2) = 19
        Consumption(3) = 119
        Consumption(4) = 319

        Call ChartScreen(12)
        :
        :
```

Now we have to indicate the *type* and *style* of chart we want. We can use one of these (predefined) constants to indicate the type of chart we want: cBar, cColumn, cLine, cScatter, cPie—we'll choose cPie to ask for a pie chart. We also have to select the style of the chart from these options for each type:

Type	Style
Bar	cPlain or cStacked
Column	cPlain or cStacked
Line	cLines or cNoLines
Scatter	cLines or cNoLines
Pie	cPercent or cNoPercent

271

For our example, let's choose the pie chart type (cPie) drawn in a style that marks each slice with the percentage it represents of the whole (cPercent). We use the Professional Edition procedure DefaultChart( ) to let the Presentation Graphics package know what our selections are:

```
' $Include: 'Font.Bi'
' $Include: 'Chart.Bi'

        Dim OurChart As ChartEnvironment
        Dim Regions(4) As String
        Dim Consumption(4) As Single
        Dim Exploded(4) As Integer

        Regions(1) = "North"
        Regions(2) = "East"
        Regions(3) = "South"
        Regions(4) = "West"

        Consumption(1) = 219
        Consumption(2) = 19
        Consumption(3) = 119
        Consumption(4) = 319

        Call ChartScreen(12)
    —>  Call DefaultChart(OurChart, cPie, cPercent)
        :
        :
```

Finally, we fill the Title fields in the data structure OurChart, and we're ready to place the chart on the screen:

```
' $Include: 'Font.Bi'
' $Include: 'Chart.Bi'

        Dim OurChart As ChartEnvironment
        Dim Regions(4) As String
        Dim Consumption(4) As Single
        Dim Exploded(4) As Integer

        Regions(1) = "North"
        Regions(2) = "East"
        Regions(3) = "South"
        Regions(4) = "West"

        Consumption(1) = 219
        Consumption(2) = 19
        Consumption(3) = 119
        Consumption(4) = 319
```

```
            Call ChartScreen(12)

            Call DefaultChart(OurChart, cPie, cPercent)

    —>      OurChart.MainTitle.Title = "Peanut Butter Consumption"
    :       OurChart.MainTitle.TitleColor = 15
            OurChart.MainTitle.Justify = cCenter
            OurChart.SubTitle.Title = "Consumption (Tons)"
            OurChart.SubTitle.TitleColor = 11
            OurChart.SubTitle.Justify = cCenter
            OurChart.ChartWindow.Border = cYes
    :
```

To actually display it, we call ChartPie( ) with these arguments:

```
Call ChartPie (OurChart, Regions( ), Consumption( ), Exploded( ), 4)
```

Here, OurChart is the ChartEnvironment variable we set up; Regions( ) holds the titles of each pie section; Consumption( ) holds the actual numerical data to plot; Exploded( ) indicates which pie slice(s) should be exploded; and the final integer, in this case 4, indicates how many data points there are. We can call ChartPie( ) and then finish up like this:

```
' $Include: 'Font.Bi'
' $Include: 'Chart.Bi'

        Dim OurChart As ChartEnvironment
        Dim Regions(4) As String
        Dim Consumption(4) As Single
        Dim Exploded(4) As Integer

        Regions(1) = "North"
        Regions(2) = "East"
        Regions(3) = "South"
        Regions(4) = "West"

        Consumption(1) = 219
        Consumption(2) = 19
        Consumption(3) = 119
        Consumption(4) = 319

        Call ChartScreen(12)

        Call DefaultChart(OurChart, cPie, cPercent)

        OurChart.MainTitle.Title = "Peanut Butter Consumption"
        OurChart.MainTitle.TitleColor = 15
```

```
OurChart.MainTitle.Justify = cCenter
OurChart.SubTitle.Title = "Consumption (Tons)"
OurChart.SubTitle.TitleColor = 11
OurChart.SubTitle.Justify = cCenter
OurChart.ChartWindow.Border = cYes

—>  Call ChartPie(OurChart, Regions( ), Consumption( ),
       Exploded( ), 4)
     Sleep
```

Notice that we placed a Visual Basic Sleep statement at the end of the code to hold the pie chart on the screen until we press a key. The result of this program appears in Figure 7-6. All this may seem like a lot of work to display a simple graph, but now that we've got the skeleton of the program working, it will be easy to adapt for other chart types.

Figure 7-6 Presentation Graphics Pie Chart

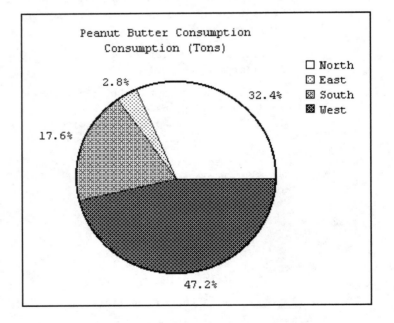

Bar Charts

For example, we can put together a bar chart example very easily from what we already have. We just need to omit the definition of

Exploded( ) (which has no use in a bar chart), and specify a plain style bar chart to DefaultChart( ):

```
' $Include: 'Font.Bi'
' $Include: 'Chart.Bi'

        Dim OurChart As ChartEnvironment
        Dim Regions(4) As String
        Dim Consumption(4) As Single

        Regions(1) = "North"
        Regions(2) = "East"
        Regions(3) = "South"
        Regions(4) = "West"

        Consumption(1) = 219
        Consumption(2) = 19
        Consumption(3) = 119
        Consumption(4) = 319

        Call ChartScreen(12)

    —>  Call DefaultChart(OurChart, cBar, CPlain)

        :
        :
```

Next, we add titles for the X and Y axes (which had no meaning, and therefore were not used, when we drew a pie chart) and call Chart( )—not ChartPie( )—to display the bar graph:

```
' $Include: 'Font.Bi'
' $Include: 'Chart.Bi'

        Dim OurChart As ChartEnvironment
        Dim Regions(4) As String
        Dim Consumption(4) As Single

        Regions(1) = "North"
        Regions(2) = "East"
        Regions(3) = "South"
        Regions(4) = "West"

        Consumption(1) = 219
        Consumption(2) = 19
        Consumption(3) = 119
        Consumption(4) = 319
```

```
                 Call ChartScreen(12)

                 Call DefaultChart(OurChart, cBar, CPlain)

                 OurChart.MainTitle.Title = "Peanut Butter Consumption"
                 OurChart.MainTitle.TitleColor = 15
                 OurChart.MainTitle.Justify = cCenter
                 OurChart.SubTitle.Title = "Consumption (Tons)"
                 OurChart.SubTitle.TitleColor = 11
                 OurChart.SubTitle.Justify = cCenter
                 OurChart.ChartWindow.Border = cYes

          —>     OurChart.XAxis.AxisTitle.Title = "Consumption"
          —>     OurChart.YAxis.AxisTitle.Title = "Region"

          —>     Call Chart(OurChart, Regions( ), Consumption( ), 4)
                 Sleep
```

The bar chart is now on the screen, as shown in Figure 7-7. Let's work
through one more type of Presentation Graphics chart—line charts.

Figure 7-7 Presentation Graphics Bar Chart

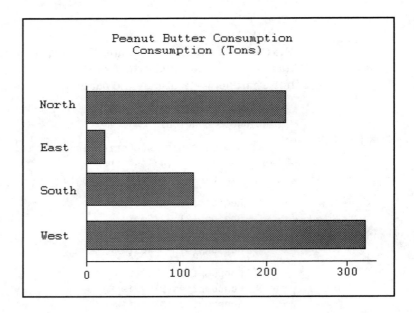

Line Charts

It's easy to adapt our example to produce a line chart, where all the displayed points are connected by a line. We just specify what we want to DefaultChart( ):

```
'  $Include: 'Font.Bi'
'  $Include: 'Chart.Bi'

        Dim OurChart As ChartEnvironment
        Dim Regions(4) As String
        Dim Consumption(4) As Single

        Regions(1) = "North"
        Regions(2) = "East"
        Regions(3) = "South"
        Regions(4) = "West"

        Consumption(1) = 219
        Consumption(2) = 19
        Consumption(3) = 119
        Consumption(4) = 319

        Call ChartScreen(12)

—>      Call DefaultChart(OurChart, cLine, cLine)
        :
        :
```

Then we call Chart( ) again (Chart( ) plots bar, column, and line charts depending on what you've asked for with DefaultChart( )):

```
'  $Include: 'Font.Bi'
'  $Include: 'Chart.Bi'

        Dim OurChart As ChartEnvironment
        Dim Regions(4) As String
        Dim Consumption(4) As Single

        Regions(1) = "North"
        Regions(2) = "East"
        Regions(3) = "South"
        Regions(4) = "West"

        Consumption(1) = 219
        Consumption(2) = 19
        Consumption(3) = 119
        Consumption(4) = 319
```

```
Call ChartScreen(12)

Call DefaultChart(OurChart, cLine, cLine)

OurChart.MainTitle.Title = "Peanut Butter Consumption"
OurChart.MainTitle.TitleColor = 15
OurChart.MainTitle.Justify = cCenter
OurChart.SubTitle.Title = "Consumption (Tons)"
OurChart.SubTitle.TitleColor = 11
OurChart.SubTitle.Justify = cCenter
OurChart.ChartWindow.Border = cYes

OurChart.XAxis.AxisTitle.Title = "Region"
OurChart.YAxis.AxisTitle.Title = "Number"

—>  Call Chart(OurChart, Regions( ), Consumption( ), 4)
    Sleep
```

Our line chart is on the screen, as shown in Figure 7-8. Now we've worked through pie charts, bar charts, and line charts; as you can see, the Professional Edition offers a good set of tools for presenting data.

Figure 7-8 Presentation Graphics Line Chart

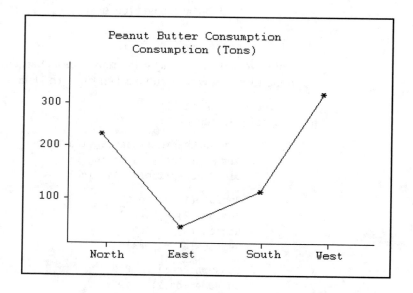

That completes our coverage of graphics. In the next chapter, we'll start working with some data-handling techniques in Visual Basic.

Data Handling and Sorting in Visual Basic

In this chapter, we'll work through nearly all the ways of organizing data in Visual Basic for DOS (and then we'll add a few of our own). Organizing your data for easy access can be crucial in program development—for speed in both program coding and execution. In fact, organizing your data at the beginning may win you more than half the battle of writing a program.

We'll work through the most helpful methods of arranging data, including arrays, data structures, linked lists, circular buffers, and binary trees; programmers should be familiar with these common methods of organizing data and not have to continually reinvent the wheel. And, at the end of the chapter, we'll examine two fast sorting methods to get the most out of our data, as well as a fast searching algorithm to search through sorted arrays.

Variables

The most elementary method of organizing data is by storing it in simple variables. Here are the standard types used in Visual Basic:

Type	Symbol	Bytes	Range
Integer	%	2	–32,768 to 32,767
Long	&	4	–2,147,483,648 to 2,147,483,647
Single	!	4	–3.402823E38 to –1.40129E-45
Double	#	8	–1.79769313486232D308 to –2.2250738585072D-308
Currency	@	8	–$922337203685477.5808 to $922337203685477.5807
String	$	32K	Strings can range up to 32K characters (bytes)

We're familiar with all of these, except perhaps the Currency type. You use that type to store amounts of money; here's an example (results are printed out to the nearest cent):

```
Sub Form_Load ()
    Savings@ = 6000.00
    Rent@ = 775.00
    Food@ = 124.50
    Bills@ = 513.72

    Savings@ = Savings@ - Rent@
    Savings@ = Savings@ - Food@
    Savings@ = Savings@ - Bills@

    Print "Money left: $"; Savings@
End Sub
```

This example prints out how much of your savings are left after paying rent and the bills. For most purposes, you can think of a Currency variable as a more accurate Long variable—with four decimal places added on to it as well (although the last two decimal places are for internal accuracy only).

The next step up in data handling is the Data statement, which you might be familiar with, and which works like this, where we calculate the sum of the numbers 1-10, stored in a Data statement (place the Data statement in the program's declaration area):

```
—>   Data 1, 2, 3, 4, 5, 6, 7, 8, 9, 10

     Form_Load()
         Sum& = 0
         Product& = 1

     For i = 1 To 10
—>           Read Number&
             Sum& = Sum& + Number&
     Next i

     Print "The sum of your data is:"; Sum&
 End Sub
```

The program prints: "The sum of your data is: 55". The Data statement is of some utility, but the next step in data handling in VB is working with something we're already familiar with: arrays.

Arrays

We're all familiar with arrays, such as the one in this example (set the form's AutoRedraw property to True so we can display text from the Form_Load( ) procedure):

```
Sub Form_Load()
    Dim DataArray(10, 2) As Currency   <—

    'Fill DataArray(n,1) with today's sales:

    DataArray(1, 1) = 10.00
    DataArray(2, 1) = 53.00
    DataArray(3, 1) = 7.17
    DataArray(4, 1) = 9.67
    DataArray(5, 1) = 87.99
    DataArray(6, 1) = 14.00
    DataArray(7, 1) = 91.19
```

```
DataArray(8, 1) = 12.73
DataArray(9, 1) = 1.03
DataArray(10, 1) = 5.04

'Fill DataArray(n,2) with yesterday's sales:

DataArray(1, 2) = 9.67
DataArray(2, 2) = 3.5
DataArray(3, 2) = 8.97
DataArray(4, 2) = 10.00
DataArray(5, 2) = 78.33
DataArray(6, 2) = 17.00
DataArray(7, 2) = 91.36
DataArray(8, 2) = 12.73
DataArray(9, 2) = 16.12
DataArray(10, 2) = 7.98

Print "     SALES (in $)"
Print "Yesterday" ; Tab(20) ; "Today"
Print "---------" ; Tab(20) ; "-----"
For loop_index = 1 To 10
        Print DataArray(loop_index, 1) ; Tab(20) ; DataArray
            (loop_index, 2)
Next loop_index
Print "---------" ; Tab(20) ; "-----"

Sum1@ = 0
Sum2@ = 0
For loop_index = 1 To 10
    Sum1@ = Sum1@ + DataArray(loop_index, 1)
    Sum2@ = Sum2@ + DataArray(loop_index, 2)
Next loop_index

Print Sum1@ ; Tab(20) ; Sum2@ ; " = Total"
End Sub
```

In this program, we're setting up an array of 10 rows and 2 columns to hold sales values for the last two days:

```
Dim DataArray(10, 2) As Currency  <—

'Fill DataArray(n,1) with today's sales:

DataArray(1, 1) = 10.00
DataArray(2, 1) = 53.00
DataArray(3, 1) = 7.17
```

Peter Norton's Visual Basic for DOS

```
DataArray(4, 1) = 9.67
DataArray(5, 1) = 87.99
DataArray(6, 1) = 14.00
DataArray(7, 1) = 91.19
DataArray(8, 1) = 12.73
DataArray(9, 1) = 1.03
DataArray(10, 1) = 5.04

'Fill DataArray(n,2) with yesterday's sales:

DataArray(1, 2) = 9.67
DataArray(2, 2) = 3.5
DataArray(3, 2) = 8.97
DataArray(4, 2) = 10.00
DataArray(5, 2) = 78.33
DataArray(6, 2) = 17.00
DataArray(7, 2) = 91.36
DataArray(8, 2) = 12.73
DataArray(9, 2) = 16.12
DataArray(10, 2) = 7.98
        :
        :
```

And this is the array produced:

Col 1   Col 2

Col 1	Col 2	
10.00	9.67	<— Row 1
53.00	3.5	<— Row 2
7.17	8.97	
9.67	10.00	
87.99	78.33	
14.00	17.00	
91.19	91.36	
12.73	12.73	
1.03	16.12	
5.04	7.98	

Now we can reach each day's column of sales just by incrementing the column index. In this format, we can perform parallel operations on parallel sets of data, such as adding the columns of sales to produce sums in our example program:

```
Sub Form_Load()
    Dim DataArray(10, 2) As Currency  <—

    'Fill DataArray(n,1) with today's sales:

    DataArray(1, 1) = 10.00
    DataArray(2, 1) = 53.00
    DataArray(3, 1) = 7.17
    DataArray(4, 1) = 9.67
    DataArray(5, 1) = 87.99
    DataArray(6, 1) = 14.00
    DataArray(7, 1) = 91.19
    DataArray(8, 1) = 12.73
    DataArray(9, 1) = 1.03
    DataArray(10, 1) = 5.04

    'Fill DataArray(n,2) with yesterday's sales:

    DataArray(1, 2) = 9.67
    DataArray(2, 2) = 3.5
    DataArray(3, 2) = 8.97
    DataArray(4, 2) = 10.00
    DataArray(5, 2) = 78.33
    DataArray(6, 2) = 17.00
    DataArray(7, 2) = 91.36
    DataArray(8, 2) = 12.73
    DataArray(9, 2) = 16.12
    DataArray(10, 2) = 7.98

    Print "      SALES (in $)"
    Print "Yesterday" ; Tab(20) ; "Today"
    Print "---------" ; Tab(20) ; "-----"
    For loop_index = 1 To 10
            Print DataArray(loop_index, 1) ; Tab(20) ; DataArray
                (loop_index, 2)
    Next loop_index
    Print "---------" ; Tab(20) ; "-----"
```

```
    Sum1@ = 0
    Sum2@ = 0
    For loop_index = 1 To 10
        Sum1@ = Sum1@ + DataArray(loop_index, 1)
        Sum2@ = Sum2@ + DataArray(loop_index, 2)
    Next loop_index

    Print Sum1@ ; Tab(20) ; Sum2@ ; " = Total"
End Sub
```

The results of this program appear in Figure 8-1.

Figure 8-1 Our Array Example

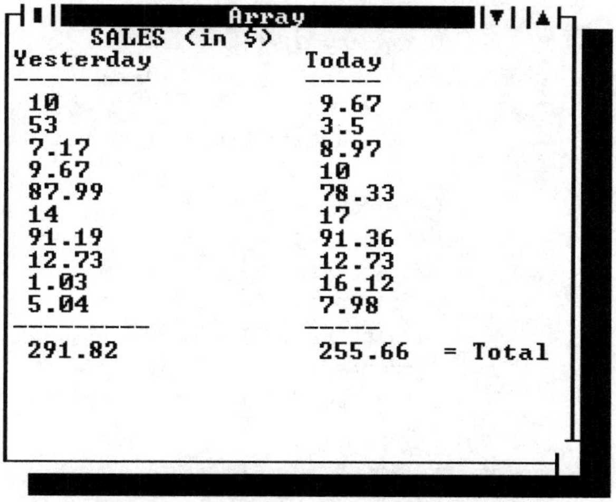

In Visual Basic, you can also declare arrays as *dynamic*, which means
that you can redimension them with the *ReDim* statement at run time.
To declare a dynamic array at the procedure level, just declare it using
Dim and with no arguments in the parentheses as follows:

```
Sub Form_Load()
    Dim DataArray() As Currency  <—
        :
```

Now you can redimension it whenever you want to, and use it as
before:

```
Sub Form_Load()
    Dim DataArray() As Currency

    ReDim DataArray(10, 2) As Currency   <—

    'Fill DataArray(n,1) with today's sales:

    DataArray(1, 1) = 10.00
    DataArray(2, 1) = 53.00
    DataArray(3, 1) = 7.17
    DataArray(4, 1) = 9.67
    DataArray(5, 1) = 87.99
    DataArray(6, 1) = 14.00
    DataArray(7, 1) = 91.19
    DataArray(8, 1) = 12.73
    DataArray(9, 1) = 1.03
    DataArray(10, 1) = 5.04

    'Fill DataArray(n,2) with yesterday's sales:

    DataArray(1, 2) = 9.67
    DataArray(2, 2) = 3.5
    DataArray(3, 2) = 8.97
    DataArray(4, 2) = 10.00
    DataArray(5, 2) = 78.33
    DataArray(6, 2) = 17.00
    DataArray(7, 2) = 91.36
    DataArray(8, 2) = 12.73
    DataArray(9, 2) = 16.12
    DataArray(10, 2) = 7.98
        :
End Sub
```

The ReDim statement initializes all elements of the array to 0; in addition, you can't use ReDim to create arrays with more than eight dimensions, and there is a limit on the size of dynamic or static arrays in Visual Basic of 64K.

That's it; arrays don't get very complex in Visual Basic—unlike in C, where array names are just pointers (and two-dimensional array names are just pointers to pointers). There you can save both time and memory by converting all array references to pointer references.

Since we've gotten about as complex as arrays get in Visual Basic, let's move on to the most advanced way of organizing data after arrays: data structures.

Data Structures

As we've seen to some extent already, we can group the standard data types together and come up with a whole new type of our own. To define a Type named Person, we can do this:

```
Type Person
    FirstName As String * 20
    LastName As String * 20
End Type
:
```

Note that we have to put this Type definition into the declaration section in VB, since that's the only place that Type is valid. In addition, we can actually use variable-length strings in Type statements (except when we're using such variables as records in a random access file, as we saw before). The data structure we've created here just stores a person's first and last names. We can set up a variable of this type— or, even more powerfully, an array of variables of this type in our procedure:

```
—> Dim People(10) As Person
    :
```

And then we reference them like this:

```
    Dim People(10) As Person

    People(1).FirstName = "Al"
    People(1).LastName = "Einstein"

    People(2).FirstName = "Frank"
    People(2).LastName = "Roosevelt"

    People(2).FirstName = "Charlie"
    People(2).LastName = "DeGaulle"

    Print People(1).FirstName
    :
```

But that's not the end to working with data structures. If there is some connection between the elements of our array, we can connect them into a *linked list*.

Linked Lists

Linked lists are good for organizing data items into sequential chains, especially if you have a number of such chains to manage and want to use space efficiently.

They work in this way: for each data item, there is also a *pointer* pointing to the next data item—that is, an index of some sort that references the next data item, as we'll see below. We find the next item in the list by referring to the pointer in the present item. At any time, you can add another data item to the list, as long as you update the current pointer to point to the new data item:

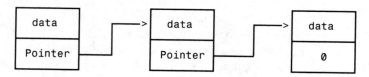

The last pointer in the chain is a null pointer with a value of 0 (so that you know the list is ended when you reach it). A prominent example of a linked list in your computer is the File Allocation Table (FAT) on disks. This is a list of the clusters allocated to files for storage. Files are stored cluster by cluster, and for each cluster on the disk, there is one entry in the FAT.

To see what clusters a file is stored in, you get its first cluster number from the internal data in its directory entry—let's say that number is 2. That means that the first section of the file is stored in cluster 2 on the disk. This number is also the key to the FAT for us. We can find the *next* cluster occupied by the file by looking in cluster 2's entry in the FAT:

```
FAT        |
           V
Entry #  2     3     4     5     6     7     8     9    10    11    12    13
```

2	3	4	5	6	7	8	9	10	11	12	13
3	4	6	32	7	End	29	10	End	0	0	0

That cluster's entry in the FAT holds 3, which is the number of the next cluster that the file occupies on the disk. To find the cluster after 3, check the entry in the File Allocation Table for that cluster:

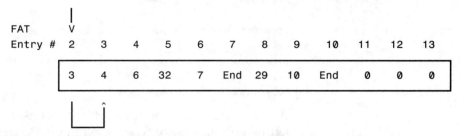

Since that holds 4, the next section of the file is in cluster 4. To continue from there, check the number in the FAT entry for cluster 4:

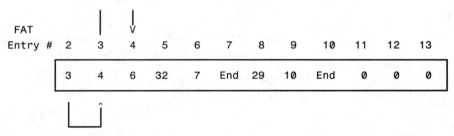

That number is 6, and you continue on until you come to the end-of-file mark in the FAT:

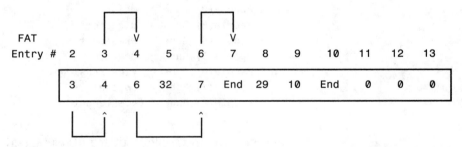

In other words, this file is stored in clusters 2, 3, 4, 6 and 7. Notice that 5 was already taken by another file, which is also weaving its own thread of clusters through the FAT at the same time. Linked lists like this are used when you want to efficiently use memory or disk space and have to keep track of a number of sequential chains of data. For example, when this file is deleted, its entries in the FAT can be written over, and those clusters can be taken by another file.

Let's see an example of a linked list in Visual Basic. For example, we might have these two distinct career paths to keep track of:

```
President        Colonel
   |                |
Vice President   Major           ^  Moving "up"
   |                |             |  the career
Director         Captain         |  track
   |                |
Supervisor       Lieutenant
```

We can connect the various levels with a linked list. We start by setting up a variable of type Person in the global module as follows:

```
—>   Type Person
—>       Rank As String * 20
—>       SuperiorPointer As Integer
—>   End Type
```

Now we fill the Rank fields—we can fill them in any order; the SuperiorPointers will keep them straight:

```
  Sub Form_Load ()

      'Linked List Example

      Dim People(10) As Person

—>    People(1).Rank = "Supervisor"
  :   People(2).Rank = "Major"
  :   People(3).Rank = "Director"
      People(4).Rank = "President"
      People(5).Rank = "Captain"
      People(6).Rank = "Vice President"
      People(7).Rank = "Colonel"
      People(8).Rank = "Lieutenant"
          :
```

For each entry in People( ), there's also a "superior" position; for example, the superior of the entry in People(1)—Supervisor—is in People(3)—Director. To link the entries in each of the two chains, we have to point to the superior rank by filling the pointers Person( ).SuperiorPointer:

```
Sub Form_Load ()

    'Linked List Example

    Dim People(10) As Person

    People(1).Rank = "Supervisor"
    People(2).Rank = "Major"
    People(3).Rank = "Director"
    People(4).Rank = "President"
    People(5).Rank = "Captain"
    People(6).Rank = "Vice President"
    People(7).Rank = "Colonel"
    People(8).Rank = "Lieutenant"

—>  People(1).SuperiorPointer = 3
 :  People(2).SuperiorPointer = 7
 :  People(3).SuperiorPointer = 6
    People(5).SuperiorPointer = 2
    People(6).SuperiorPointer = 4
    People(7).SuperiorPointer = 0
    People(8).SuperiorPointer = 5
          :
```

Now that all the items in the two lists are linked, we can choose a
number, 1 or 2, and work our way through the first or second linked
list, printing out the various Rank names as we go. In this example,
let's choose career track 1:

```
Sub Form_Load ()

    'Linked List Example

    Dim People(10) As Person

    People(1).Rank = "Supervisor"
    People(2).Rank = "Major"
    People(3).Rank = "Director"
    People(4).Rank = "President"
    People(5).Rank = "Captain"
    People(6).Rank = "Vice President"
    People(7).Rank = "Colonel"
    People(8).Rank = "Lieutenant"
```

```
                    People(1).SuperiorPointer = 3
                    People(2).SuperiorPointer = 7
                    People(3).SuperiorPointer = 6
                    People(4).SuperiorPointer = 0
                    People(5).SuperiorPointer = 2
                    People(6).SuperiorPointer = 4
                    People(7).SuperiorPointer = 0
                    People(8).SuperiorPointer = 5
                         :
      —>    Index = 1

      —>    Do
      —>          Print People(Index).Rank     'Print out results.
      —>          Index = People(Index).SuperiorPointer
      —>    Loop While Index <> 0

           End Sub
```

When this program runs, it prints out career track 1, and we see this
list on the form:

```
Supervisor
Director
Vice President
President
```

Note that we must know in advance that chain 1 starts with entry 1
and chain 2 with entry 8—we always need the first entry to use as a
key to the first position in the linked list. After that, we can work our
way up either chain of command; as we do so, we print out the
current Rank, and at the same time, get a pointer to (that is, the array
index number of) the next Rank.

Circular Buffers

There is another type of linked list that programmers often use—
a list in which the last item points to the first one, so that the
whole thing forms a circle. This is called a circular buffer. The
most well-known circular buffer in your computer is the keyboard
buffer.

While one part of the operating system is putting key codes into the keyboard buffer, another part of the operating system is taking them out. The location in the buffer where the next key code will be placed is called the "tail," and the location where the next key code is to be read from is called the "head."

When keys are typed in, the tail advances: when they are read, the head advances. As you write to and read from the keyboard buffer, the head and tail march around (each data location can be either the head or the tail). When the buffer is filled, the tail comes up behind the head, and the buffer-full warning beeps.

You can use circular buffers when some part of your program is writing data and another part is reading it—but at different times. Store the location of the head and tail positions, and after you put data into the buffer, advance the tail. When you take data out, advance the head. This way, you can use the same memory space for both reading and writing.

The primary problem with linked lists, however, is that all access to their data is sequential access. To find the last entry in a linked list, for example, you have to start at the very first one and work your way back. That's fine for files tracked through the FAT (where you need every FAT entry before you can read the whole file), but it's a terrible method if you're only looking for a specific record. A better way is to make what's called a *binary tree*.

Binary Trees

Binary trees differ from linked lists in that the data is ordered. We can start with a linked list:

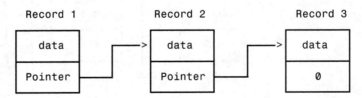

And then make it a *doubly* linked list:

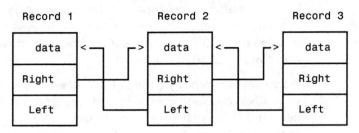

Now there are two pointers in each record—one scans up the chain, the other down. Doubly linked lists have many uses in themselves, but this is still not a binary tree. Instead, let's put in some values for the data fields, -5, 0, and 2:

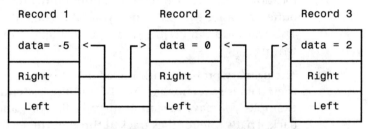

Notice that we've constructed a hierarchy based on data values, arranging them from left to right in increasing order (-5, 0, 2). The record with the data value closest to the median data value becomes the *root* of our binary tree:

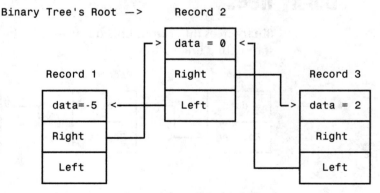

Because it has the data value closest to the middle of all three records, record 2 is the root of our binary tree. If we wanted to find a record with a data value of, say, -5, we'd start at the root—record 2, whose data value is 0. Since -5 is less than 0, we would next search the record to its left (since data values decrease to the left). This record is record 1, with a data value of -5, which means that we've found our target value. This might seem like a small gain here, but imagine having a list like this:

```
First name="Denise"
  Age=23
First name="Ed"
  Age=46
First name="Nick"
  Age=47
First name="Dennis"
  Age=42
First name="Doug"
  Age=33
First name="Margo"
  Age=27
First name="John"
  Age=41
First name="Cheryl"
  Age=28
```

Let's say that it is your job to coordinate this list and find a person with a specified age. A binary tree simply has a number of data nodes, each of which can be connected to two lower data nodes, one containing "less than" data and the other containing "greater than" data. To construct a binary tree from our data, you'd pick the person with an age as close to the median as possible (Doug) to be the binary tree's root. Then we might put the tree together something like this (note that each node itself is the root of a binary tree):

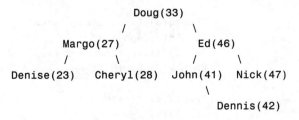

Now you can start with Doug and just keep working until you find the age you require. For example, to find the person who is 47 years old, start at Doug, who is 33. Since 47 is greater than 33, continue moving to the right, where you'll find Ed, who is 46. Since 47 is greater than 46, continue to the right once again, where you reach Nick, who is 47. Let's put this example into code. We begin by defining a new Person Type in the global module, which has two pointers, one to the next older person, and one to the next-younger:

```
Type Person
    FirstName As String * 20
    Age As Integer
    NextYoungerPerson As Integer
    NextOlderPerson As Integer
End Type
```

Now we can use that type in a Form_Load( ) Sub procedure, and we fill the NextYoungerPerson and NextOlderPerson fields like this (matching our binary tree above):

```
  Sub Form_Load ()

      'Binary Tree example.

—>    Dim People(10) As Person
  :
      People(1).FirstName = "Denise"
      People(1).Age = 23
      People(1).NextYoungerPerson = 0
      People(1).NextOlderPerson = 0

      People(2).FirstName = "Ed"
      People(2).Age = 46
      People(2).NextYoungerPerson = 7
      People(2).NextOlderPerson = 3

      People(3).FirstName = "Nick"
      People(3).Age = 47
      People(3).NextYoungerPerson = 0
      People(3).NextOlderPerson = 0

      People(4).FirstName = "Dennis"
      People(4).Age = 42
```

```
People(4).NextYoungerPerson = 0
People(4).NextOlderPerson = 0

People(5).FirstName = "Doug"
People(5).Age = 33
People(5).NextYoungerPerson = 6
People(5).NextOlderPerson = 2

People(6).FirstName = "Margo"
People(6).Age = 27
People(6).NextYoungerPerson = 1
People(6).NextOlderPerson = 8

People(7).FirstName = "John"
People(7).Age = 41
People(7).NextYoungerPerson = 0
People(7).NextOlderPerson = 4

People(8).FirstName = "Cheryl"
People(8).Age = 28
People(8).NextYoungerPerson = 0
People(8).NextOlderPerson = 0
        :
        :
```

Next, we can search for the first person who is 47 years old. First, we start at the root as follows:

```
Sub Form_Load ()

    'Binary Tree example.

    Dim People(10) As Person

    People(1).FirstName = "Denise"
    People(1).Age = 23
    People(1).NextYoungerPerson = 0
    People(1).NextOlderPerson = 0

    People(2).FirstName = "Ed"
    People(2).Age = 46
    People(2).NextYoungerPerson = 7
    People(2).NextOlderPerson = 3
```

```
            People(3).FirstName = "Nick"
            People(3).Age = 47
            People(3).NextYoungerPerson = 0
            People(3).NextOlderPerson = 0

            People(4).FirstName = "Dennis"
            People(4).Age = 42
            People(4).NextYoungerPerson = 0
            People(4).NextOlderPerson = 0

            People(5).FirstName = "Doug"
            People(5).Age = 33
            People(5).NextYoungerPerson = 6
            People(5).NextOlderPerson = 2

            People(6).FirstName = "Margo"
            People(6).Age = 27
            People(6).NextYoungerPerson = 1
            People(6).NextOlderPerson = 8

            People(7).FirstName = "John"
            People(7).Age = 41
            People(7).NextYoungerPerson = 0
            People(7).NextOlderPerson = 4

            People(8).FirstName = "Cheryl"
            People(8).Age = 28
            People(8).NextYoungerPerson = 0
            People(8).NextOlderPerson = 0
```

—>   `BinaryTreeRoot% = 5     'Doug has about the median age`

—>   `Print "Searching for a person 47 years old..."`

—>   `CurrentRecord% = BinaryTreeRoot%`
              `:`
              `:`

And check to see whether that person is 47 years old:

```
Sub Form_Load ()

    'Binary Tree example.

    Dim People(10) As Person

    People(1).FirstName = "Denise"
    People(1).Age = 23
    People(1).NextYoungerPerson = 0
    People(1).NextOlderPerson = 0

    People(2).FirstName = "Ed"
    People(2).Age = 46
    People(2).NextYoungerPerson = 7
    People(2).NextOlderPerson = 3

    People(3).FirstName = "Nick"
    People(3).Age = 47
    People(3).NextYoungerPerson = 0
    People(3).NextOlderPerson = 0

    People(4).FirstName = "Dennis"
    People(4).Age = 42
    People(4).NextYoungerPerson = 0
    People(4).NextOlderPerson = 0

    People(5).FirstName = "Doug"
    People(5).Age = 33
    People(5).NextYoungerPerson = 6
    People(5).NextOlderPerson = 2

    People(6).FirstName = "Margo"
    People(6).Age = 27
    People(6).NextYoungerPerson = 1
    People(6).NextOlderPerson = 8

    People(7).FirstName = "John"
    People(7).Age = 41
    People(7).NextYoungerPerson = 0
    People(7).NextOlderPerson = 4

    People(8).FirstName = "Cheryl"
    People(8).Age = 28
```

```
              People(8).NextYoungerPerson = 0
              People(8).NextOlderPerson = 0

              BinaryTreeRoot% = 5      'Doug has about the median age

              Print "Searching for a person 47 years old..."

              CurrentRecord% = BinaryTreeRoot%

    —>    Do
    :         If People(CurrentRecord%).Age = 47 Then
    :             Print "That person is: ";
                      People(CurrentRecord%).FirstName
                  Exit Do
              End If
    :
    :
```

If not, then we have to compare the current person's age to 47. If it's less, then we want the NextOlderPerson; if greater, then we want the NextYoungerPerson, as shown below in Form_Load( ):

```
Sub Form_Load ()

    'Binary Tree example.

    Dim People(10) As Person

    People(1).FirstName = "Denise"
    People(1).Age = 23
    People(1).NextYoungerPerson = 0
    People(1).NextOlderPerson = 0

    People(2).FirstName = "Ed"
    People(2).Age = 46
    People(2).NextYoungerPerson = 7
    People(2).NextOlderPerson = 3

    People(3).FirstName = "Nick"
    People(3).Age = 47
    People(3).NextYoungerPerson = 0
    People(3).NextOlderPerson = 0
```

```
          People(4).FirstName = "Dennis"
          People(4).Age = 42
          People(4).NextYoungerPerson = 0
          People(4).NextOlderPerson = 0

          People(5).FirstName = "Doug"
          People(5).Age = 33
          People(5).NextYoungerPerson = 6
          People(5).NextOlderPerson = 2

          People(6).FirstName = "Margo"
          People(6).Age = 27
          People(6).NextYoungerPerson = 1
          People(6).NextOlderPerson = 8

          People(7).FirstName = "John"
          People(7).Age = 41
          People(7).NextYoungerPerson = 0
          People(7).NextOlderPerson = 4

          People(8).FirstName = "Cheryl"
          People(8).Age = 28
          People(8).NextYoungerPerson = 0
          People(8).NextOlderPerson = 0

          BinaryTreeRoot% = 5     'Doug has about the median age

          Print "Searching for a person 47 years old..."

          CurrentRecord% = BinaryTreeRoot%

          Do
              If People(CurrentRecord%).Age = 47 Then
                  Print "That person is: ";
                      People(CurrentRecord%).FirstName
                  Exit Do
              End If
    —>        If People(CurrentRecord%).Age > 47 Then
    :             CurrentRecord% =
                      People(CurrentRecord%).NextYoungerPerson
    :         Else
                  CurrentRecord% =
                      People(CurrentRecord%).NextOlderPerson
```

```
                    End If
        Loop While CurrentRecord% <> 0

End Sub
```

And that's how to search through a binary tree: just keep going until
you find what you're looking for (or run out of branches). The results
of this program appear in Figure 8-2.

Figure 8-2 Our Binary Tree Example

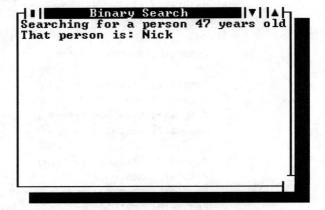

With binary trees, we've started ordering our data. That is, we've
established the relative position of a record with respect to its two
neighbors. But what if we wanted to sort all the data? Sorting data is,
of course, a very common thing to do; it's the next step in organizing
our data. And, because it's so common, we should explore it in some
detail. To do that, we'll work through two of the fastest algorithms
available—shell sorts and the Quicksort. And we'll put them to work.

Shell Sorts

The shell sort is alway popular among programmers. Ours will not
be the fastest implementation of the shell sort, but it will show
how it works (if you want a faster sorting routine, take a look at
the Quicksort, coming up later). The shell sort works as shown below.

Say you had a one-dimensional array with these values in it:

```
8 7 6 5 4 3 2 1
```

To sort this list into ascending order, divide it into two partitions like this:

```
8 7 6 5 4 3 2 1
L___J L___J
```

Then compare the first element of the first partition with the first element of the second:

```
|       |
V       V
8 7 6 5 4 3 2 1
L___J L___J
```

In this case, 8 is greater than 4, so we switch the elements, and go on to compare the next pair:

```
  |       |
  V       V
4 7 6 5 8 3 2 1
L___J L___J
```

Again, 7 is greater than 3, so we switch and go on:

```
  |       |
  V       V
4 3 6 5 8 7 2 1
L___J L___J
```

We also switch 6 and 2 and then look at the last pair:

```
    |       |
    V       V
4 3 2 5 8 7 6 1
L___J L___J
```

After we switch them too, we get the following as the new list:

```
4 3 2 1 8 7 6 5
```

While this is somewhat better than before, we're still not through. The next step is to decrement the partion size by one and to repeat the process as follows:

```
4 3 2 1 8 7 6 5 x
|__|  |__|  |__|
```

Here we compare 4 to 1:

```
 |     |
 v     v
4 3 2 1 8 7 6 5 x
|__|  |__|  |__|
```

One is less than 4, so we switch them and go on, examining the next pair:

```
   |     |
   v     v
1 3 2 4 8 7 6 5 x
|__|  |__|  |__|
```

Here, 3 is less than 8, so we do not switch them. Next comes 2 and 7:

```
     |     |
     v     v
1 3 2 4 8 7 6 5 x
|__|  |__|  |__|
```

Since 2 is less than 7, we don't switch them. Now we can move up to the next partition:

```
       |     |
       v     v
1 3 2 4 8 7 6 5 x
|__|  |__|  |__|
```

Because 4 is less than 6, we don't switch; instead, we move on to the next pair:

```
   |     |
   v     v
1 3 2 4 8 7 6 5 x
|__|  |__|  |__|
```

We do switch these. Note that because we're dividing an even number of total elements up into partitions with an odd number of elements, there is no member of the last partition. In that case, we do not perform a comparison (i.e., there is no later element that may have to be switched to an earlier place). That means that we end up with the following order:

1 3 2 4 5 7 6 8

We're almost there. The next step is to make the partition size smaller by one, as follows:

1 3 2 4 5 7 6 8
⊔ ⊔ ⊔ ⊔

Because there are no switches here, we cut the partition size down to one and compare the first pair, as follows:

```
| |
V V
1 3 2 4 5 7 6 8
```

In this case, since 1 is less than 3, we don't make a switch. Instead, we move on to the next pair:

```
  | |
  V V
1 3 2 4 5 7 6 8
```

Here, since 2 is less than 3, we do switch them, and then continue:

```
    | |
    V V
1 2 3 4 5 7 6 8
```

Since these are all right, we move up:

```
    | |
    V V
1 2 3 4 5 7 6 8
```

Again, we don't have to make a switch, nor do we have to switch the next three pairs. However, when we compare 7 to 6, as follows:

```
    | |
    V V
1 2 3 4 5 7 6 8
```

we do have to make a switch:

1 2 3 4 5 6 7 8

Since the final two elements are fine, we're done (i.e., the next partition size is 0, which is the point at which shell sorts terminate).

Now let's see this in code. We start by dimensioning an array and filling it with values (which are as out of ascending order as they can be):

```
Sub Form_Load ()

    Dim Array(9) As Integer   <—

    Array(1) = 9
    Array(2) = 8
    Array(3) = 7
    Array(4) = 6
    Array(5) = 5
    Array(6) = 4
    Array(7) = 3
    Array(8) = 2
    Array(9) = 1
        :

        :
```

We can also print those values to the form so that they can be compared to the sorted list later:

```
Sub Form_Load ()

    Dim Array(9) As Integer

    Array(1) = 9
    Array(2) = 8
    Array(3) = 7
    Array(4) = 6
    Array(5) = 5
    Array(6) = 4
    Array(7) = 3
    Array(8) = 2
    Array(9) = 1

    Print " i" ; Tab(20) ; "Array(i)"     <—
    Print "---" ; Tab(20) ; "---------"
    For i = 1 To 9
        Print i ; Tab(20) ; Array(i)
    Next i
```

```
Print
Print "Sorting..."
  :
  :
```

Now we have to implement our shell sort. In this type of sorting routine, we loop over partition size (PartitionSize% below). Let's set that loop up first, as follows:

```
Sub Form_Load ()

    Dim Array(9) As Integer

    Array(1) = 9
    Array(2) = 8
    Array(3) = 7
    Array(4) = 6
    Array(5) = 5
    Array(6) = 4
    Array(7) = 3
    Array(8) = 2
    Array(9) = 1

    Print " i" ; Tab(20) ; "Array(i)"
    Print "---" ; Tab(20) ; "---------"
    For i = 1 To 9
        Print i ; Tab(20) ; Array(i)
    Next i
    Print
    Print "Sorting..."

            NumItems% = Ubound(Array, 1)
            PartitionSize% = Int((NumItems% + 1) / 2)

    -->   Do
            :

            :
    -->   Loop While PartitionSize% > 0
                :

                :
```

Notice in particular that, since we need the number of items to sort, we can use the Ubound( ) function, which returns the dimensions of an array in Visual Basic (Ubound( ) returns an array's upper bound, and Lbound( ) returns its lower bound). In the loop, we loop over partition size, decrementing it each time:

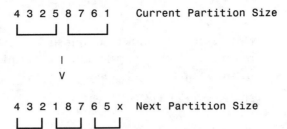

```
4 3 2 5 8 7 6 1     Current Partition Size
L___I L___I

         I
         V

4 3 2 1 8 7 6 5 x   Next Partition Size
L_I L_I L_I
```

For every partition size, however, the list is broken up into a different number of partitions, and we have to loop over the number of partitions so that we can compare elements in the current partition to the elements of the next one:

```
Current Partition __     __ Next Partition
                    I     I
                    V     V
                  4 3 2 1 8 7 6 5 x
                  L_I L_I L_I
```

The loop-over partitions appear below (note that when we're done with each partition, we decrement the partition size):

```
Sub Form_Load ()

    Dim Array(9) As Integer

    Array(1) = 9
    Array(2) = 8
    Array(3) = 7
    Array(4) = 6
    Array(5) = 5
    Array(6) = 4
    Array(7) = 3
    Array(8) = 2
    Array(9) = 1

    Print " i" ; Tab(20) ; "Array(i)"
    Print "---" ; Tab(20) ; "--------"
    For i = 1 To 9
```

```
      Print i ; Tab(20) ; Array(i)
   Next i
   Print
   Print "Sorting..."

      NumItems% = Ubound(Array, 1)
      PartitionSize% = Int((NumItems% + 1) / 2)

      Do
—>      NumPartitions% = (NumItems% + 1) / PartitionSize%
—>      Low% = 1
—>      For i = 1 To NumPartitions% - 1
            :
            :
—>      Next i
—>      PartitionSize% = PartitionSize% - 1
      Loop While PartitionSize% > 0
      :
      :
```

Finally, we have to loop over each element in the current partition, comparing it to the corresponding element in the next partition:

```
        |       |
        v       v
    4 3 2 1 8 7 6 5 x
    └─┘  └─┘  └─┘
```

This is the element-by-element comparison. We'll go from Array(Low%) to Array(High%) in the current partition, where Low% is the array index at the beginning of this partition and High% is the index of the element at the end, comparing each element to the corresponding one in the next partition:

```
Sub Form_Load ()

   Dim Array(9) As Integer

   Array(1) = 9
   Array(2) = 8
   Array(3) = 7
   Array(4) = 6
   Array(5) = 5
   Array(6) = 4
```

```
        Array(7) = 3
        Array(8) = 2
        Array(9) = 1

        Print " i" ; Tab(20) ; "Array(i)"
        Print "---" ; Tab(20) ; "--------"
        For i = 1 To 9
            Print i ; Tab(20) ; Array(i)
        Next i
        Print
        Print "Sorting..."

                NumItems% = Ubound(Array, 1)
                PartitionSize% = Int((NumItems% + 1) / 2)

                Do
                    NumPartitions% = (NumItems% + 1) / PartitionSize%
                    Low% = 1
                    For i = 1 To NumPartitions% - 1
                       High% = Low% + PartitionSize% - 1
                       If High% > NumItems% - PartitionSize% Then
                         High% =
                           NumItems% - PartitionSize%
      —>             For j = Low% To High%
      —>                 If Array(j) > Array(j + PartitionSize%)
                           Then
                              :
                              :
      —>                 End If
                      Next j
                      Low% = Low% + PartitionSize%
                    Next i
                    PartitionSize% = PartitionSize% - 1
                Loop While PartitionSize% > 0
                    :
                    :
```

If it turns out that the element in the later partition is smaller than the element in the current one, we have to swap them, which we can do this way:

```
Sub Form_Load ()

    Dim Array(9) As Integer
```

```
Array(1) = 9
Array(2) = 8
Array(3) = 7
Array(4) = 6
Array(5) = 5
Array(6) = 4
Array(7) = 3
Array(8) = 2
Array(9) = 1

Print " i" ; Tab(20) ; "Array(i)"
Print "---" ; Tab(20) ; "--------"
For i = 1 To 9
    Print i ; Tab(20) ; Array(i)
Next i
Print
Print "Sorting..."

        NumItems% = Ubound(Array, 1)
        PartitionSize% = Int((NumItems% + 1) / 2)

        Do
            NumPartitions% = (NumItems% + 1) / PartitionSize%
            Low% = 1
            For i = 1 To NumPartitions% - 1
                High% = Low% + PartitionSize% - 1
                If High% > NumItems% - PartitionSize% Then
                    High% =
                     NumItems% - PartitionSize%
                For j = Low% To High%
                    If Array(j) > Array(j + PartitionSize%)
                    Then
—>                      Temp% = Array(j)
—>                      Array(j) = Array(j + PartitionSize%)
—>                      Array(j + PartitionSize%) = Temp%
                    End If
                Next j
                Low% = Low% + PartitionSize%
            Next i
            PartitionSize% = PartitionSize% - 1
        Loop While PartitionSize% > 0
        :
        :
```

And that's all there is to it. We loop over partition sizes, over each partition, and over each element in the current partition, swapping it with its counterpart in the next partition if necessary. At the end, we can print out the newly-sorted array. Here's the whole program:

```
Sub Form_Load ()

    Dim Array(9) As Integer

    Array(1) = 9
    Array(2) = 8
    Array(3) = 7
    Array(4) = 6
    Array(5) = 5
    Array(6) = 4
    Array(7) = 3
    Array(8) = 2
    Array(9) = 1

    Print " i" ; Tab(20) ; "Array(i)"
    Print "---" ; Tab(20) ; "--------"
    For i = 1 To 9
        Print i ; Tab(20) ; Array(i)
    Next i
    Print
    Print "Sorting..."

            NumItems% = Ubound(Array, 1)
            PartitionSize% = Int((NumItems% + 1) / 2)

            Do
                NumPartitions% = (NumItems% + 1) / PartitionSize%
                Low% = 1
                For i = 1 To NumPartitions% - 1
                    High% = Low% + PartitionSize% - 1
                    If High% > NumItems% - PartitionSize% Then
                        High% =
                        NumItems% - PartitionSize%
                    For j = Low% To High%
                        If Array(j) > Array(j + PartitionSize%)
                        Then
                        Temp% = Array(j)
                        Array(j) = Array(j + PartitionSize%)
```

```
                    Array(j + PartitionSize%) = Temp%
                End If
            Next j
            Low% = Low% + PartitionSize%
        Next i
        PartitionSize% = PartitionSize% - 1
    Loop While PartitionSize% > 0

    Print
    Print " i" ; Tab(20) ; "Array(i)"
    Print "---" ; Tab(20) ; "--------"
    For i = 1 To 9
        Print i ; Tab(20) ; Array(i)
    Next i
End Sub
```

The results of this program are shown in Figure 8-3.

Figure 8-3 Shell Sort Example

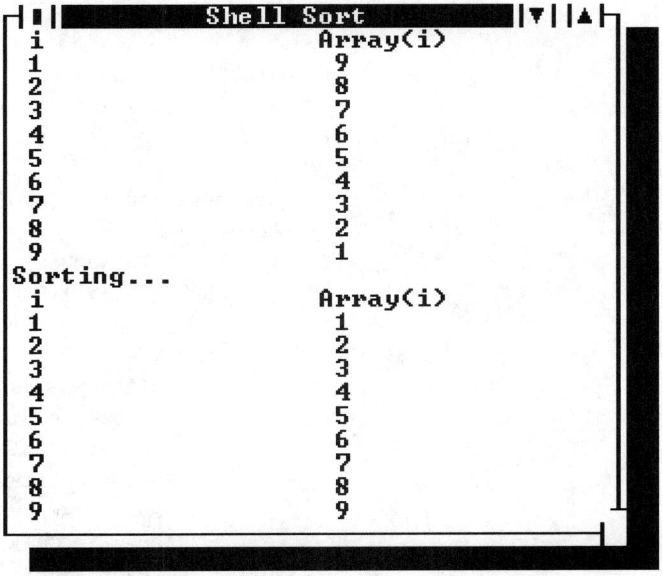

We can even do the same thing for two dimensional arrays. In that case, we simply sort the array on one of its columns. For example, we can adapt the above program to handle a two-dimensional array by adding a column index (Col%) to Array( ), as shown below:

313

```
Sub Form_Load ()

    Dim Array(9, 4) As Integer

    Array(1, 1) = 9
    Array(2, 1) = 8
    Array(3, 1) = 7
    Array(4, 1) = 6
    Array(5, 1) = 5
    Array(6, 1) = 4
    Array(7, 1) = 3
    Array(8, 1) = 2
    Array(9, 1) = 1

    Print " i" ; Tab(20) ; "Array(i,1)"
    Print "--" ; Tab(20) ; "--------"
    For i = 1 To 9
        Print i ; Tab(20) ; Array(i, 1)
    Next i
    Print
    Print "Sorting..."

        NumItems% = Ubound(Array, 1)
        PartitionSize% = Int((NumItems% + 1) / 2)
  —>   Col% = 1
        Do
            NumPartitions% = (NumItems% + 1) / PartitionSize%
            Low% = 1
            For i = 1 To NumPartitions% - 1
                High% = Low% + PartitionSize% - 1
                If High% > NumItems% - PartitionSize% Then
                  High% =
                    NumItems% - PartitionSize%
                For j = Low% To High%
  —>           If Array(j, Col%) > Array(j +
                    PartitionSize%, Col%) Then
                    Temp% = Array(j, Col%)
                    Array(j, Col%) = Array(j +
                        PartitionSize%, Col%)
                    Array(j + PartitionSize%, Col%) = Temp%
                End If
                Next j
                Low% = Low% + PartitionSize%
            Next i
```

```
                    PartitionSize% = PartitionSize% - 1
             Loop While PartitionSize% > 0

        Print
        Print " i" ; Tab(20) ; "Array(i,1)"
        Print "--" ; Tab(20) ; "----------"
        For i = 1 To 9
            Print i ; Tab(20) ; Array(i, 1)
        Next i
```

And now we're able to sort two dimensional arrays on a specified
column. That concludes our tour of shell sorts. Let's turn to QuickSorts
next.

Quicksorts

TIP: *An algorithm
sometimes chosen
is to take three values
from the array and use
the middle value as
the key.*

B esides shell sorts, another popular sorting algorithm is the
Quicksort. That sorting routine works as follows: first we find a
key, or test, value to compare values to. The best value here would
be the median value of the elements of the array, but in practice, a
random entry is usually chosen. Here, we'll choose a value from the
center of the array.

Then we divide the array into two partitions: those less than the test
value, and those greater. We move upwards in the array until we come
to the first value that is greater than the test value, and down the array
(starting from the end) until we find a number less than the test value.
Then we swap them. We keep going until all the numbers in the first
partition are less than the test value, and all the numbers in the
second partition are greater.

Next, we do the same thing to each partition: we select a new test
value from each partition and break that partition into two *new*
partitions. One of those new partitions holds the numbers that are less
than that test value, while the other holds those greater. We keep
going in that way, splitting partitions continuously until there are just
two numbers in a partition—at which point we compare and switch
them if necessary.

You may have noticed that each subsequent step is itself a QuickSort;
that is, to start, we divide the array into two partitions, less than and
greater than the test value, then take each partition and break *it* into

TIP: *If the term*
recursion is new to
you, you should know
that it just refers to a
routine that calls itself.
If a programming task
can be divided into a
number of identical
levels, it can be dealt
with recursively — each
time the routine calls
itself, it deals with a
deeper level. After the
final level is reached,
control returns through
each successive level
back to the beginning.

two partitions depending on a new test value, and so on. In this way, QuickSorts lend themselves easily to recursion, and which is the way they're usually coded. And, since Visual Basic supports recursion, the QuickSort we'll develop here is no exception. Let's see how this looks in code.

Since this routine is recursive, we will set up a subprogram called SortQuick( ) to call from the main program (this subprogram will call itself repeatedly—i.e., recursively):

```
Call SortQuick(Array(), SortFrom%, SortTo%)
```

We just pass the array name to sort, the index to start sorting from (SortFrom%) and the index to sort to (SortTo%); working this way will be useful when we have to sort a particular partition in the array. In SortQuick( ), we first handle the final case—that is, a partition of only two elements:

```
Sub SortQuick (Array() As Integer, SortFrom%, SortTo%)
      If SortFrom% >= SortTo% Then Exit Sub
      If SortFrom% + 1 = SortTo% Then   'Final case
          If Array(SortFrom%) > Array(SortTo%) Then
              Temp% = Array(SortFrom%)
              Array(SortFrom%) = Array(SortTo%)
              Array(SortTo%) = Temp%
          End If
        :
        :
```

In this case, we just compare each element to its neighbor (the only other element in this partition) and swap them if needed. That's all there is to the final case in the Quicksort algorithm.

If the partition size is greater than two, however, we have to sort the values from Array(SortFrom%) to Array(SortTo%) according to a test value, dividing the elements into two new partitions, and then call SortQuick( ) again on each new partition. Let's see how that works. First, we pick a test value, then we divide the present partition into two partitions on the basis of it.

We start by moving up from the bottom of the partition, swapping any values that we find are greater than the test value:

```
Sub SortQuick (Array() As Integer, SortFrom%, SortTo%)
```

```
If SortFrom% >= SortTo% Then Exit Sub
If SortFrom% + 1 = SortTo% Then   'Final case
    If Array(SortFrom%) > Array(SortTo%) Then
        Temp% = Array(SortFrom%)
        Array(SortFrom%) = Array(SortTo%)
        Array(SortTo%) = Temp%
    End If

Else    'Have to split problem
    AtRandom = (SortFrom% + SortTo%) \ 2
    Test = Array(AtRandom)
        Temp% = Array(AtRandom)
        Array(AtRandom) = Array(SortTo%)
        Array(SortTo%) = Temp%

—> Do
    :       'Split into two partitions
    :
    :       For i = SortFrom% To SortTo% - 1
    :               If Array(i) > Test Then Exit For
    :       Next i
    :               :
    :               :
    :       If i < j Then
    :           Temp% = Array(i)
    :           Array(i) = Array(j)
    :           Array(j) = Temp%
    :       End If
    :
—> Loop UNTIL i >= j
        :
        :
```

And we also scan from the top of the partition down in the same loop,
looking for the first value that's smaller than the test value:

```
Sub SortQuick (Array() As Integer, SortFrom%, SortTo%)

        If SortFrom% >= SortTo% Then Exit Sub
        If SortFrom% + 1 = SortTo% Then   'Final case
            If Array(SortFrom%) > Array(SortTo%) Then
                Temp% = Array(SortFrom%)
                Array(SortFrom%) = Array(SortTo%)
                Array(SortTo%) = Temp%
            End If
```

```
    Else      'Have to split problem
        AtRandom = (SortFrom% + SortTo%) \ 2
        Test = Array(AtRandom)
            Temp% = Array(AtRandom)
            Array(AtRandom) = Array(SortTo%)
            Array(SortTo%) = Temp%

        Do
            'Split into two partitions

            For i = SortFrom% To SortTo% - 1
                    If Array(i) > Test Then Exit For
            Next i

—>          For j = SortTo% To i + 1 Step -1
—>                  If Array(j) < Test Then Exit For
—>          Next j

            If i < j Then
                Temp% = Array(i)
                Array(i) = Array(j)
                Array(j) = Temp%
            End If

        Loop UNTIL i >= j
            :
            :
```

We keep going until i and j meet, at which time we've created our two new partitions. Next we can call SortQuick( ) again for each of the resulting partitions (which may be of unequal size):

```
Sub SortQuick (Array() As Integer, SortFrom%, SortTo%)

        If SortFrom% >= SortTo% Then Exit Sub
        If SortFrom% + 1 = SortTo% Then    'Final case
            If Array(SortFrom%) > Array(SortTo%) Then
                Temp% = Array(SortFrom%)
                Array(SortFrom%) = Array(SortTo%)
                Array(SortTo%) = Temp%
            End If
        Else      'Have to split problem
```

```
                 AtRandom = (SortFrom% + SortTo%) \ 2
                 Test = Array(AtRandom)
                     Temp% = Array(AtRandom)
                     Array(AtRandom) = Array(SortTo%)
                     Array(SortTo%) = Temp%
             Do
                     For i = SortFrom% To SortTo% - 1
                             If Array(i) > Test Then Exit For
                     Next i

                     For j = SortTo% To i + 1 Step -1
                             If Array(j) < Test Then Exit For
                     Next j

                     If i < j Then
                         Temp% = Array(i)
                         Array(i) = Array(j)
                         Array(j) = Temp%
                     End If

             Loop Until i >= j

                         Temp% = Array(i)
                         Array(i) = Array(SortTo%)
                         Array(SortTo%) = Temp%

    —>      Call SortQuick(Array(), SortFrom%, i - 1)
    —>      Call SortQuick(Array(), i + 1, SortTo%)
         End If
End Sub
```

And that's all there is to it; the sort will continue recursively until we get down to the final case of a partition size of 1, the final swaps will be done if necessary, and then we're finished. Here's the whole thing:

```
Sub Form_Load ()
    Dim Array(9) As Integer

    Array(1) = 9
    Array(2) = 8
    Array(3) = 7
    Array(4) = 6
    Array(5) = 5
    Array(6) = 4
```

```
                    Array(7) = 3
                    Array(8) = 2
                    Array(9) = 1


                    Print " i" ; Tab(20) ; "Array(i)"
                    Print "---" ; Tab(20) ; "--------"
                    For i = 1 To 9
                            Print i; Tab(20) ; Array(i)
                    Next i

                    Call SortQuick(Array(), 1, UBound(Array, 1))

                    Print
                    Print "Sorting..."
                    Print
                    Print " i" ; Tab(20) ; "Array(i)"
                    Print "---" ; Tab(20) ; "--------"
                    For i = 1 To 9
                            Print i; Tab(20) ; Array(i)
                    Next i

        End Sub

        Sub SortQuick (Array() As Integer, SortFrom%, SortTo%)

                    If SortFrom% >= SortTo% Then Exit Sub
                    If SortFrom% + 1 = SortTo% Then   'Final case
                        If Array(SortFrom%) > Array(SortTo%) Then
                            Temp% = Array(SortFrom%)
                            Array(SortFrom%) = Array(SortTo%)
                            Array(SortTo%) = Temp%
                        End If
                    Else      'Have to split problem
                        AtRandom = (SortFrom% + SortTo%) \ 2
                        Test = Array(AtRandom)
                            Temp% = Array(AtRandom)
                            Array(AtRandom) = Array(SortTo%)
                            Array(SortTo%) = Temp%


                        Do

                            For i = SortFrom% To SortTo% - 1
                                    If Array(i) > Test Then Exit For
                            Next i
```

```
                    For j = SortTo% To i + 1 Step -1
                            If Array(j) < Test Then Exit For
                    Next j

                    If i < j Then
                        Temp% = Array(i)
                        Array(i) = Array(j)
                        Array(j) = Temp%
                    End If

            Loop Until i >= j

                    Temp% = Array(i)
                    Array(i) = Array(SortTo%)
                    Array(SortTo%) = Temp%

            Call SortQuick(Array(), SortFrom%, i - 1)
            Call SortQuick(Array(), i + 1, SortTo%)

        End If
End Sub
```

That's it for sorting. Both the shell sort and the Quicksort are pretty fast—the one you should use will depend on your application; you might want to try them both and use the faster of the two.

Searching Your Data

Now that we've ordered our data, it becomes much easier to search through. If the data is unordered, we'd have no choice but to simply check one value after another until we found a match, as in the following example program:

```
Sub Form_Load ()

    'Unordered Search

    Dim Array(9) As Integer

    Array(1) = 9
    Array(2) = 7
```

```
Array(3) = 8
Array(4) = 3
Array(5) = 5
Array(6) = 4
Array(7) = 6
Array(8) = 2
Array(9) = 1

Print "Searching the unordered list for the value 1."

For i = 1 To Ubound(Array,1)
        If Array(i) = 1 Then
                Print "Value of 1 in element";i
        End If
Next i
```

End Sub

We just keep scanning up the list of values until we find what we're looking for. On the other hand, we can be more intelligent when searching a sorted list. For example, if our sorted array had these values in it:

1 2 3 4 5 6 7 8 9 10 11 12 13 14 15

and we were searching for the entry with 10 in it, we could start off in the center of the list:

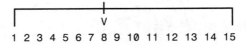

Since 10 is greater than 8, we divide the *upper* half of the array in two and check the mid point again:

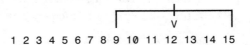

Since the value we're looking for, 10, is less than 12, we move *down* and cut the remaining distance in half:

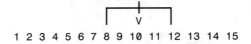

And in this way, we've zeroed in on our number, cutting down the number of values we have to check. Let's see how this looks in a program. First, we set up our array. In the following example, let's search an array of 9 elements for the entry with 8 in it:

```
Sub Form_Load()

    'Ordered Search

    Dim Array(9) As Integer

    Array(1) = 1
    Array(2) = 2
    Array(3) = 3
    Array(4) = 4
    Array(5) = 5
    Array(6) = 6
    Array(7) = 7
    Array(8) = 8
    Array(9) = 9

—> SearchValue% = 8
—> Print "Searching the ordered list for the value 8."
     :
     :
```

Now we cut the array into two partitions and check the test value which is right between them, at position TestIndex%:

```
Sub Form_Load ()

    'Ordered Search

    Dim Array(9) As Integer

    Array(1) = 1
    Array(2) = 2
    Array(3) = 3
    Array(4) = 4
    Array(5) = 5
    Array(6) = 6
    Array(7) = 7
    Array(8) = 8
    Array(9) = 9
```

```
       SearchValue% = 8
       Print "Searching the ordered list for the value 8."

—> Partition% = (Ubound(Array, 1) + 1) \ 2
—> TestIndex% = Partition%
            :
            :
```

Then we need to start searching. We will keep looping over partition size—if the partition size becomes 0 without success, then the value we're looking for isn't in the array:

```
Sub Form_Load ()

    'Ordered Search

    Dim Array(9) As Integer

    Array(1) = 1
    Array(2) = 2
    Array(3) = 3
    Array(4) = 4
    Array(5) = 5
    Array(6) = 6
    Array(7) = 7
    Array(8) = 8
    Array(9) = 9

    SearchValue% = 8
    Print "Searching the ordered list for the value 8."

    Partition% = (Ubound(Array, 1) + 1) \ 2
    TestIndex% = Partition%

—> Do
—>     Partition% = Partition% \ 2
            :
        Search this partition
            :
—> Loop While Partition% > 0
    :
    :
```

Let's first check to see whether we've found our value—and if so, we can quit:

```
Sub Form_Load ()

    'Ordered Search

    Dim Array(9) As Integer

    Array(1) = 1
    Array(2) = 2
    Array(3) = 3
    Array(4) = 4
    Array(5) = 5
    Array(6) = 6
    Array(7) = 7
    Array(8) = 8
    Array(9) = 9

    SearchValue% = 8
    Print "Searching the ordered list for the value 8."

    Partition% = (Ubound(Array, 1) + 1) \ 2
    TestIndex% = Partition%

    Do
        Partition% = Partition% \ 2
—>      If Array(TestIndex%) = SearchValue% Then
—>          Print "Value of"; SearchValue%; "in element";
                TestIndex%
—>          Exit Do
—>      End If
                :
                :
    Loop While Partition% > 0
    :
    :
```

If we haven't found our value, we have to go on to the next iteration of the loop, setting TestIndex% to the middle of either the higher or lower partition, and then dividing that partition into two new partitions. If the search value is bigger than the value at our current location in the array, we want to move to the partition at higher values, as follows:

```
Sub Form_Load ()

    'Ordered Search

    Dim Array(9) As Integer

    Array(1) = 1
    Array(2) = 2
    Array(3) = 3
    Array(4) = 4
    Array(5) = 5
    Array(6) = 6
    Array(7) = 7
    Array(8) = 8
    Array(9) = 9

    SearchValue% = 8
    Print "Searching the ordered list for the value 8."

    Partition% = (Ubound(Array, 1) + 1) \ 2
    TestIndex% = Partition%

    Do
        Partition% = Partition% \ 2
        If Array(TestIndex%) = SearchValue% Then
            Print "Value of"; SearchValue%; "in element";
                TestIndex%
            Exit Do
        End If
—>      If Array(TestIndex%) < SearchValue% Then
—>          TestIndex% = TestIndex% + Partition%
                :
                :
    Loop While Partition% > 0
        :
        :
```

But if the search value is smaller, on the other hand, we want to move to the lower partition (which holds lower values), as follows:

```
Sub Form_Load ()

    'Ordered Search
```

```
Dim Array(9) As Integer

Array(1) = 1
Array(2) = 2
Array(3) = 3
Array(4) = 4
Array(5) = 5
Array(6) = 6
Array(7) = 7
Array(8) = 8
Array(9) = 9

SearchValue% = 8
Print "Searching the ordered list for the value 8."

Partition% = (Ubound(Array, 1) + 1) \ 2
TestIndex% = Partition%

Do
    Partition% = Partition% \ 2
    If Array(TestIndex%) = SearchValue% Then
        Print "Value of"; SearchValue%; "in element";
            TestIndex%
        Exit Do
    End If
    If Array(TestIndex%) < SearchValue% Then
        TestIndex% = TestIndex% + Partition%
—>  Else
—>      TestIndex% = TestIndex% - Partition%
—>  End If
  Loop While Partition% > 0
    :
```

And that's almost all there is to do. We just keep going until we find
what we're looking for, or the partition size becomes 0, in which case
it's not there.

If we were unsuccessful, however, there are two remaining tests that
we should apply: we should check the value we're searching for
against the very first and last entries in the array. That is, our algorithm demands that all numbers that it checks be *straddled* by two

other values and that is true of every element in the array except for the first and last ones. This means that if we didn't find what we were looking for, we have to check these last two values explicitly:

```
Sub Form_Load ()

    'Ordered Search

    Dim Array(9) As Integer

    Array(1) = 1
    Array(2) = 2
    Array(3) = 3
    Array(4) = 4
    Array(5) = 5
    Array(6) = 6
    Array(7) = 7
    Array(8) = 8
    Array(9) = 9

    SearchValue% = 8
    Print "Searching the ordered list for the value 8."

    Partition% = (Ubound(Array, 1) + 1) \ 2
    TestIndex% = Partition%

Do
    Partition% = Partition% \ 2
    If Array(TestIndex%) = SearchValue% Then
        Print "Value of"; SearchValue%; "in element";
            TestIndex%
        Exit Do
    End If
    If Array(TestIndex%) < SearchValue% Then
        TestIndex% = TestIndex% + Partition%
    Else
        TestIndex% = TestIndex% - Partition%
    End If
Loop While Partition% > 0

'Can only find straddled numbers, so add these tests:
```

```
—>      If Array(1) = SearchValue% Then
:           Print "Value of"; SearchValue%; "in element 1"
:       End If
:
:       If Array(Ubound(Array, 1)) = SearchValue% Then
:           Print "Value of"; SearchValue%; "in element";
:               Ubound(Array, 1)
—>      End If
End Sub
```

And we're done with the ordered search; the result of this program appears in Figure 8-4, and the full program is in Listing 8-1.

Figure 8-4 Ordered Search Example

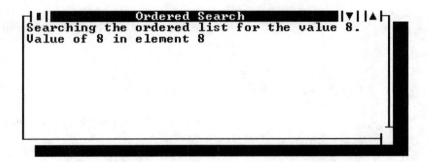

Listing 8-1 Ordered Search Example

```
Sub Form_Load ()

    'Ordered Search

    Dim Array(9) As Integer

    Array(1) = 1
    Array(2) = 2
    Array(3) = 3
    Array(4) = 4
    Array(5) = 5
    Array(6) = 6
    Array(7) = 7
    Array(8) = 8
    Array(9) = 9
```

continues

Listing 8-1 continued

```
SearchValue% = 8
Print "Searching the ordered list for the value 8."

Partition% = (Ubound(Array, 1) + 1) \ 2
TestIndex% = Partition%

Do
    Partition% = Partition% \ 2
    If Array(TestIndex%) = SearchValue% Then
        Print "Value of"; SearchValue%; "in element";
          TestIndex%
        Exit Do
    End If
    If Array(TestIndex%) < SearchValue% Then
        TestIndex% = TestIndex% + Partition%
    Else
        TestIndex% = TestIndex% - Partition%
    End If
Loop While Partition% > 0

'Can only find straddled numbers, so add these tests:

    If Array(1) = SearchValue% Then
        Print "Value of"; SearchValue%; "in element 1"
    End If

    If Array(Ubound(Array, 1)) = SearchValue% Then
        Print "Value of"; SearchValue%; "in element";
          Ubound(Array, 1)
    End If
End Sub
```

That's all there is to data handling and sorting. We've seen most of the popular ways of handling numeric data in this chapter. When we're designing code, it's always important to organize our data correctly—as mentioned earlier, that can be half the battle of writing a program. Next, let's see how to debug our programs and handle errors.

Error Handling and Debugging

Errors occur even for the best programmers. In fact, the longer the program and the more complex the code, the more likely errors are to appear. Errors come in several different types: those that cause design-time errors, those that cause run-time errors, and those that make your programs produce incorrect or unexpected results (bugs). Visual Basic handles the first type, design-time errors, by refusing to run programs until they're fixed, and Visual Basic usually offers some assistance in the form of help and help messages. The second two types are up to the user to correct. This chapter is about run-time errors and bugs.

A run-time error is what Visual Basic refers to as a *trappable error*— VB recognizes that there was an error and allows you to "trap" it, taking some corrective action if it occurs (untrappable errors usually only occur at design time). Bugs are different, because Visual Basic usually doesn't recognize that there's a problem, but the code still doesn't operate as intended. For example, if you had a function called Counter that was supposed to increment an internal counter and return its current value every time it was called, it might look like this:

```
Function Counter()
    Dim counter_value As Integer

    counter_value = counter_value + 1

    Counter = counter_value
End Function
```

There is a bug here: counter_value is not declared Static, so every time this function is called, counter_value starts at 0; the function adds 1 to it and returns that value, so the value returned is 1 every time. A function that simply returns 1 every time it is called does not generate a run-time error, but in the light of its intended purpose, it is a bug.

We'll be able to find trappable errors without difficulty, because Visual Basic generates them, knows exactly when they occur, and allows us to take some action. However, bugs are another story. In their case, we'll have to use VB's debugging capabilities to find out what went wrong, working our way through the program slowly, possibly even statement by statement. These skills are necessary for programmers, however, especially those who want to produce real applications that are subject to strict testing. And that will be our first topic—how to test the programs we write.

How To Test Programs

When programs run, they usually operate on ranges of data; for example, a program may read the value of an unsigned integer from the user, and that value can range from 0 to 65,535 (i.e., if the value couldn't vary, there would be no point in reading it in). The limits of that value, 0 and 65,535, are called its *bounds*. When you're trying to check your programs for potential problems, it's important that you cover the whole allowed range of such values. That doesn't normally mean checking every value between 0 and 65,535, but it does mean checking values at the bounds of this range, as well as some mid-range values, and any other values that are likely to give you problems.

For example, this value may represent the number of students in a class, and, having summed all their test scores, we would like to divide by this value to find the class average. There may be no problem for 15 or 20 students, but what if the user enters a value of 0? Even though it's in the allowed range for unsigned integers, dividing by 0 will result in an error. Or, what if we stored the students' test scores in another unsigned integer and found that as we went towards higher numbers of students, the division didn't give us the accuracy we want? Checking a program's bounding values like this is vitally important; generally, there will be bounds for every crucial variable, and you should check all combinations of these values when you run your program to see how they interact (this is particularly important when it comes to array indices).

Of course, you should check mid-range values as well. It may turn out that some combination of such values gives you unexpected errors as well. The longer you test your program under both usual and unusual operating circumstances, the more confidence you'll have in it. As programs get more complex, the testing period usually gets longer and longer, which is why major software companies often send out hundreds—or thousands—of preliminary versions of their software (called beta versions) for testing by programmers (the final software package is usually the gamma version).

In addition, you should attempt to duplicate every run-time problem that may occur to see how your program will react. File operations are great at generating such errors—for example, what if the disk is full and you try to write to it? What if the specified input file doesn't exist? What if the specified file to write is already read-only? What if the disk has been removed? What if the user asks you to write record –15 in a file? It's hard to generate every conceivable set of problematic circumstances, of course, but the closer you come, the more polished your application will be.

However, Visual Basic is helpful when it comes to certain types of errors, called trappable errors. Let's take a look at how to handle them first.

Handling Run-Time Errors

We already placed some error checking in our Pad program, because file handling is such a notorious source of possible errors (as is handling input from the keyboard). For example, if we asked the Pad to read a file on a disk that has been removed, we would get a message box like the one in Figure 9-1, informing us that there's been a file error. Because we were able to intercept that kind of error, let's reexamine how we did it.

Figure 9-1 The Pad Application's File Error Message

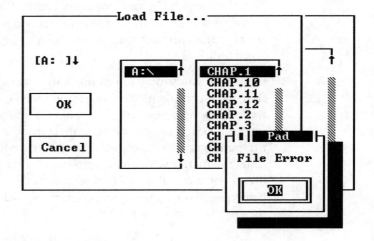

The On Error Goto Statement

The way to trap trappable errors is with an On Error Goto statement. For example, here is how we did it in the Pad application:

```
Sub OKButton_Click ()
—>    On Local Error Goto FileError

      If (Right$(Dir1.Path, 1) = "\") Then        'Get file name
          Filename$ = Dir1.Path + File1.FileName
      Else
          Filename$ = Dir1.Path + "\" + File1.FileName
      End If

      Open Filename$ For Input As # 1              'Open file
```

```
            Pad.PadText.Text = Input$(LOF(1), # 1)      'Read file in

            Close # 1                      'Close file
            LoadForm.Hide                  'Hide dialog box

            Exit Sub

—>     FileError:
            MsgBox "File Error", 0, "Pad"     'MsgBox for file error.
            Resume
        End Sub
```

When Visual Basic generates a trappable error after executing a similar
statement in a procedure, control jumps to the specified label—in our
case, that's FileError. That is exactly what the Goto statement does—it
transfers controls to a new location in the program. The general form
for such a procedure is as follows:

```
        Sub Name ()
            On [Local] Error Goto ErrorLabel
                 :
                 :

            Exit Sub

        ErrorLabel:
             :
             :

        End Sub
```

We use the Local keyword when we're dealing with a form, because we
can define only procedure-level error handlers in forms. In code-only
modules, however, you can use the On Error Goto statement (note no
Local keyword) to handle all the procedures in the module.

In the preceding procedure, we execute the On [Local] Error Goto
statement first, setting up our error-handling routine; note also that
we exit the Sub procedure before reaching that routine so that we do
not inadvertently execute the error-handling code. In this way, the
procedure is set up much like a procedure that has subroutines, which

are handled with the GoSub statement in Visual Basic just as they are in other forms of Basic—that is, as follows:

```
Sub Name ()
        :
    GoSub Label1
        :

    Exit Sub

Label1
      :
      :
    Return
End Sub
```

Note that since the code in an error-handling routine (as well as the code in a GoSub subroutine) is in the same Sub or Function procedure, it shares all the variables of the rest of the Sub or Function procedure. That means that we'll have access to variables that may be valuable to us in fixing the error.

We also can override On [Local] Error Goto statements with later statements of the same kind; this is useful if we've entered a different part of the code, with different potential errors, and want to use a different error handler. However, we haven't done much here; we've only recognized the fact that an error occurred. The next step must be to find out what the error was and then to take action if possible.

The Err and Erl Functions

In order to determine what error occurred, we can use the Err function, which returns an error number. These error numbers are predefined in Visual Basic. The most common ones appear in Table 9-1. Note that it includes such items as array subscripts out of bounds, division by zero, file not found, disk full (a very common file-writing error) and other errors—all these represent trappable errors that you can catch with some possibility of correcting them.

Table 9-1 Common Trappable Errors

Error Number	Means
1	NEXT without FOR
2	Syntax error
3	Return without GOSUB
4	Out of DATA
5	Illegal function call
6	Overflow
7	Out of memory
8	Label NOT defined
9	Subscript out of range
10	Duplicate definition
11	Division by zero
12	Illegal in direct mode
13	TYPE mismatch
14	Out of string space
16	String formula too complex
17	Can't continue
18	FUNCTION not defined
19	No Resume
20	Resume without error
24	Device timeout
25	Device fault
26	FOR without NEXT
27	Out of paper
28	Out of stack space
29	WHILE without WEND
30	WEND without WHILE

continues

Table 9-1 continued

Error Number	Means
33	Duplicate Label
35	SUB or FUNCTION not defined
37	Argument-count mismatch
38	Array NOT defined
40	Variable required
48	Error in loading DLL
50	FIELD overflow
51	Internal error
52	Bad file name or number
53	File NOT found
54	Bad file mode
55	File already open
56	FIELD statement active
57	Device I/O error
58	File already exists
59	Bad record length
61	Disk full
62	Input past end of file
63	Bad record number
64	Bad file name
67	Too many files
68	Device unavailable
69	Communication-buffer overflow
70	Permission denied
71	Disk NOT ready
72	Disk-media error

Error Number	Means
73	Feature unavailable
74	Can't rename with different drive
75	Path/File access error
76	Path NOT found
80	Feature removed
81	ISAM - Invalid name
82	ISAM - Table not found
83	ISAM - Index not found
84	ISAM - Invalid column
85	ISAM - No current record
86	ISAM - Duplicate value for unique index
87	ISAM - Invalid operation on NULL index
88	ISAM - Database inconsistent
89	ISAM - Insufficient ISAM buffers
260	No timer available
271	Invalid screen mode
272	Invalid when forms are showing
340	Control array element does not exist
341	Invalid object array index
342	Not enough room to allocate control array
343	Object not an array
344	Must specify index for object array
345	Reached limit: cannot create any more controls for this form
361	Can't load or unload this object
362	Can't unload controls created at design time
363	Custom control 'item' not found

continues

Table 9-1 continued

Error Number	Means
364	Object was unloaded
365	Unable to unload within this context
380	Invalid property value
381	Invalid property array index
382	Property can't be set at run-time
383	Property is read-only
384	Property can't be modified when form is minimized or maximized
385	Must specify index when using property array
386	Property not available at run-time
387	Property can't be set on this control
388	Can't set Visible property from a parent menu
400	Form already displayed; can't show form modally
401	Can't show nonmodal form when a modal form is being displayed
402	Must close or hide topmost modal form first
410	Property can't be modified on MDI form
420	Invalid object reference
421	Method not applicable for this object
422	Property NOT found
423	Property or control not found
424	Object required
425	Invalid object use
430	No currently active control
431	No currently active form
480	Can't create AutoRedraw image

Let's update our Pad program so that it can at least indicate what error occurred. To do that, we can use the following statement:

```
Sub OKButton_Click ()
    On Local Error Goto FileError

    If (Right$(Dir1.Path, 1) = "\") Then      'Get file name
        Filename$ = Dir1.Path + File1.FileName
    Else
        Filename$ = Dir1.Path + "\" + File1.FileName
    End If

    Open Filename$ For Input As # 1              'Open file
    Pad.PadText.Text = Input$(LOF(1), # 1)    'Read file in

    Close # 1                       'Close file
    LoadForm.Hide                   'Hide dialog box

    Exit Sub

FileError:
--> MsgBox "File Error" + Str$(Err), 0, "Pad"
    Resume
End Sub
```

We can do this for both saving and loading files; now if we select a file from a disk, remove the disk, and then try to read it, we see that our former error box now displays the message: *File Error 71*, as shown in Figure 9-2. Checking Table 9-1, we see that this error means: Disk Not Ready.

In fact, we can report more information here as well; in particular, we can report the line number that the error occurred in by using the Erl function. This function returns a number that stands for the line number in the current procedure of the statement that caused the error. To use this function, we have to use line numbers (which are no longer standard in BASIC):

```
Sub OKButton_Click ()
1   On Local Error Goto FileError

2   If (Right$(Dir1.Path, 1) = "\") Then          'Get file name
3       Filename$ = Dir1.Path + File1.FileName
4   Else
```

```
5        Filename$ = Dir1.Path + "\" + File1.FileName
6    End If

7    Open Filename$ For Input As # 1           'Open file
8    Pad.PadText.Text = Input$(LOF(1), # 1)    'Read file in

9    Close # 1                      'Close file
10   LoadForm.Hide                  'Hide dialog box

11   Exit Sub

FileError:
12   MsgBox "File Error"+Str$(Err)+" in line "+Str$(Erl), 0,
         "Pad"
13   Resume
End Sub
```

Figure 9-2 Pad Application with Error Number

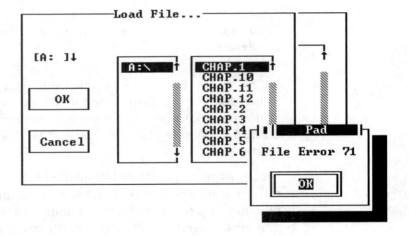

If we cause the same error as before—removing the disk with the file on it—we see a message informing us that the error occurred in line 7, which is the line in which we try to open the file. On the other hand, that information is of very little use to the user; what does it matter what line number the error occurred on? The user would prefer to know what the error was. We can print out the error number, as previously, but that's not necessarily much more help. If the user has no knowledge of Visual Basic or doesn't have the information in Table 9-1, the simple explanation that error 71 occurred is not going to help. However, there is a way to translate that information into English with a simple function. We'll explore that method next.

The Error$ Function

The Error$( ) function is a very useful function when handling errors, because it can translate the error number we get from Err into English. That means that we can change our procedure as follows:

```
Sub OKButton_Click ()
    On Local Error Goto FileError

    If (Right$(Dir1.Path, 1) = "\") Then        'Get file name
        Filename$ = Dir1.Path + File1.FileName
    Else
        Filename$ = Dir1.Path + "\" + File1.FileName
    End If

    Open Filename$ For Input As # 1              'Open file
    Pad.PadText.Text = Input$(LOF(1), # 1)    'Read file in

    Close # 1                     'Close file
    LoadForm.Hide                 'Hide dialog box

    Exit Sub


FileError:
—>    MsgBox Error$(Err), 0, "Pad"
    Resume
End Sub
```

When we run the Pad application with this new error handler (but the same error), we get this message: "Disk not ready," as shown in Figure 9-3. This is a considerable improvement over "File Error 71"—in fact, it's like having Table 9-1 built into your program, ready to be used. In general, this is a much better way to handle errors than printing out the error number, which may be meaningless and frustrating to the user. However, even this message leaves something to be desired: what action is required of the user? Does the user know what device

to use? Indicating the next step is still up to us, and we should design
our error handler around such questions.

Figure 9-3 Pad Application with English Error Message

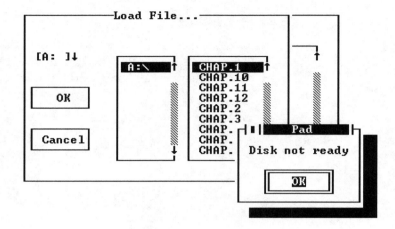

Creating Customized Error Handlers

When creating our own error handler, there's some errors
that we might anticipate occurring more than others,
and we might want to make special provisions for handling
them. For example, if we were writing files, we might anticipate error
61, Disk full. If that error occurred, we could place a message in a
message box with this message in it: "The disk is full. Please delete
some files and click the OK Button." Users might be able to clear some
more disk space (in cases like this, we should also include a Cancel
button in case the user wants to cancel the file-writing operation
instead). Then, after they clicked the OK button, they could go back
and try the operation again, as we'll see soon. Let's see an example of a
custom error handler in code. When we load files, these are some of
the errors (and the messages that Error$( ) will give) that we might
expect:

```
7            Out of memory
57           Device I/O error
61           Disk full
67           Too many files
```

```
68          Device Unavailable
70          Permission denied
71          Disk Not ready
72          Disk-media error
```

We might write our own error handler as follows:

```
Sub OKButton_Click ()
    On Local Error Goto FileError

    If (Right$(Dir1.Path, 1) = "\") Then         'Get file name
        Filename$ = Dir1.Path + File1.FileName
    Else
        Filename$ = Dir1.Path + "\" + File1.FileName
    End If

    Open Filename$ For Input As # 1              'Open file
    Pad.PadText.Text = Input$(LOF(1), # 1)    'Read file in

    Close # 1                      'Close file
    LoadForm.Hide                  'Hide dialog box

    Exit Sub

FileError:
    Msg$ = Error$(Err)
    Select Case Err      'Display our own message?
        Case 7
            Msg$ = "File is too big to open."
        Case 57, 68, 71, 72
            Msg$ = "Please check the disk and try again."
        Case 67
            Msg$ = "Too many files open. Close some and try
                again."
    End Select
—>  MsgBox Msg$, 0, "Pad"
    Resume
End Sub
```

Now, if we produce the same error as before, we'll see the message:
"Please check the disk and try again." as shown in Figure 9-4. In
general, the more information you can provide the user, the better.
(Of course, it's usually better to handle the error internally if at all

possible.) Often, we'll want the user to take some action, and then to click the OK button. When they do, we should retry the operation, such as trying to read in the file again. Let's see how to do that next.

Figure 9-4 Customized Error Message

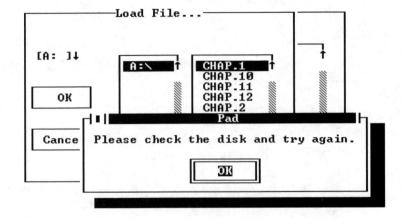

The Resume Statement

Note the line at the end of our error handler:

```
Sub OKButton_Click ()
    On Local Error Goto FileError

    If (Right$(Dir1.Path, 1) = "\") Then        'Get file name
        Filename$ = Dir1.Path + File1.FileName
    Else
        Filename$ = Dir1.Path + "\" + File1.FileName
    End If

    Open Filename$ For Input As # 1              'Open file
    Pad.PadText.Text = Input$(LOF(1), # 1)       'Read file in

    Close # 1                  'Close file
    LoadForm.Hide              'Hide dialog box

    Exit Sub
```

```
        FileError:
            Msg$ = Error$(Err)
            Select Case Err        'Display our own message?
                Case 7
                    Msg$ = "File is too big to open."
                Case 57, 68, 71, 72
                    Msg$ = "Please check the disk and try again."
                Case 67
                    Msg$ = "Too many files open. Close some and try
                        again."
            End Select
            MsgBox Msg$, 0, "Pad"
—>          Resume
        End Sub
```

This simple statement, Resume, will let us retry the operation that caused the error after the user took some corrective action. When Visual Basic encounters a Resume statement in an error handler—i.e., after an On [Local] Error Goto type of routine has been set up and entered (the error trap is said to be active at this point)—it leaves the error handler and returns to the statement that caused the error. In other words, Resume allows us to retry an operation, as follows:

```
Sub OKButton_Click ()
    On Local Error Goto FileError

    If (Right$(Dir1.Path, 1) = "\") Then         'Get file name
        Filename$ = Dir1.Path + File1.FileName
    Else
        Filename$ = Dir1.Path + "\" + File1.FileName
    End If

  > Open Filename$ For Input As # 1                'Open file
    Pad.PadText.Text = Input$(LOF(1), # 1)       'Read file in

    Close # 1                       'Close file
    LoadForm.Hide                   'Hide dialog box

    Exit Sub

FileError:
    Msg$ = Error$(Err)
    Select Case Err        'Display our own message?
```

```
            Case 7
                Msg$ = "File is too big to open."
            Case 57, 68, 71, 72
                Msg$ = "Please check the disk and try again."
            Case 67
                Msg$ = "Too many files open. Close some and try
                   again."
        End Select
        MsgBox Msg$, 0, "Pad"
        Resume
End Sub
```

If we had a problem trying to open the file, we display an error message, let the user take some corrective action, and then try opening the file again. Note, however, that this is a potential problem; if the user decides not to open the file after all, we should provide some way of exiting this Sub procedure. We can do that by using a message box that has two buttons instead of one—that is, a box with both OK and Cancel buttons. We can also read the response in the same statement with the MsgBox( ) function (i.e., you might recall that MsgBox has two forms—as a statement if you expect no reply and as a function if you want input from the user):

```
Response% = MsgBox(Msg$, 1, "Pad")
```

We're passing a message box type parameter of 1 (include both OK and Cancel buttons), and placing the user's reponse in the variable Response%. If they select the OK button, this response will equal 1; if they select the Cancel button, it will equal 2. We can modify our code to retry the problematic operation if the user selected the OK button like this:

```
Sub OKButton_Click ()
    On Local Error Goto FileError

    If (Right$(Dir1.Path, 1) = "\") Then          'Get file name
        Filename$ = Dir1.Path + File1.FileName
    Else
        Filename$ = Dir1.Path + "\" + File1.FileName
    End If

    Open Filename$ For Input As # 1               'Open file
    Pad.PadText.Text = Input$(LOF(1), # 1)     'Read file in

    Close # 1                       'Close file
```

```
            LoadForm.Hide                    'Hide dialog box

            Exit Sub

     FileError:
            Msg$ = Error$(Err)
            Select Case Err       'Display our own message?
                Case 7
                    Msg$ = "File is too big to open."
                Case 57, 68, 71, 72
                    Msg$ = "Please check the disk and try again."
                Case 67
                    Msg$ = "Too many files open. Close some and try
                         again."
            End Select
—>          Response% = MsgBox(Msg$, 1, "Pad")
—>          If Response% = 1 Then Resume
        End Sub
```

In this case, if the user chose OK, we move back to the same line that
caused the error (probably the Open statement) and try it again. On
the other hand, if the user chose the Cancel button, we want to exit
the Sub procedure entirely; to do that, however, it's not enough to rely
on the End Sub statement at the end of the procedure, as we're doing
in the preceding code. If Visual Basic is in an error handler and reaches
the end of the procedure without finding a Resume, it stops everything
and helpfully points out that you have no Resume statement in your
error handler. (It even does this in compiled code, placing a special
"No Resume" window on the screen.)

However, we really don't want to use Resume if the user chose Cancel,
because there are some errors that they can't fix at this level—for
example, if the error was that the file was too big to fit into memory,
they'll have to leave this procedure (OKButton_Click( )), select a new
file, and then select the OK button again. To leave this procedure
without messages about the lack of a Resume statement, we need to
use Exit Sub, like this:

```
Sub OKButton_Click ()
    On Local Error Goto FileError

    If (Right$(Dir1.Path, 1) = "\") Then          'Get file name
        Filename$ = Dir1.Path + File1.FileName
    Else
```

```
              Filename$ = Dir1.Path + "\" + File1.FileName
          End If

          Open Filename$ For Input As # 1              'Open file
          Pad.PadText.Text = Input$(LOF(1), # 1)       'Read file in

          Close # 1                        'Close file
          LoadForm.Hide                    'Hide dialog box

          Exit Sub

      FileError:
          Msg$ = Error$(Err)
          Select Case Err      'Display our own message?
              Case 7
                  Msg$ = "File is too big to open."
              Case 57, 68, 71, 72
                  Msg$ = "Please check the disk and try again."
              Case 67
                  Msg$ = "Too many files open. Close some and try
                      again."
          End Select
          Response% = MsgBox(Msg$, 1, "Pad")
          If Response% = 1 Then
              Resume
—>    Else
—>        Exit Sub
—>    End If
      End Sub
```

This avoids the "No Resume" messages from Visual Basic and fixes the
problem. In fact, there are other ways of handling Resume statements
as well—Visual Basic supports two variations of Resume: Resume Next
and Resume Line #.

Resume Next and Resume Line

Sometimes, you don't want to keep retrying the operation that caused
the error. We've seen that one alternate method is to simply leave the
procedure entirely and let the user select some other action. Two other
methods are Resume Next and Resume Line #. The Resume Next
statement causes Visual Basic to resume with the statement following
the one that caused the error—in effect, we are simply skipping the

statement that produced the problem. This can be useful, but it's usually not good to simply skip a line and then continue executing the rest of the code; for example, if we used Resume Next instead of Resume, and the Open statement had caused the error, we'd continue with the next statement after that, which tries to read from the file that we haven't been able to open:

```
Sub OKButton_Click ()
    On Local Error Goto FileError

    If (Right$(Dir1.Path, 1) = "\") Then          'Get file name
        Filename$ = Dir1.Path + File1.FileName
    Else
        Filename$ = Dir1.Path + "\" + File1.FileName
    End If

    Open Filename$ For Input As # 1                'Open file
    Pad.PadText.Text = Input$(LOF(1), # 1)     'Read file in

    Close # 1                          'Close file
    LoadForm.Hide                      'Hide dialog box

    Exit Sub

FileError:
    Msg$ = Error$(Err)
    Select Case Err      'Display our own message?
        Case 7
            Msg$ = "File is too big to open."
        Case 57, 68, 71, 72
            Msg$ = "Please check the disk and try again."
        Case 67
            Msg$ = "Too many files open. Close some and try
                again."
    End Select
    MsgBox Msg$, 0, "Pad"
    Resume Next
End Sub
```

However, there are times when Resume Next is exactly what we need. Let's see an example of this in code. One common method in Visual Basic of determining whether or not a file exists on disk is to create a deliberate, trappable error. You may recall that in almost all Open modes (e.g., For Random, For Binary, etc.), the file is automatically created if it doesn't already exist. On the other hand, if you open a file For Input, VB generates a trappable error if the file doesn't exist (i.e., it doesn't make sense to create the file from scratch if we're about to read from it). We can use that error to indicate whether or not the file exists. Let's write a function called Exist( ), which takes a file name as its argument and returns True if the file exists and False otherwise:

```
Sub Form_Load ()
    If Exist("C:\Autoexec.Bat") Then Print "Boot batch file
        exists."
End Sub
```

To add this function at the form level, click New Function... in the Edit menu and give it a name of Exist. This template appears:

```
Function Exist ()

End Function
```

Give this function an argument of FileName As String and set up the error handler like this:

```
Function Exist (FileName As String)
    On Local Error Goto DoesNotExist
        :
        :

        Exit Function

DoesNotExist:
        :
        :

End Function
```

If there's no error, we should return a value of True, so we set Exist to True (–1), and try to open the file:

```
Function Exist (FileName As String)
    On Error Goto DoesNotExist
    Exist = -1                      'Set to True
    Open (FileName) For Input As #200    'Unlikely to conflict
        :
        :
```

```
        Exit Function

    DoesNotExist:
              :
              :

    End Function
```

TIP: *Here, we're assuming that the error was caused because the file was not found; in a real application, however, we might not be able to open the file for a variety of reasons (disk does not respond, device I/O error, etc). To make sure that the file was simply not found, you might add a line in the error handler to make sure that Err = 53, which is the error generated when a file is not found (as shown in Table 9-1).*

Here, we open the file as #200 because that file number is unlikely to conflict with other file numbers used elsewhere in the program. If the file does not exist, we'll go to the location DoesNotExist, where we want to set Exist to False (0). Then we want to use Resume Next, not Resume (which would cause us to try to open the file again):

```
    Function Exist (FileName As String)
        On Error Goto DoesNotExist
        Exist = -1                 'Set to True
        Open (FileName) For Input As #200   'Unlikely to conflict
              :
              :

        Exit Function

    DoesNotExist:
—>      Exist = 0                  'Set to False
—>      Resume Next
      End Function
```

At this point, Exist holds the correct value, True or False; all that remains is to close the file and exit the function, which we can do like this:

```
    Function Exist (FileName As String)
        On Error Goto DoesNotExist
        Exist = -1                 'Set to True
        Open (FileName) For Input As #200   'Unlikely to conflict
—>      Close #200
        Exit Function

    DoesNotExist:
        Exist = 0                  'Set to False
        Resume Next
    End Function
```

Exist( ) is ready to go, giving us a good use for Resume Next. However, it's usually better to move to an entirely different part of the code and take some alternate action (and let the user know that you're doing so). That's what the Resume Line # statement allows us to do: with it, we can specify the line number to resume execution at. For example, we might decide that our Pad application should always try to open and load a default file named File.Txt when we start the application. To do that, we can put this code in the Form_Load( ) Sub procedure:

```
Sub Form_Load ()
    Open "File.Txt" For Input As # 1              'Open file
    Pad.PadText.Text = Input$(LOF(1), # 1)   'Read file in
    Close # 1                    'Close file
End Sub
```

On the other hand, if there was an error, we might want to pop the Load File... dialog box on the screen. First, we set up our error handler:

```
Sub Form_Load ()
—>    On Local Error Goto FileError

    Open "File.Txt" For Input As # 1              'Open file
    Pad.PadText.Text = Input$(LOF(1), # 1)   'Read file in
    Close # 1                    'Close file
    Exit Sub


—>FileError:
      :
      :


      End Sub
```

Then, we can resume with another part of the procedure entirely with a Resume Line # statement like this, in which we pop the Load File... dialog box up:

```
Sub Form_Load ()
    On Local Error Goto FileError

    Open "File.Txt" For Input As # 1                  'Open file
```

```
        Pad.PadText.Text = Input$(LOF(1), # 1)      'Read file in
        Close # 1                    'Close file
        Exit Sub


—>10  LoadForm.Show
—>    Exit Sub


  FileError:
—>     Resume 10
  End Sub
```

And that's it for Resume, Resume Next, and Resume Line #. However, there are a few more points to consider. Suppose that we're using On Error Goto (not On Local Error Goto). In that case, error handling is module-wide, which can cause problems. For example, consider the case where Proc1 calls Proc2:

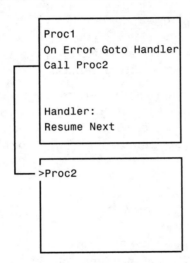

```
Proc1
On Error Goto Handler
Call Proc2



Handler:
Resume Next


>Proc2
```

If an error occurs while we're in Proc2, but it has no error handler, what happens? Visual Basic works its way back up the calling ladder, searching for an error handler. In this case, that's Proc1:

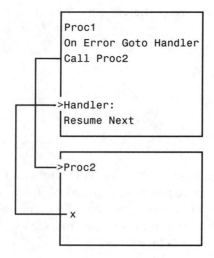

```
Proc1
On Error Goto Handler
Call Proc2


>Handler:
Resume Next


>Proc2



  x
```

In other words, Proc1 is handling Proc2's error in this way. If you leave an error handler out of Proc2, you should be aware of this point. That is, statements such as Resume Next in Proc1's error handler may cause unexpected or even disastrous results.

That completes our coverage of trappable errors in Visual Basic; as you can see, we can do a lot with the On [Local] Error Goto statement, especially when coupled with the Resume statement. However, there's more to finding and eliminating errors than this; now it's time to turn to debugging.

Debugging

As we type our program into Visual Basic, we may have errors in syntax; that is, we may type something like this:

```
Circle (x!, y!)
```

When we try to move on to the next line, Visual Basic puts a warning box on the screen, indicating that something more is expected—in this case, the circle's radius (at least). In this way, Visual Basic catches syntax errors at design time. On the other hand, we may end up with errors in run-time that are impossible to avoid at design time—out-of-memory or disk-full errors, for example; in other words, trappable errors. We've just seen that if we can anticipate errors like that, we can trap and deal with them.

TIP: *Text boxes can make excellent debugging tools if you use them to print intermediate results. Add a few extra text boxes to your application and print crucial values as your program is running. In general, temporary text boxes can provide a window into what's happening behind the scenes in your program.*

The kinds of errors that we're going to turn to next are usually harder to find: logic errors in the program. Here, an error may be buried deep in a long chain of complex statements—pages and pages of code, in fact. Fortunately, Visual Basic provides us with some debugging tools that we can use to locate and even fix errors.

For the purposes of exploring debugging, let's set ourselves the task of alphabetizing 10 or so names, as follows:

```
John
Tim
Edward
Samuel
Frank
Todd
George
Ralph
Leonard
Thomas
```

We can start by setting up an array to hold all the names in the Form_Click( ) Sub procedure:

```
Sub Form_Click ()
    Dim Names(10) As String

    Names(1) = "John"
    Names(2) = "Tim"
    Names(3) = "Edward"
    Names(4) = "Samuel"
    Names(5) = "Frank"
    Names(6) = "Todd"
    Names(7) = "George"
    Names(8) = "Ralph"
    Names(9) = "Leonard"
    Names(10) = "Thomas"
        :
```

Then we arrange them in alphabetical order with the following Basic instructions (this part of the code has three very common bugs in it):

```
Sub Form_Click ()
    Dim Names(10) As String

    Names(1) = "John"
    Names(2) = "Tim"
```

```
        Names(3) = "Edward"
        Names(4) = "Samuel"
        Names(5) = "Frank"
        Names(6) = "Todd"
        Names(7) = "George"
        Names(8) = "Ralph"
        Names(9) = "Leonard"
        Names(10) = "Thomas"

—>      For i = i To 10
  :         For j = i To 10
  :             If Names(i) > Names(j) Then
                    Temp$ = Names(i)
                    Names(j) = Names(j)
                    Names(j) = Tmp$
                End If
            Next j
        Next i
  :
```

Note here that we're using the > logical operator to compare strings with; this procedure is perfectly legal in Visual Basic, and it allows us to determine the alphabetical order of such strings. Finally, we can print out the result, name by name:

```
Sub Form_Click ()
    Dim Names(10) As String

    Names(1) = "John"
    Names(2) = "Tim"
    Names(3) = "Edward"
    Names(4) = "Samuel"
    Names(5) = "Frank"
    Names(6) = "Todd"
    Names(7) = "George"
    Names(8) = "Ralph"
    Names(9) = "Leonard"
    Names(10) = "Thomas"

    For i = i To 10
        For j = i To 10
            If Names(i) > Names(j) Then
                Temp$ = Names(i)
                Names(j) = Names(j)
```

```
                    Names(j) = Tmp$
              End If
         Next j
     Next i

—>  For k = 1 To 10
—>      Print Names(k)
—>  Next k
 End Sub
```

Unfortunately, when we execute the Form_Click( ) procedure by clicking the form, the following occurs:

```
     John
     Tim
```

```
     Todd
```

This looks a little incomplete; it's time to debug. In fact, we can start debugging without even stopping the program. To do that, click the Code button in the project window and bring up the Form_Click( ) Sub procedure. When we do, we might spot one error right away just by reading the code; in particular, when we switch elements around in the array, we load them temporarily into a variable named Temp$— but when we load them back into the array, we use a (misspelled) variable named Tmp$:

```
Sub Form_Click ()
    Dim Names(10) As String

    Names(1) = "John"
    Names(2) = "Tim"
    Names(3) = "Edward"
    Names(4) = "Samuel"
    Names(5) = "Frank"
    Names(6) = "Todd"
    Names(7) = "George"
    Names(8) = "Ralph"
    Names(9) = "Leonard"
    Names(10) = "Thomas"
```

```
        For i = i To 10
            For j = i To 10
                If Names(i) > Names(j) Then
            —>      Temp$ = Names(i)
                        Names(j) = Names(j)
            —>      Names(j) = Tmp$
                End If
            Next j
        Next i

        For k = 1 To 10
            Print Names(k)
        Next k
    End Sub
```

This is probably the most common of Visual Basic logic errors—
misspelling a variable's name. Visual Basic does not complain about
such errors, because it assumes that you're implicitly declaring a new
variable, Tmp$, and it sets that new variable to the empty string, "".
After we fix this problem, the program reads as follows:

```
    Sub Form_Click ()
        Dim Names(10) As String

        Names(1) = "John"
        Names(2) = "Tim"
        Names(3) = "Edward"
        Names(4) = "Samuel"
        Names(5) = "Frank"
        Names(6) = "Todd"
        Names(7) = "George"
        Names(8) = "Ralph"
        Names(9) = "Leonard"
        Names(10) = "Thomas"

        For i = i To 10
            For j = i To 10
                If Names(i) > Names(j) Then
                    Temp$ = Names(i)
                    Names(j) = Names(j)
            —>      Names(j) = Temp$
                End If
            Next j
        Next i
```

```
        For k = 1 To 10
          Print Names(k)
        Next k
   End Sub
```

We can let the program continue now by selecting the Continue item in the Run menu. After we do, we can click the form to see whether we've made a difference. This is the list that appears:

```
        Tim
        Tim
        Todd
        Todd
        Todd
        Todd
        Todd
```

There's been a change, but the result is clearly not right. The obvious problem in our program is that the entries in the Names( ) array are being filled incorrectly. To check what's happening, we should watch the array elements as they're filled. And we can do that by setting *breakpoint*. A breakpoint halts program execution when it is reached. For example, we can set a breakpoint by moving the cursor on the screen down to the line that reads "If Names(i) > Names(j) Then":

```
   Sub Form_Click ()
       Dim Names(10) As String

       Names(1) = "John"
       Names(2) = "Tim"
       Names(3) = "Edward"
       Names(4) = "Samuel"
       Names(5) = "Frank"
       Names(6) = "Todd"
       Names(7) = "George"
       Names(8) = "Ralph"
       Names(9) = "Leonard"
       Names(10) = "Thomas"

       For i = i To 10
           For j = i To 10
               If Names(i) > Names(j) Then   <—
                   Temp$ = Names(i)
```

```
                    Names(j) = Names(j)
                    Names(j) = Temp$
            End If
        Next j
    Next i

    For k = 1 To 10
        Print Names(k)
    Next k
End Sub
```

Now we press F9 or select Toggle Breakpoint in the Run menu. The statement we've selected appears highlighted to indicate that a breakpoint has been set, as shown in Figure 9-5.

Figure 9-5 Breakpoint Set

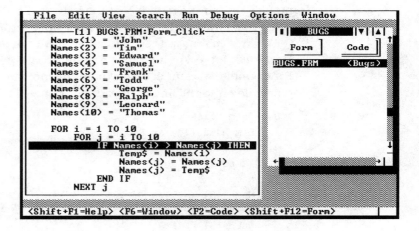

Next, we run the program by selecting Start in the Run menu. Program execution continues until we reach the breakpoint and then stops; the breakpoint line, "If Names(i) > Names(j) Then," is highlighted, as in Figure 9-6. We can check the values of Names(i) and Names(j) with Visual Basic's *immediate window*.

The immediate window lets us check the values of a program or execute Visual Basic statements while we're in a break state (i.e., which happens when you select Break in the Run menu, or the program reaches a breakpoint). To open the immediate window, select Immediate in Visual Basic's Window menu. Next, to check the value of Names(i), we only need to type ?Names(i) in the immediate window and press <Enter>. When we do, the display switches back to our program's window, and the string in Names(i) is displayed in the upper-left corner of the window (exactly as if we had executed a Print Names(i) statement). However, when we check both Names(i) and Names(j) this way, we see that they are blank and nothing appears in the upper left corner of our program's window, as shown in Figure 9-6.

Figure 9-6 Examining Immediate Values

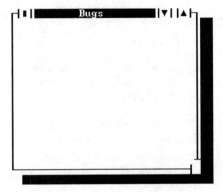

In other words, the line If Names(i) > Names(j) Then is comparing nothing; the values in Names(i) and Names(j) are not valid. At this beginning point in the program, both i and j are supposed to point at the first element in the array. That is, both i and j should be 1. We can check the value of i by executing ?i with the immediate window. When we do, we see that i = 0, which is a problem. The highlighted line in the code:

```
Dim Names(10) As String

Names(1) = "John"
Names(2) = "Tim"
Names(3) = "Edward"
Names(4) = "Samuel"
```

```
      Names(5) = "Frank"
      Names(6) = "Todd"
      Names(7) = "George"
      Names(8) = "Ralph"
      Names(9) = "Leonard"
      Names(10) = "Thomas"

—>    For i = i To 10
          For j = i To 10
              If Names(i) > Names(j) Then
                  Temp$ = Names(i)
                  Names(j) = Names(j)
                  Names(j) = Temp$
              End If
          Next j
      Next i

      For k = 1 To 10
          Print Names(k)
      Next k
```

must be changed to For i = 1 To 10, because we need to initialize i before using it. However, when we make the change and run the program (note that we can use F9 to toggle off the set breakpoint, or we can remove all breakpoints by selecting the Clear All Breakpoints in the Run menu), we still see:

```
      John
      Tim
      Tim
      Tim
      Tim
      Todd
      Todd
      Todd
      Todd
      Todd
```

Obviously, there is still a problem. Let's examine the part of the program in which the actual elements are switched, the only other part of the program. We can put a breakpoint in at the end of the element switching section as shown:

```
Dim Names(10) As String

Names(1) = "John"
Names(2) = "Tim"
Names(3) = "Edward"
Names(4) = "Samuel"
Names(5) = "Frank"
Names(6) = "Todd"
Names(7) = "George"
Names(8) = "Ralph"
Names(9) = "Leonard"
Names(10) = "Thomas"

For i = 1 To 10
    For j = i To 10
        If Names(i) > Names(j) Then
            Temp$ = Names(i)
            Names(j) = Names(j)
            Names(j) = Temp$          <—
        End If
    Next j
Next i

For k = 1 To 10
    Print Names(k)
Next k
```

Now when we execute the program, we'll stop at the breakpoint, where we'll be able to determine whether the elements really were switched. Run the program to the breakpoint. When we stop, we can check the values of Names(i) and Names(j). It turns out that there's another way besides the immediate window to do this; place the cursor over them one at a time and select Instant Watch... in the Debug menu. When you do, a dialog box opens as shown in Figure 9-7, showing the current value of the variable you want to examine. In this case, we're looking at Names(i) and Names(j); one is John, and the other is Edward.

Figure 9-7 Instant Watch with Names(i)

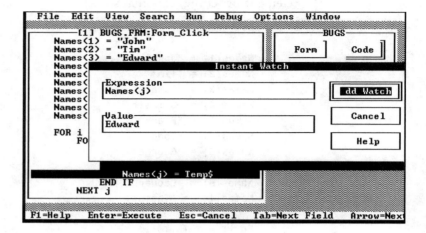

The exchange of array elements is supposed to function in a straight-forward way: we take the value in Names(i) and place it in Temp$. Then we copy the element in Names(j) and place it into Names(i). The final step is to move Temp$ into Names(j). At this breakpoint, all but the final step has been taken: we are about to move the value in Temp$ into Names(j).

In other words, we'd expect Names(i) and Names(j) to hold the same value—but they do not. Names(i) holds "John" and Names(j) holds "Edward." Something is wrong. If we look back one line in our code, we see the line with the arrow as follows:

```
Dim Names(10) As String

Names(1) = "John"
Names(2) = "Tim"
Names(3) = "Edward"
Names(4) = "Samuel"
Names(5) = "Frank"
Names(6) = "Todd"
Names(7) = "George"
Names(8) = "Ralph"
Names(9) = "Leonard"
Names(10) = "Thomas"
```

```
For i = 1 To 10
    For j = i To 10
        If Names(i) > Names(j) Then
            Temp$ = Names(i)
—>          Names(j) = Names(j)
            Names(j) = Temp$
        End If
    Next j
Next i


For k = 1 To 10
    Print Names(k)
Next k
```

It is apparent that the line with the arrow should be Names(i) = Names(j). We make the change, yielding the debugged program as follows:

```
Dim Names(10) As String

Names(1) = "John"
Names(2) = "Tim"
Names(3) = "Edward"
Names(4) = "Samuel"
Names(5) = "Frank"
Names(6) = "Todd"
Names(7) = "George"
Names(8) = "Ralph"
Names(9) = "Leonard"
Names(10) = "Thomas"

For i = 1 To 10
    For j = i To 10
        If Names(i) > Names(j) Then
            Temp$ = Names(i)
            Names(i) = Names(j)
            Names(j) = Temp$
        End If
    Next j
Next i

For k = 1 To 10
    Print Names(k)
Next k
```

This is the final result when we run the program:

```
Edward
Frank
George
John
Leonard
Ralph
Samuel
Thomas
Tim
Todd
```

The program has been debugged. We have some powerful debugging tools available to us in Visual Basic, including the immediate window and breakpoints. In fact, these tools have even more capabilities. For example, we can execute a program line by line and even change the values of variables while the program is running. Let's see how this works with an example.

Debugging an Investment Calculator

For instance, we might decide to write a small investment calculator to tell us what an investment would be worth in a certain number of years. That is, we might invest $1,000.00 at 7% for 12 years; if we did, that investment would be worth (if it was compounded annually):

$$(\$1,000.00) * (1.07)^{12} = \$2,252.19$$

Let's put this calculator together. Start Visual Basic and place three text boxes on the form to hold the three values: Investment ($1,000.00), InterestRate (7%), and Years (12). The calculation that we want to perform is:

```
Result = Investment * (1 + InterestRate / 100) ^ Years
```

Label the boxes as shown in Figure 9-8 and give them CtlNames (from the top) of InvestmentText, InterestRateText, and YearsText. Next, place a button with the caption Yields and CtlName YieldsButton under and a label at the bottom (set its BorderStyle to Fixed Single so that it looks like the text boxes), with the CtlName ResultLabel, as shown in Figure 9-9.

Figure 9-8 Our Investment Calculator Template

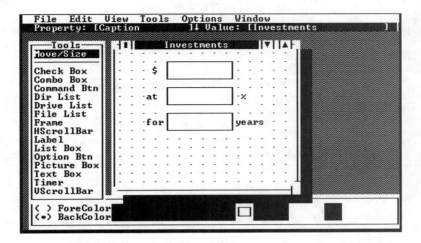

Figure 9-9 Completed Investment Calculator Template

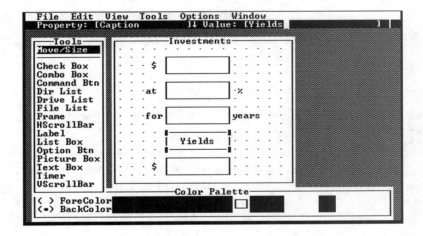

Our investment calculator template is set; all that remains is the code.
To use the calculator, the user places the investment amount in the
top text box, the interest rate in the next box, and the number of years
that the investment will last in the third text box. Then the user clicks
the Yields button to see the result in the bottom box. That means that

all the action will take place in YieldsButton_Click ( ). Now bring that up the code window:

```
Sub YieldsButton_Click()

End Sub
```

We can start by converting the text in the text boxes into numeric values as follows:

```
Sub YieldsButton_Click()
    Investment = Val(InvestmentText.Text)
    InterstRate = Val(InterestRateText.Text)
    Years = Val(YearsText.Text)
        :

End Sub
```

Next, we can perform the calculation:

```
Sub YieldsButton_Click()
    Investment = Val(InvestmentText.Text)
    InterstRate = Val(InterestRateText.Text)
    Years = Val(YearsText.Text)
—>  Result = Investments * (1 + InterestRate / 100) ^ Years
        :

End Sub
```

Finally, we display the result as follows:

```
Sub YieldsButton_Click()
    Investment = Val(InvestmentText.Text)
    InterstRate = Val(InterestRateText.Text)
    Years = Val(YearsText.Text)
    Result = Investments * (1 + InterestRate / 100) ^ Years
—>  ResultLabel.Caption = Format$(Result, "###,###,##0.00")
End Sub
```

Let's give it a try; for example, we can try the preceding calculation, $1000.00 at 7% for 12 years. However, the result is $0.00, as shown in Figure 9-10. Obviously, there's a problem; it's time to debug.

Figure 9-10 Investment Calculator, First Attempt

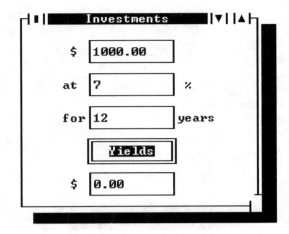

We can start by placing a breakpoint (i.e., by using F9 or Toggle Breakpoint in the Run menu) in the first line of the YieldsButton_Click ( ) procedure:

```
Sub YieldsButton_Click()
—>   Investment = Val(InvestmentText.Text)
     InterstRate = Val(InterestRateText.Text)
     Years = Val(YearsText.Text)
     Result = Investments * (1 + InterestRate / 100) ^ Years
     ResultLabel.Caption = Format$(Result, "###,###,##0.00")
End Sub
```

When we reach this point, the program will automatically break. Start the program again, place the same values in the text boxes, and click the Yields button. When you do, the program reaches the breakpoint and stops. Now we can single-step through each line of the code, one line at a time, using the F8 key. Press F8 once to execute the first line; the box around the first line (as is usual for a breakpoint) moves to the second line, indicating where we are, as shown in Figure 9-11. Note also that the text of the first line stays highlighted, indicating that there is still a breakpoint.

After executing the first line, we can check the value of Investment with an instant watch window as shown in Figure 9-12, where we see that Investment holds 1000.00, as it should.

Figure 9-11 Single Stepping in the Investment Calculator

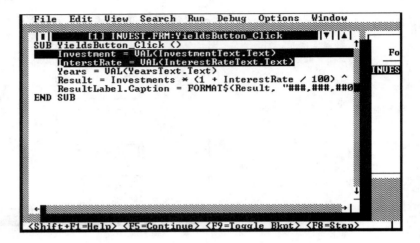

Figure 9-12 Instant Watch with Investment's Value

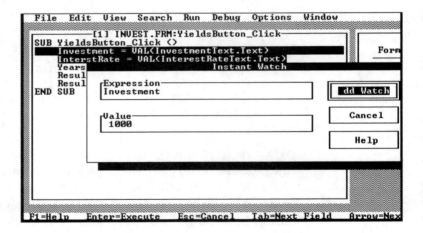

The next step is to set the interest rate; we execute the next line by pressing F8 again:

```
Sub YieldsButton_Click()
      Investment = Val(InvestmentText.Text)
—>    InterstRate = Val(InterestRateText.Text)
      Years = Val(YearsText.Text)
```

```
    Result = Investments * (1 + InterestRate / 100) ^ Years
    ResultLabel.Caption = Format$(Result, "###,###,##0.00")
End Sub
```

Then check the value of InterestRate with the immediate window by typing ?InterestRate. This value should be 7, but the result, as shown in Figure 9-13 (in the upper-left corner of the window), is 0. This is clearly a bug; by checking the code, we can see that InterestRate is misspelled in the second line (i.e., "InterstRate"). Fixing that yields this code:

```
Sub YieldsButton_Click()
    Investment = Val(InvestmentText.Text)
—>  InterestRate = Val(InterestRateText.Text)
    Years = Val(YearsText.Text)
    Result = Investments * (1 + InterestRate / 100) ^ Years
    ResultLabel.Caption = Format$(Result, "###,###,##0.00")
End Sub
```

Figure 9-13 Instant Value of InterestRate

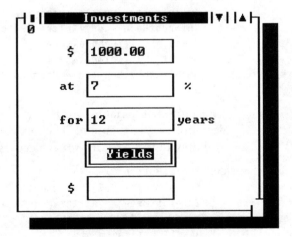

We can also fix the problem without stopping the program, by placing a value directly into InterestRate. That is, Visual Basic allows us to load values into our variables even when the program is running. In particular, we want to load a value of 7 into InterestRate; to do that, simply type the line InterestRate = 7 into the immediate window. We can then check the new value of InterestRate by typing ?InterestRate. As shown in Figure 9-14, InterestRate does indeed hold 7 now.

Figure 9-14 New Value of Investment

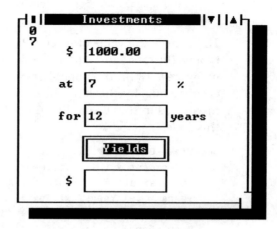

Pressing F8 once again executes the third line in the code, setting the value of the variable Years:

```
Sub YieldsButton_Click()
    Investment = Val(InvestmentText.Text)
    InterestRate = Val(InterestRateText.Text)
—>  Years = Val(YearsText.Text)
    Result = Investments * (1 + InterestRate / 100) ^ Years
    ResultLabel.Caption = Format$(Result, "###,###,##0.00")
End Sub
```

Checking that variable in the instant watch window verifies that it does hold 12, as it should. The next line does the actual calculation, and pressing F8 a fourth time executes it:

```
Sub YieldsButton_Click()
    Investment = Val(InvestmentText.Text)
    InterestRate = Val(InterestRateText.Text)
    Years = Val(YearsText.Text)
—>  Result = Investments * (1 + InterestRate / 100) ^ Years
    ResultLabel.Caption = Format$(Result, "###,###,##0.00")
End Sub
```

This line assigns the results of the calculation to a variable named Result; we can check the value of Result in the instant watch box. When we do, however, we find that it's 0. Once again, we check the code, finding that we're using a variable named Investments, not Investment, in the fourth line. Since we've already executed that line, however, we can't execute it again without reentering the YieldsButton_Click() procedure. Even so, since we have isolated that problem, we can fix the code. Change that line so that it uses the variable Investment instead of Investments:

```
Sub YieldsButton_Click()
    Investment = Val(InvestmentText.Text)
    InterestRate = Val(InterestRateText.Text)
    Years = Val(YearsText.Text)
    Result = Investment * (1 + InterestRate / 100) ^ Years
    ResultLabel.Caption = Format$(Result, "###,###,##0.00")
End Sub
```

—>

Now we can rerun the program using the same values:

$$(\$1,000.00) * (1.07)^{12} = \$2,252.19$$

And the program is debugged, as shown in Figure 9-15. Single-stepping like this can be a powerful debugging tool, giving us a picture of what our program is doing line by line. In general, then, we've gotten a good idea of the debugging capabilities of Visual Basic, which are considerable. If we suspect errors in a program's logic, we can set breakpoints inside it, stopping it at strategic locations and checking what's happening. To further locate the problem, we can even work through the code line by line.

Figure 9-15 Working Investment Calculator

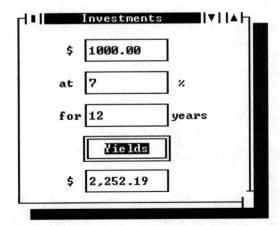

There is, however, one problem that we should mention before finishing with debugging and moving on to the next chapter. Because Visual Basic programs are event driven, there are a few considerations that we must take into account; if we place a breakpoint in a MouseDown or KeyDown event procedure and then release the mouse button or key while the program is in a break state, we may never get a MouseUp or KeyUp event when we continue. In other words, VB programs respond to the computer environment, and if we change that environment while debugging, it may result in unexpected consequences.

That's it for our coverage of debugging and error handling; let's move on to our next topic now: working with the advanced database capablilities offered in the Professional Edition of Visual Basic for DOS.

Databasing

This chapter is an exploration of the Indexed Sequential Access Method (ISAM) system in the Professional Edition of Visual Basic for DOS. If you don't have the Professional Edition, you might still want to read this chapter to get an idea of what's available—especially if you're interested in databases. The ISAM system provides an easy way to set up a database program from within Visual Basic. It's a serious system, set up for serious applications.

What is ISAM? Briefly, it's a method of quickly changing the apparent order of records in a file. For example, you may be a careful person who prefers to order your friends by height or age. Towards that end, you may have devised a new data type to hold information about each friend:

```
Type Friend
        Name As String * 50
        Age As Integer
        Height As Integer
        HomeTown As String * 50
End Type
```

Each variable in this type is a *field* in database terminology, and, together, all these fields make up a *record*. After defining a data type, we can set up a variable of this type named FriendRecord like this:

```
Type Friend
        Name As String * 50
        Age As Integer
        Height As Integer
        HomeTown As String * 50
End Type
```

—>   Dim FriendRecord As Friend

Then fill all the fields in this record with values as follows:

```
Type Friend
        Name As String * 50
        Age As Integer
        Height As Integer
        HomeTown As String * 50
End Type

Dim FriendRecord As Friend
```

```
—>    FriendRecord.Name = "Doug"
—>    FriendRecord.Age = 33
—>    FriendRecord.Height = 70      'Inches
—>    FriendRecord.HomeTown = "Redlands"
```

You can even make a file of such records, similar to the following one:

```
Name :      "Doug"
Age :       33            Record 1
Height :    70
HomeTown :  "Redlands"
```

```
Name :      "Ed"
Age :       44            Record 2
Height :    69
HomeTown :  "San Pedro"
```

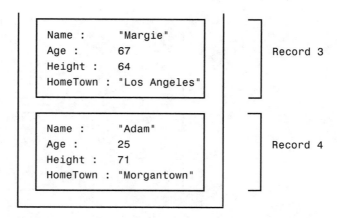

This file is a database. The records in it are in the order in which we inserted them into the file, one after the other, which is called *1insertion order.*

If we were to make this an ISAM file (which we would have to specify when we first create the file), the ISAM system would automatically begin the file with an index of the records, as follows:

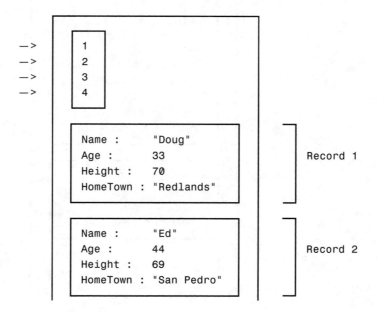

```
Name :        "Margie"
Age :         67
Height :      64
HomeTown :    "Los Angeles"
```
Record 3

```
Name :        "Adam"
Age :         25
Height :      71
HomeTown :    "Morgantown"
```
Record 4

This index just lists the record numbers in the order in which they were inserted into the file. In the ISAM system, this index is referred to as the Null index:

```
1
2
3
4
```
Null Index

```
Name :        "Doug"
Age :         33
Height :      70
HomeTown :    "Redlands"
```
Record 1

```
Name :        "Ed"
Age :         44
Height :      69
HomeTown :    "San Pedro"
```
Record 2

```
Name :        "Margie"
Age :         67
Height :      64
HomeTown :    "Los Angeles"
```
Record 3

```
Name :       "Adam"
Age :        25
Height :     71
HomeTown :   "Morgantown"
```
                                                    Record 4

The Null index is the default index of the records in the file. It is always created when you open a file for ISAM output and put records into it.

However, the crux of the ISAM system is that you can build other indices as well. For example, we can (and will) instruct the ISAM system to create an index of the records in your file by age. For easy reference, we can even give this index a name: "FriendsByAge":

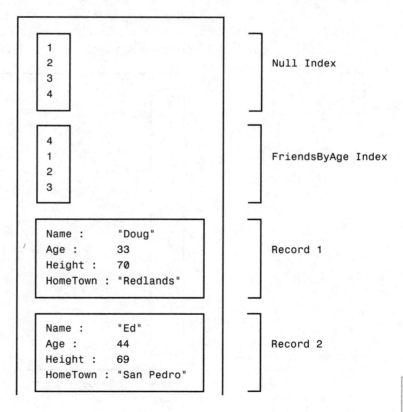

```
1
2
3
4
```
                                                    Null Index

```
4
1
2
3
```
                                                    FriendsByAge Index

```
Name :       "Doug"
Age :        33
Height :     70
HomeTown :   "Redlands"
```
                                                    Record 1

```
Name :       "Ed"
Age :        44
Height :     69
HomeTown :   "San Pedro"
```
                                                    Record 2

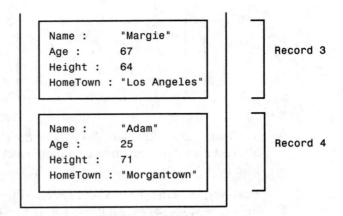

```
Name    :     "Margie"
Age     :     67                      Record 3
Height  :     64
HomeTown :    "Los Angeles"


Name    :     "Adam"
Age     :     25                      Record 4
Height  :     71
HomeTown :    "Morgantown"
```

Note that the order in this index is different from that in the Null index. Here, the records are listed in terms of increasing age.

The way we'll create indices with ISAM is through the new Visual Basic statement, CreateIndex. Similarly, we can create another index on the height of your friends, which we can call FriendsByHeight:

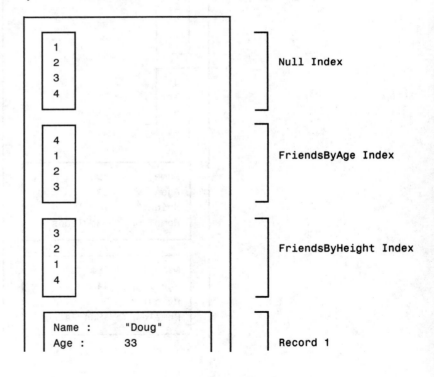

```
1
2                                      Null Index
3
4


4
1                                      FriendsByAge Index
2
3


3
2                                      FriendsByHeight Index
1
4


Name    :     "Doug"
Age     :     33                       Record 1
```

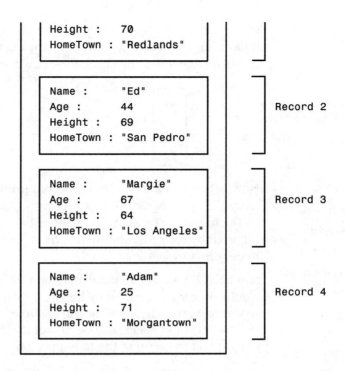

```
Height :    70
HomeTown : "Redlands"


Name :     "Ed"
Age :      44                              Record 2
Height :   69
HomeTown : "San Pedro"


Name :     "Margie"
Age :      67                              Record 3
Height :   64
HomeTown : "Los Angeles"


Name :     "Adam"
Age :      25                              Record 4
Height :   71
HomeTown : "Morgantown"
```

The Current Index

These indices themselves actually become part of the file (ISAM handles all this automatically when you create an index). However, only one index at a time can be the *current index.* Whenever you make an index to the current index, the apparent order of the records in the file is changed to match its ordering.

Before you've created any indices, the Null index is the current index:

```
1
2
3
4
```

If you ask for the first record in this file, you'll get record 1; the next record will be record 2, and so forth, exactly following the insertion order of the records.

On the other hand, you can select which index is to be the current index with the SetIndex statement. For example, you may make the FriendsByAge index the current index with SetIndex, as follows:

```
4
1
2
3
```

TIP: *The file has not really been resorted. The ISAM system uses pointers to point to each record. It is these pointers that are actually sorted.*

Now, when you ask for the first record from this file, you'll get the entry that's really record 4, not record 1 (Adam has the lowest age of all the friends). The next record after that will really be record 1, followed by record 2, and then 3. In other words, the file now appears to be sorted by age.

Similarly, if you made FriendsByHeight the current index, the file would appear to be sorted by height. When you retrieve the first record from the file, it will be the record of the person with the lowest height. The next record will be that of the person with the next lowest height, and so on up to the tallest person.

Ordering records in this way can be very useful. For example, if you wanted to exclude all people below the age of 30, you would order your file by age, giving you the following ordering of ages, record by record:

```
25      (Adam)
33      (Doug)
44      (Ed)
67      (Margie)
```

You would then scan up the file for the first age above 30 (this can be done with the Seek statement, as we'll see). The first record to meet this requirement is Doug's, as shown below:

```
        25      (Adam)
—>      33      (Doug)
        44      (Ed)
        67      (Margie)
```

Because the records are ordered, you know that all records before this one are of people under 30 and can be discarded. All records after this point can be preserved. Handling data in this way is the fundamental part of a database program. Next let's put this all into code.

A Database Program

Before actually writing any Visual Basic, you'll need a little preparation in order to work with ISAM. This time, you don't need to load new Quick libraries. Instead, you have to load a TSR (Terminate-and-Stay-Resident) program that holds the ISAM code. The short version of this program is Proisam.Exe; this program contains all the code needed to run *most* database programs. Run it once before using any ISAM routines. Then you can start Visual Basic for DOS as usual.

On the other hand, Proisam.Exe omits a few ISAM routines (including CreateIndex), all of which can be found in another program named Proisamd.Exe. Therefore, you might want to run Proisamd.Exe before running your own program to make sure that you've covered all possibilities.

Now we're free to do some programming. Our database program will do some of the things we've been talking about, and we can even use the list of friends we've developed. We can start by creating a form named Isam.Frm and by structuring our data records with Type:

```
Type Friend
        Name As String * 50
        Age As Integer
        Height As Integer
        HomeTown As String * 50
End Type
```

Next, we can set up a variable FriendRecord of this type in the Form_Load( ) Sub procedure:

```
Type Friend
    Name As String * 50
    Age As Integer
    Height As Integer
    HomeTown As String * 50
End Type

Form_Load()

—>  Dim FriendRecord As Friend
    :
    :
```

Now we can create our ISAM file. To do that, we simply say Open "Friends.Dat" For ISAM (as opposed to opening it under other Basic options such as Append), as following:

```
Type Friend
    Name As String * 50
    Age As Integer
    Height As Integer
    HomeTown As String * 50
End Type

Form_Load()

    Dim FriendRecord As Friend

—>    Open "Friends.Dat" For ISAM Friend "Pals" As #1
      :
      :
```

Let's take a look at this Open statement. We start with Open "Friends.Dat" For ISAM, which is clear enough—we want this file to be an ISAM file. The next keyword, Friend, indicates the Type of the records we'll be using so that ISAM can structure each record in the file. The following keyword, "Pals" is the *table* name, and the number, #1, is the file number as is normal in BASIC.

All the records of a particular data type (such as Type Friend) make up a table in the database file. For example, when we've filled Friends.Dat with all our friends, all the records will be in a single table, which we're naming "Pals":

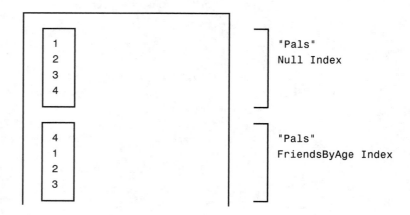

Peter Norton's Visual Basic for DOS

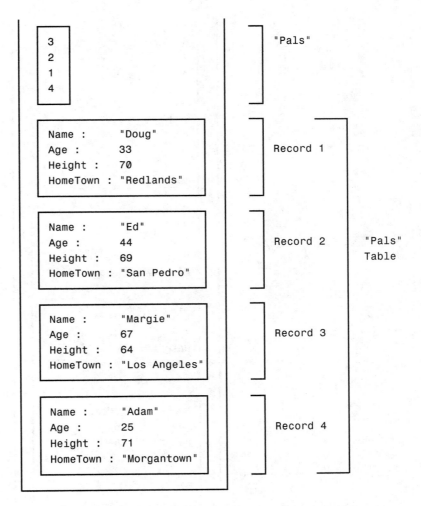

```
3
2
1
4
```
"Pals"

```
Name :      "Doug"
Age :       33
Height :    70
HomeTown : "Redlands"
```
Record 1

```
Name :      "Ed"
Age :       44
Height :    69
HomeTown : "San Pedro"
```
Record 2

```
Name :      "Margie"
Age :       67
Height :    64
HomeTown : "Los Angeles"
```
Record 3

```
Name :      "Adam"
Age :       25
Height :    71
HomeTown : "Morgantown"
```
Record 4

"Pals"
Table

But we might also have another table, with a different record type—say Type Enemy—in the same file, and this would make up a new table which we can call "NotPals":

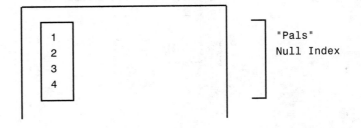

```
1
2
3
4
```
"Pals"
Null Index

```
┌─────────┐                              ┐  "Pals"
│ 4       │                              │  FriendsByAge Index
│ 1       │                              │
│ 2       │                              │
│ 3       │                              ┘
└─────────┘

┌─────────┐                              ┐  "Pals"
│ 3       │                              │  FriendsByHeight Index
│ 2       │                              │
│ 1       │                              │
│ 4       │                              ┘
└─────────┘

┌─────────────────────────────┐         ┐
│ Name    :    "Doug"         │         │  Record 1
│ Age     :    33             │         │
│ Height  :    70             │         │
│ HomeTown :  "Redlands"      │         ┘
└─────────────────────────────┘

┌─────────────────────────────┐         ┐                  ┐
│ Name    :    "Ed"           │         │  Record 2        │  "Pals"
│ Age     :    44             │         │                  │  Table
│ Height  :    69             │         │                  │
│ HomeTown :  "San Pedro"     │         ┘                  │
└─────────────────────────────┘                            │

┌─────────────────────────────┐         ┐                  │
│ Name    :    "Margie"       │         │  Record 3        │
│ Age     :    67             │         │                  │
│ Height  :    64             │         │                  │
│ HomeTown :  "Los Angeles"   │         ┘                  │
└─────────────────────────────┘                            │

┌─────────────────────────────┐         ┐                  │
│ Name    :    "Adam"         │         │  Record 4        │
│ Age     :    25             │         │                  │
│ Height  :    71             │         │                  ┘
│ HomeTown :  "Morgantown"    │         ┘
└─────────────────────────────┘

┌─────────┐                              ┐  "NotPals"
│ 1       │                              │
│ 2       │                              ┘
└─────────┘
```

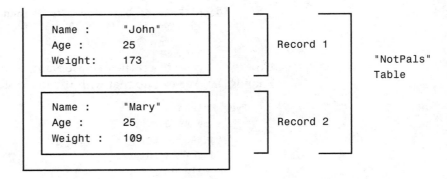

If we wanted to work with the "NotPals" table, we'd open up the *same* file again, but this time we'd specify a different record Type (Enemy), and a different file number:

```
Open "Friends.Dat" For ISAM Friend "Pals" As #1
Open "Friends.Dat" For ISAM Enemy "NotPals" As #2
```

What's referred to in normal Visual Basic as a file number (i.e., 1 and 2 as we've opened them so far) are really *table numbers* in ISAM. When we create indices, search for matches, or perform other operations in ISAM, we have to specify the table number as well.

We can have multiple tables in ISAM to avoid the need for relational databases, in which we have to tie records from different files together. Here, we can put all data, even data that would normally go into different files, into the same file. And ISAM files can be huge; the upper limit is 128 megabytes.

On the other hand, to avoid confusion, we're going to limit ourselves to one table ("Pals") in this chapter. And our table number is going to be 1, as follows:

```
Type Friend
    Name As String * 50
    Age As Integer
    Height As Integer
    HomeTown As String * 50
End Type


Form_Load()

    Dim FriendRecord As Friend
```

```
—>     Open "Friends.Dat" For ISAM Friend "Pals" As #1
       :
       :
```

Now, we have to insert the data we want, record by record, into Friends.Dat. We can do that with the Insert statement, like this:

```
Type Friend
    Name As String * 50
    Age As Integer
    Height As Integer
    HomeTown As String * 50
End Type

Form_Load()

    Dim FriendRecord As Friend

    Open "Friends.Dat" For ISAM Friend "Pals" As #1

    FriendRecord.Name = "Doug"
    FriendRecord.Age = 33
    FriendRecord.Height = 70      'Inches
    FriendRecord.HomeTown = "Redlands"
—>  Insert 1, FriendRecord

    FriendRecord.Name = "Ed"
    FriendRecord.Age = 44
    FriendRecord.Height = 69      'Inches
    FriendRecord.HomeTown = "San Pedro"
—>  Insert 1, FriendRecord

    FriendRecord.Name = "Margie"
    FriendRecord.Age = 67
    FriendRecord.Height = 64      'Inches
    FriendRecord.HomeTown = "Los Angeles"
—>  Insert 1, FriendRecord

    FriendRecord.Name = "Adam"
    FriendRecord.Age = 25
    FriendRecord.Height = 71      'Inches
    FriendRecord.HomeTown = "Morgantown"
—>  Insert 1, FriendRecord
    :
    :
```

It's an easy process: we just fill the fields in FriendRecord with the data we want and then Insert FriendRecord into the file Friends.Dat (which we've opened as #1). So far, the database file Friends.Dat has all four records loaded, and the Null index has been automatically set up by ISAM:

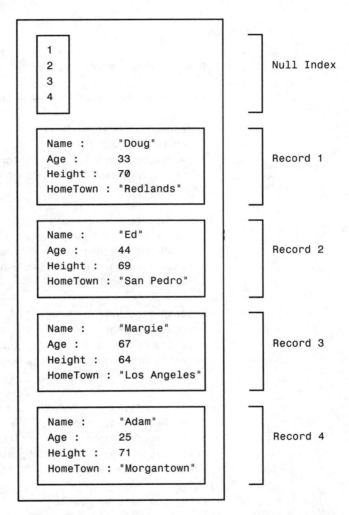

Now, we can go on to create the other two indices, FriendsByAge and FriendsByHeight. To do so, we use CreateIndex, passing it the file number, the name we want to give to this index, a parameter named *unique%*, and the name of the field we want to sort on ("Age"):

```
Type Friend
    Name As String * 50
    Age As Integer
    Height As Integer
    HomeTown As String * 50
End Type

Form_Load()

    Dim FriendRecord As Friend

    Open "Friends.Dat" For ISAM Friend "Pals" As #1

    FriendRecord.Name = "Doug"
    FriendRecord.Age = 33
    FriendRecord.Height = 70      'Inches
    FriendRecord.HomeTown = "Redlands"
    Insert 1, FriendRecord

    FriendRecord.Name = "Ed"
    FriendRecord.Age = 44
    FriendRecord.Height = 69      'Inches
    FriendRecord.HomeTown = "San Pedro"
    Insert 1, FriendRecord

    FriendRecord.Name = "Margie"
    FriendRecord.Age = 67
    FriendRecord.Height = 64      'Inches
    FriendRecord.HomeTown = "Los Angeles"
    Insert 1, FriendRecord

    FriendRecord.Name = "Adam"
    FriendRecord.Age = 25
    FriendRecord.Height = 71      'Inches
    FriendRecord.HomeTown = "Morgantown"
    Insert 1, FriendRecord

    Print "Sorting by age..."

—>  CreateIndex 1, "FriendsByAge", 0, "Age"
        :
        :
```

The unique% field indicates whether or not ISAM will tolerate the insertion of records with the same value in this field as one that already exists in the database. For example, if we set unique% to 1, demanding unique entries only and then tried to enter a record for Pete, whose age is 33—the same as Doug's—a trappable error would be generated (i.e., use On Local Error Goto...). In this chapter, we are not going to worry about the uniqueness of records. Therefore, we'll set this value to 0. Now the database file has the following appearance:

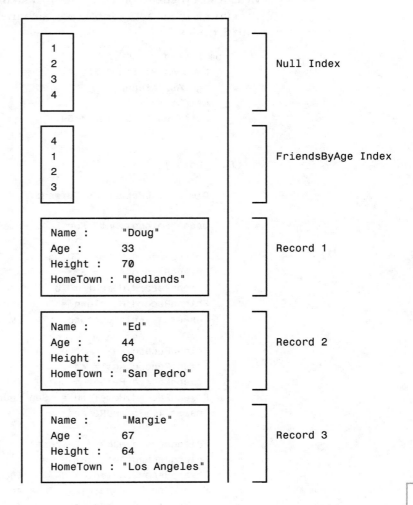

```
Name :        "Adam"
Age :         25
Height :      71
HomeTown :    "Morgantown"
```
Record 4

We know in what order we've inserted the records into the file; now we can sort them according to age by making the FriendsByAge index the current index and printing out each friend's name. We start off with SetIndex:

```
Type Friend
    Name As String * 50
    Age As Integer
    Height As Integer
    HomeTown As String * 50
End Type

Form_Load()

    Dim FriendRecord As Friend

    Open "Friends.Dat" For ISAM Friend "Pals" As #1

    FriendRecord.Name = "Doug"
    FriendRecord.Age = 33
    FriendRecord.Height = 70      'Inches
    FriendRecord.HomeTown = "Redlands"
    Insert 1, FriendRecord

    FriendRecord.Name = "Ed"
    FriendRecord.Age = 44
    FriendRecord.Height = 69       'Inches
    FriendRecord.HomeTown = "San Pedro"
    Insert 1, FriendRecord

    FriendRecord.Name = "Margie"
    FriendRecord.Age = 67
    FriendRecord.Height = 64       'Inches
    FriendRecord.HomeTown = "Los Angeles"
    Insert 1, FriendRecord

    FriendRecord.Name = "Adam"
    FriendRecord.Age = 25
```

```
            FriendRecord.Height = 71      'Inches
            FriendRecord.HomeTown = "Morgantown"
            Insert 1, FriendRecord

            Print "Sorting by age..."

            CreateIndex 1, "FriendsByAge", 0, "Age"

    —>      SetIndex 1, "FriendsByAge"
            :
            :
```

This is easy enough—we're just making the FriendsByAge index the current index for file 1 (actually, Table 1). Now we can print out the names in this new order. The ISAM system supports a number of statements for moving around in a database file. A list of the ones we'll find useful follows:

```
        MoveFirst FileNumber
                MoveLast FileNumber
                MoveNext FileNumber
                MovePrevious FileNumber
                EOF(FileNumber)
                BOF(FileNumber)
```

Keep in mind that what is listed in the ISAM documentation as FileNumber, as in the preceeding code, is really the table number. In other words—confusing as it may be—we can actually have as many file numbers for a specific file as there are tables in that file. The Move statements are self-explanatory; EOF(FileNumber) returns True if we're at the end of the table; BOF(FileNumber) returns True if we're at the beginning—otherwise, they return False.

With all this in mind, here's how to print the new ordering of the records in Friends.Dat, now sorted by age:

```
Type Friend
    Name As String * 50
    Age As Integer
    Height As Integer
    HomeTown As String * 50
End Type

Form_Load()
```

```
Dim FriendRecord As Friend

Open "Friends.Dat" For ISAM Friend "Pals" As #1

FriendRecord.Name = "Doug"
FriendRecord.Age = 33
FriendRecord.Height = 70      'Inches
FriendRecord.HomeTown = "Redlands"
Insert 1, FriendRecord

FriendRecord.Name = "Ed"
FriendRecord.Age = 44
FriendRecord.Height = 69      'Inches
FriendRecord.HomeTown = "San Pedro"
Insert 1, FriendRecord

FriendRecord.Name = "Margie"
FriendRecord.Age = 67
FriendRecord.Height = 64      'Inches
FriendRecord.HomeTown = "Los Angeles"
Insert 1, FriendRecord

FriendRecord.Name = "Adam"
FriendRecord.Age = 25
FriendRecord.Height = 71      'Inches
FriendRecord.HomeTown = "Morgantown"
Insert 1, FriendRecord

Print "Sorting by age..."

CreateIndex 1, "FriendsByAge", 0, "Age"

SetIndex 1, "FriendsByAge"
```

```
—>    MoveFirst 1

—>    Do
—>        Retrieve 1, FriendRecord
—>        Print FriendRecord.Name
—>        MoveNext 1
—>    Loop While Not EOF(1)
      :
      :
```

Next we move to the first record in the file:

```
MoveFirst 1
        :
```

And then we enter a Do loop, which loops over each record in the file by continually using MoveNext until EOF(1) becomes True:

```
MoveFirst 1

    Do
        :
        :
        MoveNext 1
    Loop While Not EOF(1)
```

When we're at the beginning of the file, the first record in the current index is the *current record*. When we use MoveNext 1, the next record in that index becomes the current record. We can look at the current record by retrieving it, using Retrieve, into a variable of type Friend, such as FriendRecord:

```
MoveFirst 1

    Do
        Retrieve 1, FriendRecord
        :
        MoveNext 1
    Loop While Not EOF(1)
```

Retrieve 1, FriendRecord reads the current record from the database file and places it into FriendRecord. That means that we can print the name of the person in the current record with Print like this:

```
MoveFirst 1

    Do
        Retrieve 1, FriendRecord
—>      Print FriendRecord.Name
        MoveNext 1
    Loop While Not EOF(1)
```

And that's the way to loop over the ordered records of an ISAM file; the result appears in Figure 10-1.

Figure 10-1 Sorting Our ISAM Records by Age

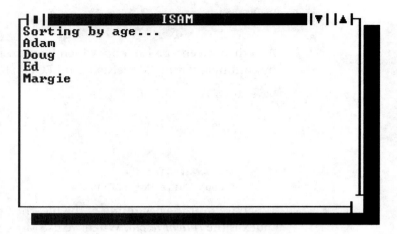

We can also create our second index, FriendsByHeight, as follows:

```
Type Friend
    Name As String * 50
    Age As Integer
    Height As Integer
    HomeTown As String * 50
End Type

Form_Load()

    Dim FriendRecord As Friend

    Open "Friends.Dat" For ISAM Friend "Pals" As #1

    FriendRecord.Name = "Doug"
    FriendRecord.Age = 33
    FriendRecord.Height = 70     'Inches
    FriendRecord.HomeTown = "Redlands"
    Insert 1, FriendRecord

    FriendRecord.Name = "Ed"
    FriendRecord.Age = 44
```

```
FriendRecord.Height = 69      'Inches
FriendRecord.HomeTown = "San Pedro"
Insert 1, FriendRecord

FriendRecord.Name = "Margie"
FriendRecord.Age = 67
FriendRecord.Height = 64      'Inches
FriendRecord.HomeTown = "Los Angeles"
Insert 1, FriendRecord

FriendRecord.Name = "Adam"
FriendRecord.Age = 25
FriendRecord.Height = 71      'Inches
FriendRecord.HomeTown = "Morgantown"
Insert 1, FriendRecord

Print "Sorting by age..."

CreateIndex 1, "FriendsByAge", 0, "Age"

SetIndex 1, "FriendsByAge"

MoveFirst 1

Do
    Retrieve 1, FriendRecord
    Print FriendRecord.Name
    MoveNext 1
Loop While Not EOF(1)

Print "Sorting by height..."

-->  CreateIndex 1, "FriendsByHeight", 0, "Height"
     :
     :
```

The structure here is exactly parallel to the creation of "FriendsByAge," except that now we sort on the "Height" field and give the index a different name. At this point, the database file has the following appearance:

```
┌─────────────────────────────────────┐
│   ┌─────┐                           │
│   │ 1   │                           ┐
│   │ 2   │                            │  Null Index
│   │ 3   │                           ┘
│   │ 4   │                           │
│   └─────┘                           │
│                                     │
│   ┌─────┐                           │
│   │ 4   │                           ┐
│   │ 1   │                            │  FriendsByAge Index
│   │ 2   │                           ┘
│   │ 3   │                           │
│   └─────┘                           │
│                                     │
│   ┌─────┐                           │
│   │ 3   │                           ┐
│   │ 2   │                            │  FriendsByHeight Index
│   │ 1   │                           ┘
│   │ 4   │                           │
│   └─────┘                           │
│   ┌─────────────────────────────┐   │
│   │ Name    :     "Doug"        │   ┐
│   │ Age     :     33            │    │  Record 1
│   │ Height  :     70            │   ┘
│   │ HomeTown : "Redlands"       │   │
│   └─────────────────────────────┘   │
│   ┌─────────────────────────────┐   │
│   │ Name    :     "Ed"          │   ┐
│   │ Age     :     44            │    │  Record 2
│   │ Height  :     69            │   ┘
│   │ HomeTown : "San Pedro"      │   │
│   └─────────────────────────────┘   │
│   ┌─────────────────────────────┐   │
│   │ Name    :     "Margie"      │   ┐
│   │ Age     :     67            │    │  Record 3
│   │ Height  :     64            │   ┘
│   │ HomeTown : "Los Angeles"    │   │
│   └─────────────────────────────┘   │
│   ┌─────────────────────────────┐   │
│   │ Name    :     "Adam"        │   ┐
│   │ Age     :     25            │    │  Record 4
│   │ Height  :     71            │   ┘
│   │ HomeTown : "Morgantown"     │   │
│   └─────────────────────────────┘   │
└─────────────────────────────────────┘
```

We can make FriendsByHeight the current index and print the records in that order, just as we did for FriendsByAge:

```
Type Friend
    Name As String * 50
    Age As Integer
    Height As Integer
    HomeTown As String * 50
End Type


Form_Load()

    Dim FriendRecord As Friend

    Open "Friends.Dat" For ISAM Friend "Pals" As #1

    FriendRecord.Name = "Doug"
    FriendRecord.Age = 33
    FriendRecord.Height = 70     'Inches
    FriendRecord.HomeTown = "Redlands"
    Insert 1, FriendRecord

    FriendRecord.Name = "Ed"
    FriendRecord.Age = 44
    FriendRecord.Height = 69     'Inches
    FriendRecord.HomeTown = "San Pedro"
    Insert 1, FriendRecord

    FriendRecord.Name = "Margie"
    FriendRecord.Age = 67
    FriendRecord.Height = 64     'Inches
    FriendRecord.HomeTown = "Los Angeles"
    Insert 1, FriendRecord

    FriendRecord.Name = "Adam"
    FriendRecord.Age = 25
    FriendRecord.Height = 71      'Inches
    FriendRecord.HomeTown = "Morgantown"
    Insert 1, FriendRecord

    Print "Sorting by age..."

    CreateIndex 1, "FriendsByAge", 0, "Age"

    SetIndex 1, "FriendsByAge"
```

```
        MoveFirst 1

        Do
            Retrieve 1, FriendRecord
            Print FriendRecord.Name
            MoveNext 1
        Loop While Not EOF(1)

        Print "Sorting by height..."

        CreateIndex 1, "FriendsByHeight", 0, "Height"

 —>     SetIndex 1, "FriendsByHeight"
   :
   :    MoveFirst 1

        Do
            Retrieve 1, FriendRecord
            Print FriendRecord.Name
            MoveNext 1
        Loop While Not EOF(1)
        :
        :
```

The result of the program so far appears in Figure 10-2. That's it for reordering the whole file. Now let's start searching through our database for specific values.

Figure 10-2 Sorting Our ISAM Records by Height

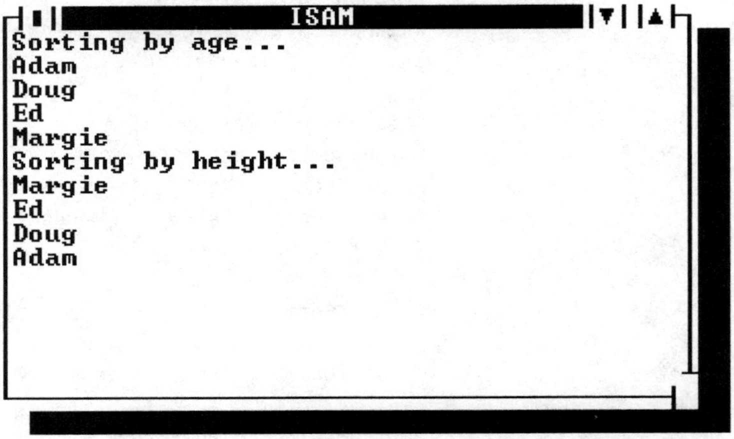

Seeking Records

A major part of working with a database is the ability to rapidly find records meeting a certain criterion. For example, we may want to search for a person 33 years old.

To perform this and other operations, ISAM provides the Seek statements: Seekgt, Seekge, and Seekeq. Using them is simple: if you wanted to find a person with age 33 in our table, Table 1, you would make FriendsByAge the current index (so that ISAM knows what field you're interested in examining) and then use the statement Seekeq 1, 33. The coding follows:

```
Type Friend
    Name As String * 50
    Age As Integer
    Height As Integer
    HomeTown As String * 50
End Type


Form_Load()

    Dim FriendRecord As Friend

    Open "Friends.Dat" For ISAM Friend "Pals" As #1

    FriendRecord.Name = "Doug"
    FriendRecord.Age = 33
    FriendRecord.Height = 70     'Inches
    FriendRecord.HomeTown = "Redlands"
    Insert 1, FriendRecord

    FriendRecord.Name = "Ed"
    FriendRecord.Age = 44
    FriendRecord.Height = 69     'Inches
    FriendRecord.HomeTown = "San Pedro"
    Insert 1, FriendRecord

    FriendRecord.Name = "Margie"
    FriendRecord.Age = 67
    FriendRecord.Height = 64     'Inches
    FriendRecord.HomeTown = "Los Angeles"
    Insert 1, FriendRecord
```

```
                    FriendRecord.Name = "Adam"
                    FriendRecord.Age = 25
                    FriendRecord.Height = 71      'Inches
                    FriendRecord.HomeTown = "Morgantown"
                    Insert 1, FriendRecord

                    Print "Sorting by age..."

                    CreateIndex 1, "FriendsByAge", 0, "Age"

                    SetIndex 1, "FriendsByAge"

                    MoveFirst 1

                    Do
                        Retrieve 1, FriendRecord
                        Print FriendRecord.Name
                        MoveNext 1
                    Loop While Not EOF(1)

                    Print "Sorting by height..."

                    CreateIndex 1, "FriendsByHeight", 0, "Height"

                    SetIndex 1, "FriendsByHeight"

                    MoveFirst 1

                    Do
                        Retrieve 1, FriendRecord
                        Print FriendRecord.Name
                        MoveNext 1
                    Loop While Not EOF(1)

        —>          Print "Seeking a person with age of 33..."

        —>          SetIndex 1, "FriendsByAge"

        —>          MoveFirst 1

        —>          Seekeq 1, 33
                        :
                        :
```

If there is no match, EOF(1) will be set true; if EOF(1) is not true, however, there was a match that was the current record. We can print it with Retrieve, as follows:

```
Type Friend
    Name As String * 50
    Age As Integer
    Height As Integer
    HomeTown As String * 50
End Type


Form_Load()

    Dim FriendRecord As Friend

    Open "Friends.Dat" For ISAM Friend "Pals" As #1

    FriendRecord.Name = "Doug"
    FriendRecord.Age = 33
    FriendRecord.Height = 70      'Inches
    FriendRecord.HomeTown = "Redlands"
    Insert 1, FriendRecord

    FriendRecord.Name = "Ed"
    FriendRecord.Age = 44
    FriendRecord.Height = 69      'Inches
    FriendRecord.HomeTown = "San Pedro"
    Insert 1, FriendRecord

    FriendRecord.Name = "Margie"
    FriendRecord.Age = 67
    FriendRecord.Height = 64      'Inches
    FriendRecord.HomeTown = "Los Angeles"
    Insert 1, FriendRecord

    FriendRecord.Name = "Adam"
    FriendRecord.Age = 25
    FriendRecord.Height = 71      'Inches
    FriendRecord.HomeTown = "Morgantown"
    Insert 1, FriendRecord

    Print "Sorting by age..."
```

```
                    CreateIndex 1, "FriendsByAge", 0, "Age"

                    SetIndex 1, "FriendsByAge"

                    MoveFirst 1

                    Do
                        Retrieve 1, FriendRecord
                        Print FriendRecord.Name
                        MoveNext 1
                    Loop While Not EOF(1)

                    Print "Sorting by height..."

                    CreateIndex 1, "FriendsByHeight", 0, "Height"

                    SetIndex 1, "FriendsByHeight"

                    MoveFirst 1

                    Do
                        Retrieve 1, FriendRecord
                        Print FriendRecord.Name
                        MoveNext 1
                    Loop While Not EOF(1)

                    Print "Seeking a person with age of 33..."

                    SetIndex 1, "FriendsByAge"

                    MoveFirst 1

                    Seekeq 1, 33

         —>        If EOF(1) Then
         —>                Print "No Match."
         —>        Else
         —>            Retrieve 1, FriendRecord
         —>            Print FriendRecord.Name
         —>        End If
                    :
                    :
```

The result of this appears in Figure 10-3. In a similar way, we can search for a person with a height over seven feet (that is, 84 inches) with Seekgt:

```
Type Friend
    Name As String * 50
    Age As Integer
    Height As Integer
    HomeTown As String * 50
End Type

Form_Load()

    Dim FriendRecord As Friend

    Open "Friends.Dat" For ISAM Friend "Pals" As #1

    FriendRecord.Name = "Doug"
    FriendRecord.Age = 33
    FriendRecord.Height = 70      'Inches
    FriendRecord.HomeTown = "Redlands"
    Insert 1, FriendRecord

    FriendRecord.Name = "Ed"
    FriendRecord.Age = 44
    FriendRecord.Height = 69      'Inches
    FriendRecord.HomeTown = "San Pedro"
    Insert 1, FriendRecord

    FriendRecord.Name = "Margie"
    FriendRecord.Age = 67
    FriendRecord.Height = 64      'Inches
    FriendRecord.HomeTown = "Los Angeles"
    Insert 1, FriendRecord

    FriendRecord.Name = "Adam"
    FriendRecord.Age = 25
    FriendRecord.Height = 71      'Inches
    FriendRecord.HomeTown = "Morgantown"
    Insert 1, FriendRecord

    Print "Sorting by age..."

    CreateIndex 1, "FriendsByAge", 0, "Age"
```

```
SetIndex 1, "FriendsByAge"

MoveFirst 1

Do
    Retrieve 1, FriendRecord
    Print FriendRecord.Name
    MoveNext 1
Loop While Not EOF(1)

Print "Sorting by height..."

CreateIndex 1, "FriendsByHeight", 0, "Height"

SetIndex 1, "FriendsByHeight"

MoveFirst 1

Do
    Retrieve 1, FriendRecord
    Print FriendRecord.Name
    MoveNext 1
Loop While Not EOF(1)

Print "Seeking a person with age of 33..."

SetIndex 1, "FriendsByAge"

MoveFirst 1

Seekeq 1, 33

If EOF(1) Then
        Print "No Match."
Else
    Retrieve 1, FriendRecord
    Print FriendRecord.Name
End If

—>    Print "Seeking people with height over seven feet..."

SetIndex 1, "FriendsByHeight"
```

```
        MoveFirst 1

        Seekgt 1, 84

        If EOF(1) Then
                Print "No Match."
        Else
            Retrieve 1, FriendRecord
            Print FriendRecord.Name
        End If
        :
        :
```

Figure 10-3 Searching Our ISAM Records by Age

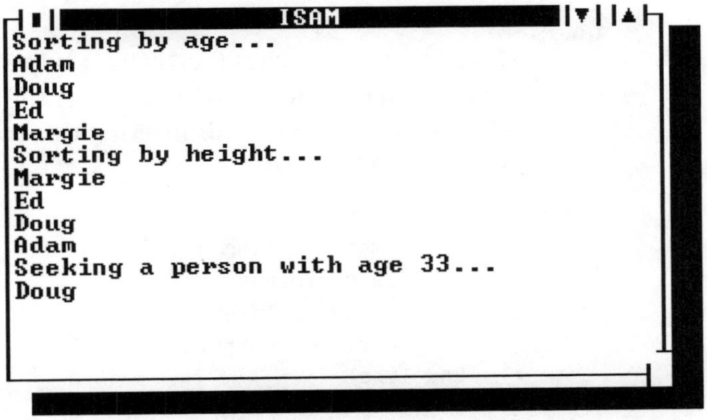

Because there is no match, EOF(1) is True, and "No Match." is printed, as shown in Figure 10-4. ISAM provides other ways of managing records besides inserting them as we've seen—we can also delete them or change the values in them. Let's start by deleting some records.

Deleting Records

Say that we wanted to delete all records of friends whose age was over 40. We could seek these records out by making FriendsByAge the current index (with SetIndex) and then using a Seekgt 1, 40 statement.

Figure 10-4 Searching Our ISAM Records by Height

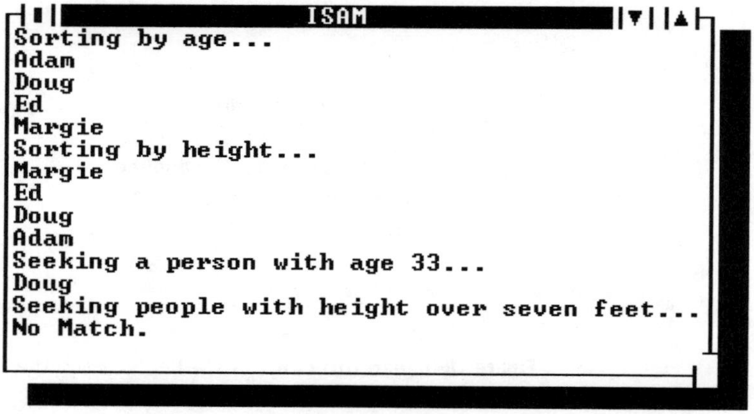

```
┤▪│▌              ISAM              │▼│ │▲├
Sorting by age...
Adam
Doug
Ed
Margie
Sorting by height...
Margie
Ed
Doug
Adam
Seeking a person with age 33...
Doug
Seeking people with height over seven feet...
No Match.
```

If we find any matches (i.e., EOF(1) is False), we can delete them with the statement Delete 1, which deletes the current record in Table 1. After removing all records meeting this criterion, we can print the remainder as follows:

```
Type Friend
    Name As String * 50
    Age As Integer
    Height As Integer
    HomeTown As String * 50
End Type

Form_Load()

    Dim FriendRecord As Friend

    Open "Friends.Dat" For ISAM Friend "Pals" As #1

    FriendRecord.Name = "Doug"
    FriendRecord.Age = 33
    FriendRecord.Height = 70      'Inches
    FriendRecord.HomeTown = "Redlands"
    Insert 1, FriendRecord

    FriendRecord.Name = "Ed"
    FriendRecord.Age = 44
```

```
FriendRecord.Height = 69      'Inches
FriendRecord.HomeTown = "San Pedro"
Insert 1, FriendRecord

FriendRecord.Name = "Margie"
FriendRecord.Age = 67
FriendRecord.Height = 64      'Inches
FriendRecord.HomeTown = "Los Angeles"
Insert 1, FriendRecord

FriendRecord.Name = "Adam"
FriendRecord.Age = 25
FriendRecord.Height = 71      'Inches
FriendRecord.HomeTown = "Morgantown"
Insert 1, FriendRecord

Print "Sorting by age..."

CreateIndex 1, "FriendsByAge", 0, "Age"

SetIndex 1, "FriendsByAge"

MoveFirst 1

Do
    Retrieve 1, FriendRecord
    Print FriendRecord.Name
    MoveNext 1
Loop While Not EOF(1)

Print "Sorting by height..."

CreateIndex 1, "FriendsByHeight", 0, "Height"

SetIndex 1, "FriendsByHeight"

MoveFirst 1

Do
    Retrieve 1, FriendRecord
    Print FriendRecord.Name
    MoveNext 1
Loop While Not EOF(1)
```

```
                Print "Seeking a person with age of 33..."

                SetIndex 1, "FriendsByAge"

                MoveFirst 1

                Seekeq 1, 33

                If EOF(1) Then
                        Print "No Match."
                Else
                    Retrieve 1, FriendRecord
                    Print FriendRecord.Name
                End If

                Print "Seeking people with height over seven feet..."

                SetIndex 1, "FriendsByHeight"

                MoveFirst 1

                Seekgt 1, 84

                If EOF(1) Then
                        Print "No Match."
                Else
                    Retrieve 1, FriendRecord
                    Print FriendRecord.Name
                End If

    —>          Print "Deleting everyone over 40..."
     :
     :          SetIndex 1, "FriendsByAge"

                Do
                    Seekgt 1, 40

                    If Not EOF(1) Then
                        Retrieve 1, FriendRecord
                        Delete 1
                    End If

                Loop Until EOF(1)
```

```
Print "Here's who's left..."

MoveFirst 1

Do
    Retrieve 1, FriendRecord
    Print FriendRecord.Name
    MoveNext 1
Loop While Not EOF(1)
    :
    :
```

The result of this program appears in Figure 10-5. Deleting records is easy, but we must be careful, because it's impossible to get them back. Also, we shouldn't expect an ISAM file (in this case, Friends.Dat) to get any smaller when we delete records. The minimum size of an ISAM file is 64K, which includes 32K of overhead and 32K of space for records.

Figure 10-5 Deleting ISAM Records

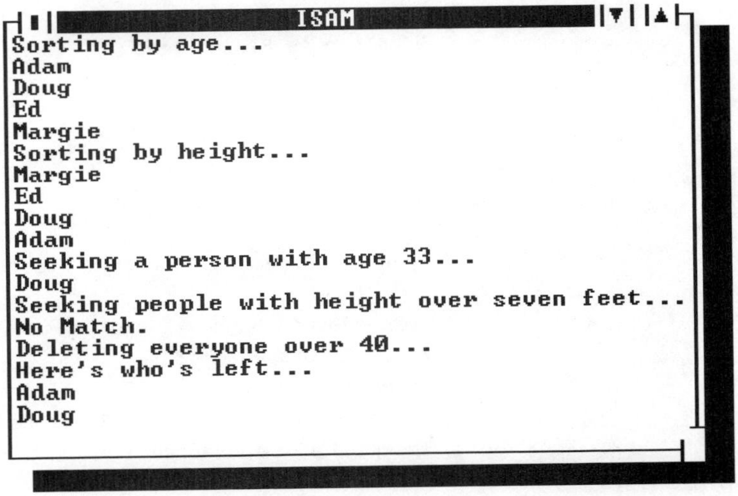

TIP: *If you have deleted many records and really want to compact an ISAM file, use the utility program ISAMPACK, but keep in mind that it works in 32K chunks—and, therefore, can only compact a file if more than 32K has been freed.*

When the data space is used up, the ISAM system adds more space in 32K chunks (it does so because its internal searching algorithms work better with data chunks of this size). When we delete a record, the file is not compacted; instead, that record's space is made available. A new record may be written there in the future.

Besides deleting records, we can change the individual fields inside them.

Updating ISAM Files

Let's say that Doug has a birthday, and his age changes from 33 to 34; we could delete his record in Friends.Dat and then insert a new one to correct his record, but the ISAM system provides a far easier method.

To update records, we can use the Update statement. In this case, all we have to do is make Doug's record the current record, read it into a variable of Type Friend—for example, FriendRecord—with Retrieve, and change the Age field to 34. Then use the statement Update 1, FriendRecord to update Friends.Dat. This statement updates the current record in file 1 using the values in FriendRecord. The entire process looks like this:

```
Type Friend
    Name As String * 50
    Age As Integer
    Height As Integer
    HomeTown As String * 50
End Type

Form_Load()

    Dim FriendRecord As Friend

    Open "Friends.Dat" For ISAM Friend "Pals" As #1

    FriendRecord.Name = "Doug"
    FriendRecord.Age = 33
    FriendRecord.Height = 70      'Inches
    FriendRecord.HomeTown = "Redlands"
    Insert 1, FriendRecord

    FriendRecord.Name = "Ed"
    FriendRecord.Age = 44
    FriendRecord.Height = 69      'Inches
    FriendRecord.HomeTown = "San Pedro"
    Insert 1, FriendRecord
```

```
FriendRecord.Name = "Margie"
FriendRecord.Age = 67
FriendRecord.Height = 64      'Inches
FriendRecord.HomeTown = "Los Angeles"
Insert 1, FriendRecord

FriendRecord.Name = "Adam"
FriendRecord.Age = 25
FriendRecord.Height = 71      'Inches
FriendRecord.HomeTown = "Morgantown"
Insert 1, FriendRecord


Print "Sorting by age..."

CreateIndex 1, "FriendsByAge", 0, "Age"

SetIndex 1, "FriendsByAge"

MoveFirst 1

Do
    Retrieve 1, FriendRecord
    Print FriendRecord.Name
    MoveNext 1
Loop While Not EOF(1)

Print "Sorting by height..."

CreateIndex 1, "FriendsByHeight", 0, "Height"

SetIndex 1, "FriendsByHeight"

MoveFirst 1

Do
    Retrieve 1, FriendRecord
    Print FriendRecord.Name
    MoveNext 1
Loop While Not EOF(1)

Print "Seeking a person with age of 33..."

SetIndex 1, "FriendsByAge"
```

```
MoveFirst 1

Seekeq 1, 33

If EOF(1) Then
        Print "No Match."
Else
    Retrieve 1, FriendRecord
    Print FriendRecord.Name
End If

Print "Seeking people with height over seven feet..."

SetIndex 1, "FriendsByHeight"

MoveFirst 1

Seekgt 1, 84

If EOF(1) Then
        Print "No Match."
Else
    Retrieve 1, FriendRecord
    Print FriendRecord.Name
End If

Print "Deleting everyone over 40..."

SetIndex 1, "FriendsByAge"

Do
Seekgt 1, 40

If Not EOF(1) Then
    Retrieve 1, FriendRecord
    Delete 1
End If

Loop Until EOF(1)

Print "Here's who's left..."

MoveFirst 1
```

```
        Do
            Retrieve 1, FriendRecord
            Print FriendRecord.Name
            MoveNext 1
        Loop While Not EOF(1)

—>     Print "Changing Doug's age to 34..."
  :
  :     CreateIndex 1, "FriendsByName", 0, "Name"

        SetIndex 1, "FriendsByName"

        Seekeq 1, "Doug"

        Retrieve 1, FriendRecord
        FriendRecord.Age = 34

        Update 1, FriendRecord
        :
        :
```

Then we can print everyone's name and age to make sure that the change was effective. The final program follows:

```
Type Friend
    Name As String * 50
    Age As Integer
    Height As Integer
    HomeTown As String * 50
End Type

Form_Load()

    Dim FriendRecord As Friend

    Open "Friends.Dat" For ISAM Friend "Pals" As #1

    FriendRecord.Name = "Doug"
    FriendRecord.Age = 33
    FriendRecord.Height = 70     'Inches
    FriendRecord.HomeTown = "Redlands"
    Insert 1, FriendRecord
```

```
                        FriendRecord.Name = "Ed"
                        FriendRecord.Age = 44
                        FriendRecord.Height = 69      'Inches
                        FriendRecord.HomeTown = "San Pedro"
                        Insert 1, FriendRecord

                        FriendRecord.Name = "Margie"
                        FriendRecord.Age = 67
                        FriendRecord.Height = 64      'Inches
                        FriendRecord.HomeTown = "Los Angeles"
                        Insert 1, FriendRecord

                        FriendRecord.Name = "Adam"
                        FriendRecord.Age = 25
                        FriendRecord.Height = 71      'Inches
                        FriendRecord.HomeTown = "Morgantown"
                        Insert 1, FriendRecord

                        Print "Sorting by age..."

                        CreateIndex 1, "FriendsByAge", 0, "Age"

                        SetIndex 1, "FriendsByAge"

                        MoveFirst 1

                        Do
                             Retrieve 1, FriendRecord
                             Print FriendRecord.Name
                             MoveNext 1
                        Loop While Not EOF(1)

                        Print "Sorting by height..."

                        CreateIndex 1, "FriendsByHeight", 0, "Height"

                        SetIndex 1, "FriendsByHeight"

                        MoveFirst 1

                        Do
                             Retrieve 1, FriendRecord
                             Print FriendRecord.Name
```

```
        MoveNext 1
Loop While Not EOF(1)


Print "Seeking a person with age of 33..."


SetIndex 1, "FriendsByAge"


MoveFirst 1


Seekeq 1, 33


If EOF(1) Then
        Print "No Match."
Else
    Retrieve 1, FriendRecord
    Print FriendRecord.Name
End If


Print "Seeking people with height over seven feet..."


SetIndex 1, "FriendsByHeight"


MoveFirst 1


Seekgt 1, 84


If EOF(1) Then
        Print "No Match."
Else
    Retrieve 1, FriendRecord
    Print FriendRecord.Name
End If


Print "Deleting everyone over 40..."


SetIndex 1, "FriendsByAge"


Do
Seekgt 1, 40


If Not EOF(1) Then
    Retrieve 1, FriendRecord
    Delete 1
End If
```

```
        Loop Until EOF(1)

        Print "Here's who's left..."

        MoveFirst 1

        Do
            Retrieve 1, FriendRecord
            Print FriendRecord.Name
            MoveNext 1
        Loop While Not EOF(1)

        Print "Changing Doug's age to 34..."

        CreateIndex 1, "FriendsByName", 0, "Name"

        SetIndex 1, "FriendsByName"

        Seekeq 1, "Doug"

        Retrieve 1, FriendRecord
        FriendRecord.Age = 34

        Update 1, FriendRecord

        SetIndex 1, "FriendsByAge"

        Do
            Retrieve 1, FriendRecord
            Print Rtrim$(FriendRecord.Name);"'s age is: ";
              FriendRecord.Age
            MoveNext 1
        Loop While Not EOF(1)

        Close #1
```

At the end, note that we close this table (and therefore the file, because there's only one table in it) with Close 1. The final result appears
in Figure 10-6. That completes our database—it's not exactly a general-
purpose database (because it has no user interface) but it has enabled
us to explore the ISAM system.

Figure 10-6 Updating Our ISAM Records

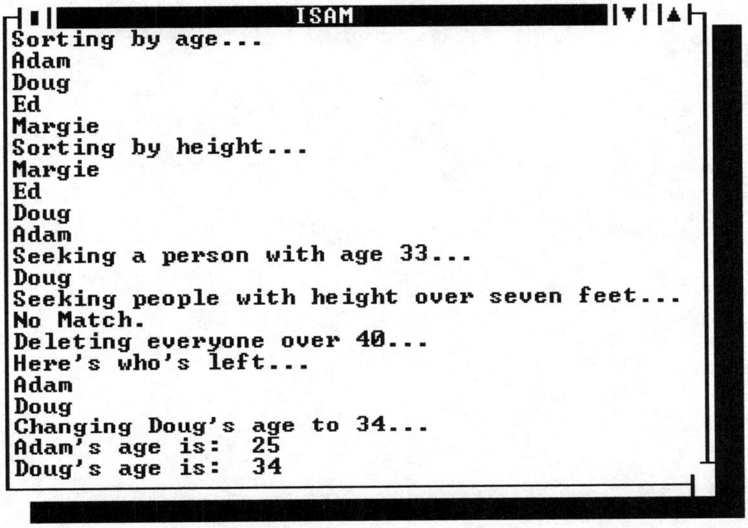

```
┌─■┌──────────────── ISAM ────────────────■▼││▲┐
│Sorting by age...
│Adam
│Doug
│Ed
│Margie
│Sorting by height...
│Margie
│Ed
│Doug
│Adam
│Seeking a person with age 33...
│Doug
│Seeking people with height over seven feet...
│No Match.
│Deleting everyone over 40...
│Here's who's left...
│Adam
│Doug
│Changing Doug's age to 34...
│Adam's age is:  25
│Doug's age is:  34
└──────────────────────────────────────────────┘
```

In this book, we've gone far with Visual Basic: from the most elementary forms up through buttons, menus, dialog boxes, and file handling. From there, we continued with graphics and the mouse, adding more power to our applications. Finally, we saw how to handle errors, some advanced data-handling techniques, and databasing. Now all that remains is putting all this power to work. (Happy programming.)

About the Diskette

The diskette contains programs from this book, and also includes three additional programs. Copy them to Visual Basic for DOS' \BIN area before running them. For some of these programs, as noted, you'll have to load additional QuickLibraries, such as Chart.Qlb. To load this file, you would use the /L switch along with the name Chart : "/L Chart". Otherwise, just load the .Mak file into Visual Basic with the Open Project menu item. A list of the projects on the diskette follows.

Project	Explanation
Alarm.Mak	Alarm clock example. Enter the time you want the alarm to go off in the box marked: Alarm Setting, and indicate whether you want the alarm on or off with the option buttons. Chapter 2.
Array.Mak	Example showing how to use arrays. Chapter 8.
Ascii.Mak	ASCII graphics example, which draws a graphic figure using ASCII box-drawing characters. Chapter 6.
Bar.Mak	Bar chart, Professional Edition Example. Load with /L Chart. Chapter 7.

Project	Explanation
Binary.Mak	Binary Tree example, showing how to use this important programming construct. This program fills a binary tree with the names of people and then searches through it for a specified entry (a person with a specific age). Chapter 8.
Calc.Mak	Windowed calculator. Place numbers in the top two text boxes and click the = button to see the result of the addition in the bottom box.Chapter 2.
Clock.Mak	Vector graphics example, draws a clock on the screen that shows the current time (does not update as time goes on, however). Chapter 7.
Db.Mak	Database example. There are three text boxes in the main form: Product, Number, and Comment. Fill in these values as you wish, and select Add Item in the File menu to add the current data to the database. After loading all data, you can retrieve records by selecting Find Item... in the File menu, and clicking the appropriate record name in the sorted dialog box that appears. You can also save and load the data to and from disk. Chapters 4-5.
Dosshell.Mak	A DOS Shell example. Lets you launch DOS programs by selecting Run... in the File menu and typing the name of a DOS program. If you do not type anything (i.e., just click OK), a new version of Command.Com runs, starting a new DOS session. To leave it, type Exit and <Enter>. Chapter 4.
Isam.Mak	Indexed Sequential Access Method (ISAM) Database example. A fast method of data-basing, using pointers to store and retrieve data from a relational database on disk. Requires Visual Basic for DOS Professional Edition; run Proisamd.Exe before running Visual Basic. Chapter 10.

Project	Explanation
Line.Mak	Line chart, Presentation Graphics example. Use /L Chart when loading; graphics data in a line chart. Chapter 7.
Mourel.Mak	Graphics mouse- and keyboard-handling example. Uses interrupt &H33 to interface to the mouse. This example program asks you to position the mouse cursor, press and release the left mouse button a few times. When you do, it reports all mouse information. Uses Interrupt( ); load with /L (no parameters, just /L). Chapter 6.
Pad.Mak	Full notepad application, complete with editing functions including Cut and Paste. Can also store its contents to disk and read them back in. Automatic word wrap, the works. Chapters 2-5.
Paint.Mak	Graphics paint program. Allows you to draw dots, lines, boxes, circles, and fill in figures. Can even save your work on disk and read it back in later. Chapter 7.
Panel.Mak	Pop-up control panel example. Using the control panel, you can set the main window's caption, height, width, and color. Chapter 4.
Phone.Mak	Phonebook example; adds names to the main menu (i.e., changes a menu's contents at run time). Selecting them pops up the person's name and number again. To use it, enter a person's name and number in the text boxes. Next, add that person to the File menu with the Add Name menu item. After adding all names, you can select the one(s) you wish to see redisplayed by selecting it in the File menu. Chapter 3.
Pie.Mak	Pie chart, Presentation Graphics example. Load with /L Chart. Presents data in a pie chart. Chapter 7.
Qsort.Mak	Quicksort example. Shows how to use the very fast Quicksort. Chapter 8.

Project	Explanation
Sort.Mak	Shell sort example. Chapter 8.
Tictac.Mak	Tic-tac-toe program; a demonstration only. Requires two players (i.e., the computer does not play against you). Chapter 2.

The following programs are BONUS programs, covering material NOT in the book.

Project	Explanation
Altfont.Mak	Alternate font graphics example; load with /L Chart; shows how to load and use courier fonts in all sizes. This program loads in the file Coura.Fon. Since these programs are supposed to be used in the Visual Basic \BIN area, the file loaded is loaded as "..\LIB\COURA.FON" in the code; you can change that file specification to the other Visual Basic font files as well.
Animate.Mak	Graphics animation example. Draws a rocket ship on the screen and then sends it flying upwards. Uses graphics mode.
Hyper.Mak	Hypertext example. Clicking highlighted words switches you to another window; clicking them there switches you back (which is how hypertext works).

Index

L

M

O

Object not an array run-time error, 339
Object required run-time error, 340
Object was unloaded run-time error, 339
object-oriented programming, 6
offset addresses, 244
On Error Goto statement, 334-344
On Local Error GoTo statement, 159
Open Project... option, 26
Open statement, 158, 386
opening files, 156
   errors, handling, 159
   random access, 158
   sequential, 157-158
operations
   file, 333
   parallel, 284
option buttons, 69-70
options
   Add Function..., 214
   Clear All Breakpoints, 364
   Continue, 361
   Event Procedures..., 19, 28
   Find Item..., 139
   Immediate, 363
   Instant Watch..., 365
   Load File..., 162-163
   Make Exe File..., 23, 56
   New Form..., 8
   New Function..., 203

New Module..., 25, 40
Open Project..., 26
Save File, 27
Save File As..., 27
Save File..., 154
Save Project, 27, 43
Save Text...., 27
Start, 22, 43
Toggle Breakpoint, 362
toggle, 103
Ordered Search Example application, 329-330
Out of DATA run-time error, 337
Out of memory run-time error, 337
Out of paper run-time error, 337
Out of stack space run-time error, 337
Out of string space run-time error, 337
OutRegs structures, 213
Overflow run-time error, 337

P

Pad application, 49-52, 61, 173-175
   Code Version 1, 94-95
   Code Version 2, 96-97
   menu system, 86
Pad.Mak application, 425
Paint sample program
   DrawBox subroutine, 255-256
   DrawCircle subroutine, 256-257

DrawLine subroutine, 252-255
DrawPaint subroutine, 257-278
DrawPixel subroutine, 249-252
GetLeftButtonPress subroutine, 235-236, 239-240
Initialization subroutine, 237-239
Initialize subroutine, 235
menu-bar options, 238-240
MenuChoice subroutine, 236-237, 240-249
starting code, 234-237
Paint statement, 257
Paint.Bas application, 259-265
Paint.Mak application, 425
Panel.Mak application, 425
parallel operations, 284
Paste button, 57-58
Path list box property, 167
Path NOT found run-time error, 339
Path/File access error run-time error, 339
Pattern list box property, 167
Permission denied run-time error, 338
perpetual loops, setting up, 235
Phone Book application, 109-110
Phone.Mak application, 425

W

X-Z